Siamese Tears
THE KINGDOM'S STRUGGLE AGAINST
THE COLONIAL SUPERPOWERS

Siamese Tears

THE KINGDOM'S STRUGGLE AGAINST THE COLONIAL SUPERPOWERS

Claire Keefe-Fox

RIVER
BOOKS

First published and distributed in 2016 by
River Books
396 Maharaj Road, Tatien, Bangkok 10200
Tel. 66 2 622-1900, 224-6686
Fax. 66 2 225-3861
E-mail: order@riverbooksbk.com
www.riverbooksbk.com

Editor: Narisa Chakrabongse
Production supervision: Paisarn Piemmettawat
Design: Ruetairat Nanta

ISBN 978 616 7339 75 7

Printed and bound in Thailand
by UPadd International Co., Ltd.

Contents

Old men talk to themselves.

I am an old man, *ergo*, that is what I do, cursing my knees for being stiff and painful when I get up from my chair, asking myself where my spectacles might have gone to, muttering about the state of the world as I read the newspapers sent up from Bangkok, and which nowadays take less than a week to reach me, and offering my wisdom to no one in particular.

In other words, I have become the kind of doddery old bore I took such pains to avoid when I was young and witty, and knew — oh, how I knew! — that life would never allow me to become as I now am.

Today, after slapping down the *Bangkok Times* in despair, I shuffle towards the garden, and announce to the rolling dark clouds that a war is coming, and that Europe is done for. The Hun is on the march again, I say, and if you thought that the last war meant the end of civilization, well, just wait until Herr Hitler has his way, which, from my experience as a diplomat, should not take more than a couple of years, knowing the backbone of governments who seem to be good only at blustering and then giving in.

Everyone is frantic to avoid another war, the people and their leaders alike, and indeed who can forget the years of seeing young men scythed down or returning poisoned from gas, burned, scarred and broken forever?

But if they think that they will buy protection by surrendering yet another land, or another people, they are sorely mistaken. Do they not know that to be a bully is to never be satisfied? What have they learned?

Can I blame them, and really, who am I to judge?

It is so easy to criticize from the safety of this little haven of golden spires and misty hills. I did not serve in the Great War, I was posted in China at the time, and enough of a coward to be thankful rather than attempt, as other, braver, colleagues did, to be sent to serve the Crown in the trenches.

Once again, I am truly and desperately afraid of the future, not for myself this time, Heaven knows, but for all of mankind.

I will not say this out loud, and certainly not to the few planters and teak wallahs I sometimes share a beer with in our un-official club here. Afraid for all mankind, they would mutter behind my back. Listen to the pretentious old faggot...

Somboon heard me and offered to bring some tea.

I suppose he is aware of my mood, he always is, but never asks the cause. At times, I find his total lack of curiosity hurtful, at others I cannot help but bless him for it. His serene, somewhat toothless smile never wavers, never changes. As long as he knows I love him, and truly I do, he is content.

So I am lucky, as was underlined by my young cousin Lawrence, when he visited here last year.

"How many men do you know who are so loved and cared for?" he asked.

A rather surprising comment, coming from one so young and who has been so surrounded by love all his life.

But, he said, as an aspiring novelist, he needed to cultivate reality, and reality so far showed him love is not that plentiful a commodity when one is — how did he put it? Ah, yes — "when one is not quite so comely as a barely ripe peach."

He, however, is as comely as that, or perhaps even more.

In fact, when he first stepped into my garden, heralded by the gardener's son who kept on squealing "*Farang! Farang! Farang!*" as if he had never seen a European before, I felt the old twist to the heart and gut that used to make my life a delight and a misery both in Oxford.

But something in the way he met my eye, an absence of guile, perhaps, or of.... understanding, or knowing, or whatever it is that enabled me to say, in the old days, "ah, yes, he is one of us..." now enabled me to recognize that young Lawrence Gallet was not, and loved women.

And so, I was ashamed — for Heaven's sake, this was Louis' son! — and embarrassed and flustered... what would he think of this pathetic old relative living with a native man who was beaming at him, and ushering him in with clucking sounds in Siamese?

His visit was announced by a letter from his father, Louis, one of those men whose souls and bodies were scoured and scarred in the trenches and, who, according to his mother, had rarely smiled since.

He is now a rather well-known Harley Street surgeon, but I remember him as a fat and fussy baby, then as a singularly appealing child, the playmate of princes and beggar children, and who spoke Siamese as well as any guttersnipe.

He is the son of a cousin who was also my dearest friend, and I always considered him as the child I never had, just as, for many years, he saw me me (..) as his father.

Ties such as this one cannot forget, although I have not seen him since he married — his wife, one gathers, does not approve of the likes of me...

His letter was as he apparently has become, somewhat terse with all emotions contained, but painfully evident.

"My son passionately admires an adventurer turned novelist named Malraux — have you heard of him? — and wishes to become a writer. I have given up the hope of seeing him follow in my footsteps and study medicine.

Apparently, to write, one must now go around the world. It is useless, as I have discovered, to mention Jane Austen or the Brontës, because he then lobs Kipling back at me.

And I admit I would rather have him roaming the East than continuing at Oxford and getting embroiled in politics.

My dear Michael, would you mind very much putting him up, and, perhaps, talking some sense into him as you did for me?"

Yes indeed, not only had I heard of Malraux, but actually met the man in Phnom Penh, some 10 years or so ago. Some say he is a brilliant writer, my French is no longer good enough to enable me to judge, but as a flamboyant and self-serving thief of antiquities, I can vouch for his impeccable taste, if not morals.

So I was to talk some sense into this demi-god from Balliol with his newly minted degree in philosophy, his wide-eyed and naïve gaze, his skin tender as a girl's and his yen to see the world?

Well, I could start by explaining Somboon.

Far too often, when Europeans come to visit me — I have the impression I am now mentioned in Baedeker as one of the must-see attractions of Chiang Mai, the old Brit who knows everything about Siamese antiquities, and people actually expect me to have them on display, as if I were the local museum — their eyes glide over poor Somboon pretending to not see or register his presence, and I never know which of the two of us is most humiliated.

But Lawrence waved my halting introduction away, and performed a fairly competent *wai* — he obviously had been tutored by his father.

So many farang think they can just carelessly bring their hands together to greet someone and only manage to look silly, but he did it with just the right amount of respect and a half-bow from the waist. "I know, cousin Michael, Somboon is your companion. Father told me."

Did Louis know about Somboon, all those years ago, and did he assume I moved back to Siam to be with him and carve out whatever happiness was still possible in what we so depressingly refer to as the twilight of my life?

In my yearly Christmas letter to what little family I still have in England, I am very discreet, more to save them embarrassment than for my own sake. But I suppose gossip circulates between Bangkok and London.

How late into the night did we talk?

We were drinking the whisky Lawrence had so thoughtfully brought, such a treat and a lovely change from the local rice hooch. Well, late enough for the bullfrogs to become silent, and Somboon to have fallen asleep on the floor, propped up against the wall.

He wanted me to tell him everything about Siam as I and his grandmother, my dearest, dearest Julie knew it.

What really happened when Britain and France almost went to war over this poor, struggling and lovely land? What was the king like? How long did it take me to learn Siamese, and was it very difficult? What about his grandmother, where did she live in Bangkok, and what was his father like as a child?

All he, Lawrence, knew, was that he had a pet gibbon named Pouan...

I chided him gently. This was almost fifty years ago...

I was not sure I could really remember... although, yes that gibbon, my God, it was years since I'd thought of him, what a rascal! But did Julie not share some of her memories before her death?

"Grandmother died when I was twelve, so.... She left some albums with photographs – there were some extraordinary ones, of her in a ball gown, one of you as a toreador, I believe, at a fancy dress evening, and a framed one of all these ladies in Siamese dress – and newspaper clippings.

"But she hardly ever mentioned her life in Bangkok.

"Well, she did, but only in the bedtime stories she told me, until I felt too grown up to have my grandmother come to say good night, and, of course, it took me years to realize she was actually telling me about things she had seen and known.

"She always started the same way: 'Once upon a time, in a beautiful kingdom far, far away, on the other side of the world, there was a king who lived in a palace with roofs made of gold, and giants guarding the gates.' Once, I remember, she said the king was very sad because the Queen of the Serpents who lived in the river stole his wife and daughter from him because she was jealous of their beauty and happiness, and dragged them down to live with her in the reeds and mud.

"I remember being terrified and having nightmares for days, and my mother was furious. In another story, she talked about the king riding an elephant to war. I loved those stories..." His voice trailed away, and we sat in silence.

I was remembering Julie, and mourning her death anew, as I have ever since I learned of her passing, some ten years ago. I hardly ever saw her at the end of her life, and for me she is, and will always be, the young woman who arrived in Bangkok on a stormy monsoon morning with dripping hair, sodden clothes and a ridiculous pith helmet.

And then, Somboon spoke. He had woken up and been following our conversation; I am always surprised by how well he understands English, though he is far too shy to ever try and speak it.

"Why do you lie and say you do not remember?

"You know you remember everything, and it would be good for you to tell your stories to one who has not yet heard them. And there are Madame Julie's notebooks. Give them to the boy."

And so, I confessed to Julie's grandson that I had her journals, written over several years, and which she gave me before embarking for England, never to return.

"I am starting a new life," she said, "and don't think I want to be reminded of the one I am leaving behind. I don't want to live in the past." She had not told me to keep them a secret, but I always assumed she did not want them to fall into the hands of someone who might not understand. But still, she did not want them destroyed...

Somboon was right, and Lawrence should have them.

The notebooks were kept in a Burmese chest and wrapped in a length of oiled silk with sandalwood to protect them from termites. I had not read them in years, it always seemed to me that I was treading in forbidden territory, all the more so when I compared the Julie I knew in Bangkok to the society lady I used to see on my later visits to London.

There were tears in my eyes when I put the parcel in Lawrence's hands, and I think in his as well. Somboon disappeared into the house and came back with a large blue leather pouch, and thrust it towards Julie's grandson.

"Letters," he said in English, trying hard to enunciate, "From Maem Chuli." Then he turned back to me with a stubborn look and added in Siamese. "You need them no longer. They are engraved in your heart."

The remaining days of Lawrence's stay were devoted to the past, but also the future, as it was seen from the enviable vantage point of being young, wealthy, and fresh from Oxford.

"It's a future I want no part of," I said, "choosing between fascism and communism is to choose between evil and evil. Why do you think I have come to live here, where nothing ever happens?"

Lawrence was kind enough not to point out that I have no future, just a series of present moments, the glint of the morning sun on a temple spire, the music of the falling rain on the banana leaves in the garden at night, or the pleasure of the frangipani perfume as I open my windows.

When he left, we all felt bereft, even the house seemed to sulk under the monsoon skies, and the rains went on for weeks.

A few days ago, I received a sheaf of neatly typewritten pages and a cover note.

"*Dear Michael*" — I had insisted he drop the "cousin" I told him it made me feel like a character out of a Victorian novel — "*this is your story, and Julie's.*

I hope you feel I have done it justice.

Your Lawrence"

Seeing my mood is somber, Somboon has just brought Lawrence's opus to me, because he knows that it is the fate of old men to seek refuge in what has passed, so as not to face what will come to pass.

So be it.

Chapter I

For a young and ambitious diplomat, Siam was not really the ideal posting.

Nothing ever seemed to happen in this glittering, somewhat gaudy and backward little kingdom and if glitter was what you wanted, then Paris, or Vienna or even Rome or Saint Petersburg were of course far preferable.

The climate was debilitating, but, as the Honourable French — for such, amusingly and confusingly, was the name of Her Majesty's Consul General in Siam — always said, it was certainly no worse than Singapore or Penang.

Ah, but Singapore or Penang were part of the Empire, one was, as it were, *chez soi,* and did not have to deal with the Royal Household and Court with its all-encompassing, rigid, incomprehensible protocol, and its charming, slippery and mysterious officials.

Wives did not like it here, they became yellow, and sour and they were bored, balls were but paltry, small affairs, there was no theatre, no concerts, servants hardly spoke English, and no one, really no one, should have to try to learn Siamese if one wanted a properly boiled egg or a stew that was not smothered in chillies.

And if Siam had not the strategic position it occupied between British Burmah and Malaya to the West and South and the constantly encroaching, ever greedier French ambitions in Indochina to the East, then the Kingdom would have been treated with even less consideration. For the future fate of Siam was certainly not in the hands of the Kingdom itself, but plotted and planned in secret in London and Paris by those two great friendly but rival colonial powers in their ruthless game of global chess.

So the members of the British Legation in Bangkok wrote their reports, composed coded telegrams recounting the latest news, or rumours – the King was ailing again, or so it was understood, the French had sent a so-called scientific and map-making mission to Laos, and new troops had arrived in Tonkin – then shed their coats and ties with relief and went off to play tennis at the Surawongse Road courts.

Michael Crawfurd, First Secretary at Her British Majesty's Legation, did not share the general views of his colleagues, but would never have dared admit to it.

He was resting against the wooden railing above the deck at Custom House, and gazed at the russet and roiling waters of the great river below.

He was early, the *Independent*, bound from Singapore would not arrive before another hour at least, according to the Customs official. The tides, he explained with a knowing, self-important look, as if he controlled them himself.

The sky had turned the colour of soot; there would be a downpour in a short while, which would certainly cool the suffocating temperatures.

But Michael had never seen a country such as this, where whatever good always seemed to have unpleasant consequences. Humidity would become unbearable, shoes covered in mould, varnished furniture would become sticky under one's fingers and newspapers would simply seem to disintegrate when one tried to open them, getting ink all over one's hands. One would toss and turn for hours at night under the net listening to the mosquitoes buzzing, and seeking sleep in vain, because during the monsoon, the Legation slowed down and afternoons were devoted to napping.

At least the older diplomats napped of an afternoon, the younger, unmarried ones abandoned themselves to the ministrations of the Siamese girl they all seemed to have in their household, and whom they described with raunchy laughs after checking there was no British wife within earshot.

But not Michael. He never discussed what he did in the afternoon.

The small boat of a floating food seller was moored close to the deck, and the short stiff waves risen by the quickening wind seemed to toss it about, threatening to upset the boiling cauldron over the brazier the old man had balanced at the stern. A woman was standing up to her waist in the water, dreamily washing her hair. She plunged down and emerged streaming, still modestly wrapped in the length of cotton cloth worn here by the poorer people, men and women alike.

With the mounting heat, a heavy mist was forming over the river, the landscape had suddenly become a study in dark, sombre hues, the trees were almost black under the pewter sky, and the only touch of colour was the orange and green roof of a nearby temple. It brought to mind a painting he once saw in Venice, done in ink with just a detail in watercolour to highlight the pearly beauty of the scene.

"To think that Bangkok is called the Venice of the East," Stringer, the Legation wit, always said with his nasal, snorting, snigger. "Can one imagine that Venetians would enjoy being called denizens of the Bangkok of the West?"

Michael sighed and unfolded a letter from his mother, the reason for his presence here so early in the morning and smiled as he started to read. It was just like seeing her in the morning room surrounded by her books, paintings and needlework, and listening to that dear voice.

Chapter I

"London, 12 of February, 1890

My beloved Son,
As a good mother, I shall of course inquire about your health, your sleep, your appetite and your general well being, but first, I must make a confession: I gave your address to my cousin Daphne Lucas-Sauvain.

I can see you raising both your eyebrows and your shoulders, which makes you look just like your father. Yes, you do know her, I often speak of her, she married a Frenchman with extremely impressive mutton-chop whiskers.

Very, very wealthy, which of course made his nationality somewhat more acceptable. In foundries I seem to remember, or something equally grimy.

We spent a summer at her seaside villa in Biarritz, you were eight, it was just before you went off to school and you built a sand fortress on the beach with her son Victor. You see, you do remember!

Why did I give her your address, you ask, and please, do bring your eyebrows down. It is because her daughter Julie is to arrive in Bangkok sometime in the spring to be closer to her husband who is part of a scientific mission looking for rare plants or some as yet unknown insects somewhere in Laos.

It would seem that life there is not possible for a young woman, and therefore she will patiently wait for him to join her occasionally in Bangkok when he is not discovering a giant carnivorous flower or a new breed of butterfly.

If only all women could have such a start to married life! In England, we wait for our husbands to come home from their club, but unfortunately, they are back every evening.

Seriously though, Daphne's letter was curious, a bit too — breathless and effervescent, I suppose. I believe she must have been desperately opposed to the match, and her daughter stood firm, and of course she must be of age and does have her own money, I remember her grandfather — Daphne's father, of course, no idea who her French grandfather was — had settled quite a bit on all of the girls, unless — but no, I do not see how she could have been in an interesting condition, the wedding was six months ago and, to quote Daphne, 'was celebrated in some haste, as Louis (the husband, I suppose) had to be in Saigon early October to join the mission.'

My darling, is this letter too jumbled for you? You must learn to bear with your poor rattle-brained mother.

In any case, there is some mystery here, otherwise it seems to me I would have been invited to the wedding, or at least been informed, if only for the silver saltcellar from Asprey's I always send in such cases. Do try and find out more, you know how I adore other people's scandals, which, I suppose, is only due to my regrets for having led such a blameless life myself.

I must say I rather envy today's young women, in my day we never did anything interesting, not even get married in haste.

I suppose you will receive a letter from Daphne, giving you the details. Strangely, I cannot remember this Julie at all, can you?

Otherwise my dear son, I hope you are still enjoying life in Siam, your letters are full of balls, picnics and billiard parties, and I wonder that you are able to dance wearing evening dress in the awful heat.

When next I meet our Foreign Secretary-cum-Prime Minister — Does Lord Salisbury still manage to do it all? How clever of him — I shall tell him that our diplomats have very difficult lives.

There are purple and yellow crocuses all about, it is so very pretty, my cat Simone just had a litter of five darling kittens that I refuse to have drowned. When you return I shall be a smelly old woman surrounded by cats.

You father is also well.

My fondest love to you Michael and do see to Julie at least at first.

Your mother,

Zinnia Crawfurd."

His mother was mistaken; he remembered that summer very well, the sand fortress on the beach, his fights with Victor, and the handfuls of sand they viciously threw at each other's eyes. They both had to wear the most ridiculous striped scratchy bathing costumes, which he hated, and what had annoyed him more than anything was this way Victor had of slipping from the English he spoke to his mother and nanny to French, a slippery, affected language, when he spoke to his sister, a mousy child who must have been this Julie he had come to fetch today.

In fact, if he and Victor agreed on one thing, it was to keep Julie out of their games, so she went back crying to her nanny or her mother, to be told that proper young ladies did not play at war, or, for that matter, with boys.

He also recalled her mother, whom he called Auntie Daphne, her slightly tired beauty, the shawls she draped herself in at the slightest breeze, and her lavender eyes, which somehow seemed larger, with far darker lashes than his mother's. There was a baby as well, a fat gurgling girl carried about by a nurse with a ruddy face and huge feet.

They never returned to Biarritz. "I dearly love my cousin, but she has become rather French, and the train journey is much too long and tiring," his mother had said when they were back home.

He was to understand much later that although Auntie Daphne's side of the family was far wealthier than his own, they were looked down on a bit, being "in trade", Daphne's mother having married the heir to a cotton mill fortune, and her sister the profligate youngest son of an earl, his own grandfather. And so, both branches of the family drifted apart, except for weddings, funerals, a letter at Christmas and of course that summer so long ago.

"Trade is the lifeblood of the Empire," he was told one day by his father, "but it takes people like us to make sure there is an Empire for the blood to circulate."

The skies opened with a startling clap of thunder. A huge drop fell on to the letter, blurring the ink, and forcing him inside the Custom House building, the river had vanished, hidden from view by a dense curtain of rain that obscured the landing deck below. What a day to start a new life, he thought, as the door opened with a gust of wind, the passengers started to arrive, and porters dashed around with parcels or offering their services.

It was the usual mix for the Singapore packet: a few prosperous looking Chinese in Western dress, greeted by a covey of bowing and scraping servants, a group of very red-faced and rather loud Englishmen, box-wallahs no doubt, a young woman attended by an amah bearing a baby — so, no, that could not be Julie, a middle-aged couple speaking either Danish or Swedish, followed by a girl, their daughter no doubt but who was looking around scanning faces and smiled with relief coming up to him.

"Cousin Michael?"

He peered down at her, he had not expected his relative to be as small as a Siamese girl, she looked about fourteen. She was not wearing a hat, but carried a pith helmet and was so wet that the hem of her completely inappropriate blue serge dress was dripping and forming a puddle at her feet.

"I recognized you, at least, I think I did."

"And I you."

She smiled slightly. "Really? Just let me say good-bye and thank you to the Larssens who looked after me during the journey."

"Of course, and I must thank them as well."

They smiled and shook the hands of the Danish lady and her husband who bade them farewell with a dour look and opened huge black umbrellas before going out into the raging downpour.

Julie turned back to him and said dryly: "Actually, they were both very sick during the crossing, and I never saw them before breakfast this morning. Not that I needed to be looked after, but my friends in Singapore know them and thought it better to entrust me to someone."

Well, Michael thought, she seemed very self-assured for a blushing bride, but thank Heaven, her English was perfect, she barely had any accent. He had worried about that somewhat.

"What about you? Have you had a good journey? It must have been fairly rough in the gulf with the storm, come, come, I have the Legation barouche, it is bigger than my own buggy, is this your only bag? And give me your topi helmet, you will certainly not need it in the monsoon. Actually, no one wears them here. What about your trunks? I have a bearer with me, give him the ticket, he will have them brought to my house, now if you could bear to face the rain again, really, it's just a few steps."

He realized he was sounding flustered, but confident young women always made him feel that way. How was he going to manage for several months of having her around?

He handed her into the horse drawn carriage, made sure the leaking black oil cloth cover was as tightly fastened as it could be and rapped on the window to get the coachman to start.

She still had not said much, except to thank him when he helped her up, and was looking around, trying to make out her surroundings through the misted windows.

"This is the main street," he explained, "it is called New Road, but the Siamese have another name for it, this is where most of the embassies and big hotels are, and look, can you see, that large building, that's the post office. I have forms if you want to write a telegram for your parents later on today.

"We now have electric streetlights on New Road, it is very pretty at night, and really so much safer, you never knew when your carriage was going to ram into a cart, they hardly ever have any lights. Behind that garden there, yes, where the tall trees are, is the French Consulate, you will have to drop off your card sometime this week, a bit further up is the famous Oriental Hotel. The British Legation is very near, but behind us, upriver a bit from Customs House."

She wiped the window with her gloved hand, and peered

out as the barouche attempted to turn left, making its way through push carts, wheelbarrows, rickshaws, and a bustle of men and women hunched against the driving rain and gusty wind, carrying heavy loads on their backs or with baskets hanging from poles on their shoulders.

It was exactly as described in the book written by Mrs Leonowens, the English governess of the King's children, exactly as she had dreamed it would be, so why was she not more excited, she asked herself, trying to bring back that lovely state of tremulous anticipation she appeared to have lost.

Was it just the rain beating mercilessly down on the deck of the ship that had made her see everything in this despondent light since this morning, when she awoke telling herself that today, yes, today, she was finally arriving in Bangkok, and found herself wishing she were back home in Paris?

She could see small makeshift kitchens and food shops, where people huddled under canvas awnings around smoky fires, she heard shrill voices shouting and the smell of frying fish wafted into the carriage as it lurched forward and the crowds eased away. Here, tall trees arched and dripped over a narrow street, one could only guess at the gardens and houses behind the high walls bordering it.

"This is my *soi*, it means lane in Siamese. The gardener will open the gate, wait till we reach the verandah steps to get down, the path is very muddy.

"As you can see, it is not far from the Legation, and on sunny mornings, I actually walk there. Otherwise, there is a tram, and little carriages called box-gharries, but I don't advise you to use them, they're fairly dirty. Here we are!"

A servant in a white jacket, blue skirt and turban was rushing to greet them with an open umbrella, but Michael waved him away.

"Too late, Pon, we're almost in. Give me your hand, the stairs are slippery in the rain."

And then he finally looked at her, and was suddenly reminded of himself when his mother first took him to his school, a small stoic figure with stiff shoulders and chin raised, trying to look less terrified than he actually was.

He squeezed her hand in its sodden glove and gave her his first real smile. "Is it very awful?" he asked. "All of this information you cannot have taken in yet, and having to live with an unknown cousin? I think you are very brave." He suddenly flushed, embarrassed, and released her fingers.

Julie smiled back at him, but did not answer. She looked about at the dark hallway, trying to conceal her feelings of acute homesickness and disappointment at seeing this house and at the idea of living here for... how long? Several weeks, at best, before she could find a house, and then, somewhere as damp and depressing as this?

What would she not give to be back Boulevard Malesherbes, in the comfortable familiar townhouse, with a novel on her lap, a cup of tea at her elbow, and Darling Mama telling her that if she wanted to find a husband it might be best to lift her nose out of her book, pin up her hair and accept the invitation to tea, or a dance, or a musical soirée that she had just received.

Well, I found my husband, she thought, and this is where it has taken me, to this dark and shabby house, this oppressive heat and this sandy-haired and balding cousin who kept on babbling, telling the servant to bring her bag upstairs, to please light the lamps in the drawing room, the trunks were coming, did she want tea, or perhaps lemon juice? And this was her house, she was to make herself at home, and treat the servants as her own.

He waved a hand at the manservant.

"Pon understands and speaks a fair amount of English. Just don't be offended if he calls you 'Sir' that is how they translate '*Khun*' which is the title given to both men and women."

Pon beamed and bowed with his hands joined before his face, and Julie clumsily tried to return the greeting. "I have asked Pon to hire a maid for you. I gather her name is Fie, and she has worked for an English family. But if she is no good, don't worry, he will find you another."

She followed around in a bit of a daze, to her left a parlour with faded chintz-covered furniture, two oil lamps that threw light on a dusty book case with what seemed to be a collection of well-worn and often-read volumes, a few pieces of greenish pottery and some strange and rather threatening looking bronze idols.

To her right off the hall was the dining room with an immense reddish wood table displaying a tarnished silver tea set, and at least twelve mismatched chairs.

"The kitchen is outside the house, which means the food is never hot when it is brought to the table. It's because of the risk of fire, the house is made of wood you see and you cannot imagine, my dear, how many Siamese houses go up in flames during the dry season. Of course, they are never really careful with oil lamps."

Her room was upstairs, and she would be brought water for her bath. The house was always dark, he added, because of the wire mesh screens to keep mosquitoes out, but of course, it did not really work.

"I must get back to the Legation now but I shall return for tiffin — that is lunch, you must get used to the way we say things here.

"You'll see, the rain will stop soon, and things should look brighter. But if you go into the garden, do watch out for snakes."

He took her hand again, and looked at her earnestly. "Try not to feel too overwhelmed."

Watch out for snakes, she repeated to herself, when she had been shown to her room, which had a wide bed shrouded in mosquito netting, a table with a greenish brass lamp and very little else. Try not to feel too overwhelmed.

Easier said than done. She peeled off her gloves, sat on the bed and began struggling with the buttons on her boots as tears started to run down her cheeks.

She was hot, but her wet clothes felt cold and clammy, and she had never been so lonely in her life. The door opened a crack, and a nutmeg coloured creature leaned in, bearing a tray with a cup and teapot. "Maem Lili? Fie". The woman, who despite her short and spiky hair, appeared to be her maid, advanced into the room on her knees, put the tray on the bed table and kowtowed.

Oh no! Flashes from Mrs Leonowens' memoirs about subservient slaves went through Julie's head, and she recoiled, surely, surely, this woman had not been bought for her, like an animal? "Please Fie, do get up," but Fie grabbed her ankle and began to nimbly wrestle the boot buttons off without using the hook that Julie was offering her, clucking disapprovingly at her footwear and shaking her cropped head at her sodden stockings. Then she motioned that she was to turn around, unfastened the buttons of her bodice and began to unlace her corset.

Julie sighed with relief. "You cannot imagine how good that feels, I had no one to help me on the ship from Singapore, and I had to sleep with my corset."

Fie smiled as if she understood, then went to open the door to a procession of servants who crouched through to the bathroom with cans of water, smiling shyly and bobbing their heads at her as she sat there with her dress and stays undone and trying to cover herself up as best she could. How many were there? Julie wondered helplessly, losing track of the blue turbans and white jackets. Five, at least.

Meanwhile, Fie was rummaging through her travel case, pulling out underclothes, commenting loudly at each garment and shaking her head. Finally she found a muslin dressing gown, shooed out the last of the servants, none too gently stripped Julie of her dress and pushed her into the tin bathtub, and began soaping her with a huge sponge as if she were still a child.

Strangeness, Julie decided in surrendering herself, was probably the best cure for silly tears.

*BANGKOK, MAY 4*TH *1890*

Darling Mama, Mon cher Papa,
I trust you received the telegram I sent you to announce I arrived safely, Cousin Michael very thoughtfully provided me with a form and one of his servants took it to the post office.

He has been kindness itself, and his house is very comfortable. I have my own maid, called Fie, so Darling Mama, you must rest assured that I am well looked after, although she does not, from what I have gathered, approve of my clothes. So you see, there really was no need for me to bring a maid along, and Michael was right when he said in his letter that it would be easy to find one here.

As I said in my short and hurried note from Singapore, Mrs Bowers invited me to stay at her lovely house for five days before I caught the steamer to Bangkok, and she and her husband both insisted in seeing me off and entrusted me to a Danish couple they know who were travelling on it. I shall write to Aunt Rose to thank her and ask her to convey my gratitude to their common friend for introducing me to Mrs Bowers who could not have been a more attentive travelling companion.
Julie grinned wryly as she wrote.

In fact, Charlotte Bowers, a modern and rather flighty young woman who had travelled to England to settle her son in his boarding school and was returning to join her husband back in Singapore, was certainly not a chaperone Darling Mama would have approved of, but when she was not flirting with sweaty and stammering young colonial officials in white duck suits, she was a fascinating and outspoken source of information on a variety of subjects, from married life — "Of course, most men have a native girl on the side, but if your husband does, just ignore it." — to life in general in the colonies. "Never wear your stays at home, you'll get prickly heat before you can say the words" or, "Most women are cats, so beware of them, all the more so as you are French, and will be scrutinized and gossiped about. Some, however, can be great fun, just be careful in your choice of friends."

I told you when I wrote from Port Said that I had suffered from seasickness in the Mediterranean, and I must say that it was blissful to sail the Suez Canal where the water is so very calm, and after that, I seem to have found my sea legs, as they say on board.

I did not have an opportunity to see much in Singapore, although Mr Bowers insisted that I try the famous curry dinner at the Raffles Hotel, followed by a dance and it was indeed very pleasant. I was quite entranced by the gardens of the hotel, with curious trees which, I am told, are called "traveller's palms." I shall ask Louis if we might not be able to send you some young plants for the villa in Biarritz.

Mrs Bowers invited me to visit again, perhaps at Christmas, which she thinks is not much celebrated in Siam. I was a bit disappointed that there was no news from Louis awaiting me on my arrival, but I expect he is far from any post office and cannot write.

Michael has just arrived and I must go down for tiffin — you see, I am becoming a true colonial lady!

My beloved parents, I miss you very much, as well as Victor and Augusta, but I beg you not to worry about me. And when you are tempted to, just remember that I am happy!
Your daughter,
Julie Gallet

Chapter II

It was to be a dinner party just like any other, and probably more tedious than most. Certainly, Daphne Lucas-Sauvain expected no great pleasure from the evening, the Boisenfray who were hosting it were very much a part of this new, rich and brash Paris society she could not help but find rather vulgar.

But Henri Boisenfray was a banker, actively involved in political circles, and keeping on the right side of power was of the greatest importance to Auguste, her husband.

And one never knew, did one, whom Julie, their bookish, rather difficult and as yet unmarried daughter, might meet at such a soirée?

After all, if a man were clever enough to dismiss her prickly manner, he might notice that she had the most lustrous grey eyes, and a lovely smile — when she did smile, of course. And the fact that she was a very wealthy young woman should certainly atone for her unconventional ways.

Of course, Auguste spoiled the girl outrageously, and just laughed when she claimed that all of the suitable gentlemen she had been introduced to thus far bored her to tears, and that, frankly, she would rather remain single than mince and preen and simper to attract someone she could not imagine spending an evening with, much less a lifetime.

"She is just like you," he said fondly, "a woman of strong opinions. But you will see, someone is bound to change her mind one day."

To which his wife always replied irritably that her strong opinion was that women should marry, and marry well, and certainly before the age of twenty-four, although, to be fair, Julie barely looked a day over eighteen, a saving grace which Daphne certainly ensured was made the most of. And she often behaved as if she were even younger than that. Her chignons collapsed, she walked too fast and put her heels through her hems, bumped into furniture, dropped things, spoke too loud, and disregarded all of her mother's patient lessons in deportment.

All in all, she took after her father's side of the family, although, naturally Auguste disagreed. "There are no bookish women on my side," he shrugged. "To me, Julie is the perfect eccentric English lady."

Really, how ridiculous...

She sighed. Well, perhaps this evening. After all, the Boisenfray were known to attract the wealthy and fashionable, and there was sure to be a smattering of intellectuals, writers or artists and such, and conversation should be lively, although, perhaps, not entirely *comme il faut.*

And they kept an excellent table, as Auguste always said.

So she prepared herself with her usual care and made sure Julie wore the cream silk chiffon dress the seamstress had delivered last week, and of which Julie had said despairingly at the last fitting that it made her look like a ridiculous schoolgirl. "Nonsense," was her mother's retort, "it makes you look young and innocent."

"A truly remarkable achievement, as I am neither."

To which Daphne snapped "When you speak thus, you think you sound worldly but actually sound very foolish. Remember that, Julie, when you are tempted to talk too much."

Thankfully, this evening, Julie was not inclined to be her usual stubborn self. She merely rolled her eyes and put down her book when she was told about the invitation, and how she was to dress. "But I shall lend you my pearl combs for your hair," her mother called from her boudoir to her retreating back.

With her mind still on the novel she had been reading in the afternoon, Julie let the maid put up her hair, and resigned herself to waste another evening on uninteresting chitchat with uninteresting and fatuous young men who would all seem to be wearing the same grey silk cravats, tight coats and shiny boots.

At the last dinner party she attended, having rapidly exhausted her neighbour's opinions on music or literature — he had none, except that he disapproved of Zola, but rather enjoyed some of Victor Hugo's poetry — she had taken perverse delight in stating her views on women's suffrage, which had led to a general and acrimonious discussion around the table, and several days of reproaches on Mama's part and sulking on hers.

This evening, she would try to keep to safer subjects.

The Boisenfray dining room was extremely grand, with modern gaslights and heavy silver candelabras illuminating the old-fashioned oil paintings of still-lifes and village scenes their hostess had waved at vaguely when the conversation had turned to the new wave of the so-called Impressionists. She herself admired Monsieur Monet's paintings, she said with a tinkling laugh, though they always made her feel her eyesight was failing. "And one of Monsieur Cézanne's landscapes would bring summer to this dark old house all year round." But her husband refused to replace these depressing somber Flemish things, claiming it was better to have a horse or a flower look like a horse or a flower. Every one chuckled politely.

After exchanging some halting sentences with her right-hand neighbour, an ageing journalist who only wanted to talk about plays she had not seen, Julie decided to concentrate on the first crayfish of the season. As she struggled with the slippery shells, she overheard some quiet words to her left, which were not even addressed to her ".... and which of course is better known as 'Siamese tears' ".

She dropped her fish fork on her plate with a clatter of china and turned to the speaker, putting a hand on his arm to attract his attention. "I beg your pardon? Siamese tears? What *are* Siamese tears?"

The young man smiled at the interruption.

He had a blond moustache, and must have been as unimportant as she was, as he had been placed next to her, at the far end of the long table. She had barely given him a look so far, except to note that his jacket seemed very new. For that matter, he had hardly acknowledged her except for some perfunctory words as they sat down, which she thought rather rude.

She was probably louder than she had intended, or perhaps it was the noise of her fork, because all of a sudden, all the other diners had fallen silent and were staring at her in the shimmering light of the many white candles.

"She is quite charming", she heard Madame Boisenfray whisper to Mama behind her fan, with an approving look taking in her face bare of even the merest dusting of powder, not to mention rouge — it makes a girl look fast, Mama had decreed, and really Julie, your freckles are not so visible. Of course, if you will go out in the summer without a parasol — as well as her silly girlish gown with its modest high-pleated collar and tight sleeves. She, Julie, personally thought that at twenty-four, she could certainly have a bit of a décolleté, though perhaps not as much as their hostess whose plump and bared bosom encased in cascading ruffles of grey silk trimmed with pink lace irresistibly brought to mind a preening pigeon-hen.

"Yes, Mademoiselle, I was talking about the ancient art

of perfume making, Siamese tears is the common name for benzoin, a resin that has been used since Antiquity. The name comes from the way the resin runs down the trunk as if the tree were crying.

"Ah, I can see that, as most ladies, you are more interested in perfumes than in the way they are made…"

She was starting to stammer that it was the name that had attracted her, when her Papa cut in and asked in his usual blunt and hearty way: "Are you in the perfume business young man?"

Mama winced — she would no doubt ask later in the carriage driving them home "Really, Auguste? In the perfume business? Must you always be so coarse?" — while Madame Boisenfray was hastening to explain that Louis Gallet, her nephew, was actually a botanist — "he is leaving soon with the Pavie Mission"— whose father, her brother—in—law, had a perfume laboratory, "although," she added in some embarrassment and a tight smile at having to admit the connection, "he is a pharmacist. As we have no children, Louis is as a son to us."

But Auguste Lucas-Sauvain ignored his wife's disapproval and their hostess's explanations, and was musing aloud. Hmm, the perfume business must be very profitable nowadays, with all those young shop girls and seamstresses and whatnot who were earning money, and were probably as willing to spend it on fripperies as our own wives.

"Women are all the same whatever their station in life, aren't they?" he asked with a knowing laugh.

As the ladies exclaimed and protested, the young man turned to Julie and commented very low that his aunt probably did not know whether to be more offended about being compared to a shop girl or being called a spendthrift.

"And what about Madame, your mother?" he asked.

Her mother was English, Julie said quenchingly. She was not prepared to engage in banter of that sort.

"Ah, England, our great friend, and even greater rival in Asia, though to whom we owe so much," Louis enthused, oblivious to her put-down. "Did you know that it was the Royal Geographical Society that financed Mouhot's expedition to rediscover the extraordinary ruins in Angkor?

"Angkor, in Cambodia?

"Come, you have surely heard of it!"

Of course she knew of Angkor, she did read *L'Illustration*, in fact there was an article with lovely sketches of the temples quite recently, she said, but there was no mention of the British support for whoever it was. Anyway, they were straying from the subject.

"About Siam, Monsieur, you mentioned procuring benzoin, I think you called it, from Siam? Forgive me, but I had not really heard what you were saying."

"Not from Siam, Mademoiselle, from Laos.

"Calling benzoin Siamese tears is actually misleading. Styrax trees, from which the resin is extracted, mainly grow in Laos."

Benzoin was his passport to freedom, he added in a dreamy voice. It was only when he had promised to procure some in Laos at a good price for his father that he finally obtained his blessing to join the Pavie Mission, and he was embarking for Saigon in three months and from there, Laos.

It was through his dear uncle's political connections that he had secured a place as a member of the expedition. "Because, as you can imagine, I am not a well-known scientist yet, and so many who are worthier than I were clamouring to be part. Strings needed to be pulled."

Her mouth half open in wonderment, Julie was gazing at him. Imagine, she had barely ever thought of Laos as someplace real, it was but a name she sometimes saw in newspapers, and here was someone who was announcing as if it were the most normal thing in the world that he was going there in three months.

She did not want him to stop talking. What was the Pavie Mission?

"A scientific and map-making exploration of the Mekong basin. I hope to be able to find new species of plants so as to describe and catalogue them, and perhaps send samples to the Natural History Museum, because the climate and geology of the highlands and northern plains of Laos are very different from Tonkin and therefore the variety of plant life is bound to be different as well."

Around them, conversations had also turned to Asia, the gentlemen were noisily debating the need to extend French colonies in Indochina, Julie's father being of the opinion that colonies generated more trouble than money.

"Remember the war in Tonkin, and what that cost us, including the downfall of Jules Ferry? Do you want a return of the riots we had two years ago, when people took to the streets against our presence in Asia?

"Mark my words, beware of Deloncle and the Colonial Party diehards, they shall ruin France!"

Monsieur Deloncle was a friend of his, retorted Monsieur Boisenfray coldly, and to his mind, the people could see no further than the tips of their noses. France needed colonies in Asia to counterbalance the influence of England, which he insisted on calling "perfidious Albion" despite his wife's ever more insistent coughs and the hard stares coming from Mama who was not enjoying the way the evening was unfolding.

"Please, please God," thought Julie intently, "please do not make her want to leave as soon as we get up from the table. I am actually enjoying a conversation with a young man, for once. Although, a botanist and the son of a pharmacist... really, it's hopeless."

He would never be wealthy enough for her father, or well-born enough for her mother, Daphne née Cartwright, daughter to a cotton mills empire in Manchester and boasting several titled relatives.

While summering in Biarritz, she had met, then married, a man who had made a fortune in the foundry industry and discovered only once they were officially engaged that he was "self-made", as he explained earnestly but in broken English to her father. He naturally omitted that only recently had he become "Lucas-Sauvain" by tacking his father's Christian name to his surname, which was far more impressive than plain old "Sauvain".

He started in life as a smelter of brass and iron scrap and then, with hard work, cunning and luck, had gradually expanded his business to become a supplier of France's Imperial army. The latest war, although by God's will France was defeated by Prussia, had nonetheless been good to him.

"Nothing wrong with making your money yourself," was the view of Mr Cartwright, who reminded his wife that her own grandfather had been a spinner at one of the family's mills.

And by then, Daphne had fallen in love with this kind, gruff man who was in awe of her, although she never could shake the feeling that she had married beneath her, and had resolved to certainly never let her daughters make the same mistake.

"Are you particularly interested in Asia, Mademoiselle?"

Julie hesitated. What should she answer?

Her mother and her governess had always told her that gentlemen feared and avoided blue-stockings and constantly mentioned her younger sister Augusta who, according to Julie, had never had a single thought in her head but at eighteen had recently married an impoverished and charming young baron from Normandy seeking a dowry to keep the roof on his rather damp and depressing manor.

On the other hand, she also thought of her brother Victor's disparaging comments about the empty-headed young ladies he danced with at cadet balls, and decided that as she was neither empty headed or a true blue stocking, she might as well be truthful, and shook her head.

Not really, it was just the word Siam. She had recently read a book by an Englishwoman who was governess to the children of the King of Siam, and had found it fascinating. Also, her mother had a cousin whose son had just been sent to Bangkok as a diplomat.

"That is why, when you said…"

But he was not listening to her. Staring at her face, he suddenly ran a finger along her cheek, and whispered that she seemed to be sprinkled with pollen.

"You look like a lily when it is in full bloom, Mademoiselle."

Startled, Julie looked around to see whether anyone had noticed such a forward gesture, all the while blessing her Mama for having ruled against powder. Never had she been compared to a flower.

Aware of her embarrassment, he sat back and gave her a longer, more considered look: "Actually, you are more like an owl, with your huge serious grey eyes. Please, no, I didn't mean to offend you." And seeing her stricken face, he grabbed her hand under the table.

"Don't be offended, please, owls are lovely. What about a cat? Cats have huge grey eyes as well. Is a cat better?"

Wordlessly, she nodded. Cats were indeed better.

Of course, she *would* be teased by both her parents in the carriage going home, but nonetheless, it was better than being upbraided for speaking loudly at the table, or devoting herself only to her left-hand dinner partner while ignoring the gentleman to her right.

"He was looking at you as if you were a rare breed of flower!" and "Did he invite you to go on plant collecting walks with him, carrying a magnifying glass and a flower press?"

Was it really that extraordinary for a young man to be interested in her? Strangely, it never seemed to occur to anyone that she in turn had been interested in him.

And the following Saturday when Victor came to lunch, he looked down at her and said: "I hear my little sister has made a conquest. A herbalist no less!"

Julie barely raised her eyes up from Kipling's latest book, *The Man who would be King*, which her cousin Iris had sent her from Manchester.

"He's a botanist", she replied in a cool voice.

"But the son of a perfume maker", her father added thoughtfully. "There's money in perfume nowadays, with all those shop girls having money to spend. And, Boisenfray said he was as a son to them... The Boisenfray have money as well. Pity he is leaving for the colonies."

The colonies, now that was the way of the future, Victor commented approvingly, stroking his moustache. So, her new swain would soon be steaming away to the Orient?

No herbalist in the family, then. Their Julie deserved better, even though she still seemed to prefer books to real life. And what was this one about? Adventures in India?

"Really, kitten, do grow up!"

He took it out of her hands, and waltzed her across the living room.

Her heart swelling with love, his mother watched him dance.

Fortunate would be the girl who took his heart, and please God may he never be sent to the colonies, not even Algeria although it was so very close.

"No," she said firmly, "no herbalist — oh, very well, Julie, no 'botanist' in the family. Nothing to worry about."

So little to worry about, in fact, that when a letter arrived that very day inviting Mademoiselle Lucas-Sauvain to accompany Louis Gallet and his sister Marie to hear a Berlioz concert at the Châtelet the following afternoon, no one objected, although Victor did hoot with laughter.

Better still, when they were ushered into the drawing room, both Mama and Papa seemed to make every effort to welcome Louis and his sister and to put them at ease, well, put Marie at ease, Louis was as perfectly confident as he had been at his aunt's table, and was chatting easily with Papa about shipping benzoin from Saigon to avoid Siamese taxes versus shipping it from Bangkok to avoid heavy overland transport costs, "because, as you know sir, the Mekong is not navigable along its full course and it is necessary to bypass the rapids and the waterfalls."

Auguste Lucas-Sauvain, who did not know, nodded sagely.

Marie was complimented on her choice of hat, a small, maroon bonnet trimmed in black to match her dress. "I do think it rude to block the view of other people with those huge plumed affairs." Mama said, though Julie could tell from her narrowed eyes taking in the unbecoming colour of Marie's outfit that she found the sister's attire perhaps lacking in elegance. The Boisenfray patronage obviously did not extend to this rather mousy young woman. But she was not showy, Julie was relieved to note.

Mama hated showy dress.

Louis was advised by Mama to enjoy the concert, he would not hear anything comparable in the years to come, she had read in Mrs Leonowens' memoirs that Asiatic music was unbearable to western ears.

Although perhaps in Saigon, there might be concerts, Marie dared to venture, but Papa opined with a laugh that Saigon was a city of reprobates, cutthroat adventurers and however many missionaries needed to attend to their souls and make converts. He could not imagine Berlioz being performed for them!

In any case, he would not spend more than a week in Saigon, Louis answered pleasantly, as Marie blushed and went back to playing with her reticule.

Julie jumped to her feet and started pulling on her gloves to put an end to the conversation as her mother began quizzing Louis about sleeping on pirogues and campsites.

"The son of a dear friend of mine, Sophie Meadows, that is Lady Arneys now, is an officer in India, and she writes that at times, with the heat, they must sleep under the stars...", but with a apologetic smile, Julie firmly hustled them out of the door before Mama had finished her sentence.

When they were finally seated in the hansom cab that was waiting at the curb, Louis turned to her and said: "I could not leave without trying to seeing you again, but I did not imagine your Mama would let you come this afternoon."

Julie could not meet his gaze, and mumbled that she had been surprised as well, but "you see, it is because they know you are leaving. Otherwise..." She looked up in embarrassment as Marie politely peered out of the window.

His parents had said the same, when they heard that he was proposing to invite Mademoiselle Lucas-Sauvain to a concert, Louis said with a smile, thinking of the conversation over breakfast that day. "How old is the girl? Twenty-four or twenty-five? Why is she not married yet? What are her parents thinking of?" his father wanted to know. And his mother, who had been talking to her Boisenfray sister, replied that the answer was obvious: she was rich enough to be choosy, but not quite enough to restore the fortunes of a duke or an earl, and rather spoiled by her parents, *n'est-ce pas*? Was she pretty?

She looks like an owl, he had said, huge grey eyes and freckles.

"My parents asked what you were like, I told them you look like a lily."

Julie did not really like Berlioz, she thought his music was shallow, and facile, with no real romantic breadth, and would have much preferred Mendelssohn, or Schumann, or Saint-Saëns at a stretch, but was so happy she could have even sat through Wagner. She replied to Marie's questions that indeed, she played the piano, although badly, but loved music. Particularly Berlioz. From their front row at the balcony, they peered down as Marie busied herself reading the programme.

Would Louis not miss all this? Julie asked, showing the red and gold of the concert hall, the crystal and bronze chandeliers, the elegant women filing in, some wearing inconsiderate huge plumed hats.

"Yes, probably, in fact how could I not?... But getting a place on this mission, or on one like it, has been a dream of mine since childhood. I am so tired of the lives our parents lead, focussed only on trade, and profit, and money — No, do not misunderstand me, I was not thinking of your family more than of mine. But I would like history to record that I did something more with my life than invent a new scent or hair tonic, even if it is only to give my name to some species of creeper or fern.

"So, as you say, it might be a sacrifice to leave all this, but a very small one."

"How I envy you!" she whispered passionately.

He gave an incredulous laugh. Envy?

She envied his future life with none of the comforts of civilization, no music, or balls, or real conversation? With only the food they could carry or catch, and nothing but a few books to keep him company at night?

Yes, she envied him, she countered stubbornly. She could not imagine a more beautiful life, a more useful or interesting one, devoted to learning and...

She faltered somewhat, (she could just hear her Mama, "Must you always show such emotion in conversation, Julie, really? It is most unattractive in young ladies.") and rather self-conscious continued that it made her realize how dull her own life would be, but what was she to do?

A woman could do nothing.

The lights were being dimmed, and Marie was putting away her programme as he grasped Julie's hand and whispered in her ear that she could bring comfort and love and the blessing of her presence at the campsite to a lonely explorer, and be by his side.

By the end of the intermission they were engaged.

Two months later they were married.

"So," Julie concluded, "that is how I find myself here, whereas I was to marry a Wendell, at least, according to my father, or a genuine, albeit penniless, Count according to my mother.

"Of course, they both realized it was not to happen, not at my age. But still, to have me go so far away... I didn't exactly break their hearts, but I certainly dashed their dreams.

"They resisted the match as long and as hard as they could, but finally, it was Papa who gave in first. He said to Mama that he wanted two things for me, that I should find happiness in marriage, and that I should be wealthy enough never to have to depend on a husband — yes, that was rather modern of him, wasn't it? And that already having the second, he was not about to prevent me from having the first. And that I would not be gone for more than a couple of years.

"So Mama, after two weeks of taking to her room with

smelling salts, reluctantly and with misgivings, finally gave me her blessing."

She drank a sip of water — she was not to worry, the servants boiled it carefully, Michael had told her — and added with a laugh:"Of course Papa turned my marriage into an opportunity and invested in Louis' father's perfume business. And Mama is now devoting her energy to finding a suitable fiancée for Victor, someone who will produce sons to take over the foundries.

"But Victor will not marry yet, he claims he is much too young, and that an officer's life is too unsettled.

"Nor will he leave the army, which is what both our parents would love him to do. Poor Mama and Papa, they do seem to have been lucky only with Augusta..."

Michael smiled back at her. "I could have predicted Victor would be a soldier from the way he fought me on the beach all those years ago.

"And as to you, I am certain your dear Mama rued the day someone gave you a book by Isabella Bird to read — *The Golden Chersonese*, I wager?"

"Oh, *Unbeaten tracks in Japan* as well? I never read that one.

"Mrs Bird has a great deal to answer for, although I am convinced most of her readers just sigh and wish they could travel, and you are probably one of the very first young ladies able to follow in her footsteps.

"I am amazed that you should have wanted to come to Siam though, after reading Mrs Leonowens' memoirs, with her descriptions of a tyrannical king, downtrodden slaves, and a benighted and destitute country.

"Of course, you realize she invented a great deal of what she wrote, including her own influence over the king."

She raised her eyebrows in amusement, no she hadn't known, and pushed away a stray lock of hair blown out of place by what Michael had explained was called a punkah, a dusty cloth curtain hanging from the ceiling above the table and that was pulled to and fro to create a breeze. The source of the motion, Julie saw, was a child seated cross-legged on the floor tugging on a long cord.

How strange and shabby everything was, she thought, chipped china, dull and dusty crystal glasses, butter sitting melted to an oily orange puddle in its tin, the sticky bottles of Major Grey chutneys, and the careless table setting on the stained cloth despite the many servants serving the food ... Would she ever feel comfortable here?

He fell silent, and they both looked away from each other, at a loss for something to say, aware of weeks ahead of sharing countless dinners and wondering if they would ever become friends as they toyed with the rice pudding and jam Pon had just put before them.

Finally, when for want of any other subject he asked how she seemed to have escaped the idiotic family tradition of giving girls only flower names, she brightened and giggled.

"Yes, my Papa put his foot down and refused to have my sister or myself called Poppy or Violet or Iris... He said it was ridiculous and unchristian, particularly your mother's name, Zinnia... I'm sorry."

"No, don't apologize, my mother thinks the same, she has always hated her name. But nonetheless, she was not brave enough to buck family tradition, and as you know, I have a sister called Dahlia.

"And now, my dear girl, let us organize your life here, shall we?

"You said you expect your husband before the end of the month, and then what?"

Well.... Julie hesitated. She had received no news from Louis to confirm or cancel his arrival sometime in the next three weeks. What she had hoped would be to find a house, where she could live for a year or two, and where

Louis could join her when he was in Bangkok. Was it possible?

It was not impossible, Michael mused. Of course, proper houses a European could live in were costly, but there were some to be had. However, he suggested, would she not prefer to stay here?

It would be certainly safer — not that there ever had been any attack against a western woman in Siam, he hastened to add. But her husband might prefer to have her live with a relative, and certainly her parents...

"Oh, certainly my parents, and I must say your letter was a godsend, thank you so much for writing to Mama, it made the departure so much less fraught and dramatic... But, and I really do not want to sound ungrateful as I am most touched by your invitation, I must confess that I was rather looking forward to being mistress of my own household.

"And would you not rather have this unknown French cousin safely at arm's length?"

He gave her a long, considering look. She certainly did not seem what his mother would have called "missy", by which she meant affected, simpering, arch young women. She wore no rouge, her hair was simply braided and coiled on her head — but that might be due to deficiencies in her maid rather than to her simplicity — and her tea gown, from what he could judge, did not appear excessively Parisian and fashionable.

Nonetheless, he decided it was somewhat early in their acquaintance to be entirely honest.

"Nonsense... It would be quite pleasant to have the company," he lied.

However, there were some things that she should know about the way the French presence in Siam was perceived.

"The French are suspected of no less than attempting to gain control over the country, after having taken both

Annam and Tonkin. And, just so you know to speak carefully about your husband when you meet people here, the Pavie Mission is seen as a spearhead of a military invasion of Laos. Why do you think its main purpose is mapmaking?

"Of course, I believe, as you do, that Louis is a scientist and only interested in his research. But unfortunately, I cannot say the same of Monsieur Pavie. "

Feeling stunned, she put down her spoon and stared at him.

"What are you saying? That it is unwise for you to have me as a houseguest?"

He shook his head with a reassuring laugh. "No, because in everybody's eyes, if you stay with me here, you shall be seen as being also — in fact, mainly — British.

"But it might be preferable to play down the Pavie mission, and to highlight the benzoin export, that's all. Of course, it is up to you to decide.

"There is no problem here with French businessmen or priests. Incidentally, there are quite a few of *them,* good men as a rule, and very devoted to their flocks. It is the colonialists in Paris, and their tools — and I think Pavie definitely is one — who are viewed with mistrust.

"Come, old girl, do not look so downcast!

"It is really not important, and way above your head and mine....

"But as we are invited to dine at the Legation Friday evening, I just wanted you to be as well informed as possible, so as not to put a foot wrong.

Do you really not want to finish your pudding? It is not very good, is it?"

She did not answer at first, feeling confused and uneasy at what she had just heard, but strangely pleased at having been treated as someone who could be told such things, as an equal, as Louis treated her. At home, her Mama and Papa would have just told her what to say or not say without giving her any explanation.

She realized suddenly that this was the beginning of a new life, where she could, and would, speak and think as an adult woman, which of course, more often than not, meant keeping her own council.

So she nodded her understanding, picked up her spoon again, then discouraged by the stone-like stewed rice, pushed away the dish.

"Really, I am sorry to have to say, it is quite awful. And if I am to stay here —and mind you, I have not said I would, I would like to discuss it with Louis when he comes — if I do stay, I could teach your cook to do something better."

BANGKOK, MAY 10TH 1890

My dear Amélie,
I have hardly had any time since my arrival, and I wanted to write a long letter, not a mere note, to tell you all about my new life here.

It is not that I have been exceedingly busy, but everything takes so much time, just obtaining a cup of tea — the servants are most attentive, and willing, but making oneself understood is difficult.

Where shall I start?

Very well, I shall begin with the crossing.

As you know, I boarded the ship of the Peninsular and Oriental Company, or the P. and O. as the habitués call it, in Liverpool, after spending a fortnight in Manchester with my Aunt Rose and cousin Iris. (My Aunt made me buy the most ridiculous tropical helmet, which apparently nobody uses here, and which I shall burn as soon as it dries, it got soaked when I arrived!)

The ship was rather splendid, and most of the passengers were English headed for Singapore. I was entrusted to a friend of a friend of my Aunt, a very amusing lady who invited me to stay with her at her beautiful house on Orchard Road, and I was quite entranced at the comfort of life in the tropics! Imagine vast, cool rooms, a myriad of Chinese servants, and lovely dark, exotic furniture. (Which was why, as I shall describe later, I was all the more disappointed on arriving here…)

I had a most spacious and airy cabin, a stewardess saw to my every need, and life on board is very sociable. There was dancing every night, concerts, even a fancy dress ball. I went as a gypsy, but unfortunately, it was not a very original idea, as three other ladies did the same.

My first impression of Bangkok was not very favourable, it was raining, I had not slept on the ship from Singapore, and everything seemed strange and frightening. I confess I almost regretted not giving in to Mama and Papa's entreaties to stay and wait for Louis' return at home with them, but once I was rested, I felt much better.

My cousin Michael is kind, and hospitable, he seems older than his years, for he cannot be more than thirty, but there is a freshness and a lack of pretension that appear at unexpected moments, and makes for interesting conversations. His house…. Well! It is as unlike the house I stayed at in Singapore as can be. It is large, with a most pleasant screened verandah on both floors, which means I have a terrace opening from my room where I am served my morning tea, and is situated in a spacious, overgrown garden, full of unknown shrubs and flowers — unknown to me at least, but Louis, I am sure, will be able to tell me their names. Michael says there are snakes as well, though I have yet to see any.

But, despite the six or seven servants he has at least, everything is in a state of neglect, dust covers every surface, and my dear, you cannot imagine the food served at his table! Tasteless, overcooked, and thoroughly English. I have volunteered to teach his cook some more palatable dishes. But oh! Amélie, the state of the kitchens… It is not that they are dirtier than the rest of the house, in fact, but the meat is stored in canvas bags dripping with blood hanging from hooks, to protect it from the flies and avoid it being carried off by rats and the legs of tables and chairs all rest in pans of kerosene so as not to have everything covered in ants. Nonetheless, the flies and ants are everywhere else. Ice, which is delivered daily, is kept in a huge tin-lined box, with the fresh fish resting on it, and staring up at you as you raise the lid. Everything reeks of fish, actually, as dried and salted fish and rice are the staple of the servants' food. The cooking is done in an enormous pan directly on the flame, and the heat in the room is quite overpowering. The cook, a small, swarthy, smiling man offered me a huge cleaver when I tried to make him understand I wanted to see to the way dishes are prepared, and I fled. Evidently, I shall need to learn some Siamese if I want to effect any change there.

It has rained every evening since my arrival, except for the first day when I arrived in a violent storm, but the mornings and afternoons are sunny, and very hot.

Yesterday, we were invited to dinner at the British Legation, The Minister-Resident, Captain Jones, is a very old-fashioned, hearty gentleman who was most welcoming, although I cannot say the same of his wife, who looked me up and down disapprovingly, perhaps because I had used rouge?

Most of the ladies were dressed in locally-made silk, which is very beautiful, but stiff, and does not drape well. I was wearing my sea-green peau-de-soie, which was perhaps a bit decolletée for the event (all the more so as I was seated next to the French Bishop, Monseigneur Vey, who kept twisting his head so as not to have to gaze down my bosom) but I was complimented on looking so Parisienne by a French lady, Madame Malherbe, whose husband is agent for a large ship insurance company. She is very pleasant, and has offered to take me to visit Bangkok in her landau. Her name is Léonie, and although she is much older — she has two daughters at school in France — I believe we shall become good friends.

There were also two Siamese princes, who spoke perfect English, and seemed very grand — or perhaps they were just shy — along with their tutor, a young English gentleman named Joseph Caulfield James who was most attentive until Michael whispered to him that I am married.

The food, once again, was inedible, sardines on toast — indeed, Amélie, can you imagine? — were served as a savoury after the pudding, which was a blanc-mange and even worse than what we ate at the convent. Madame Malherbe and I exchanged secret smiles when this quite extraordinary titbit was brought to the table.

Remember when you and I were girls and talking about our future life,

and homes, and how we would arrange them, the food we would serve at
our tables, and how we would do everything differently from our Mamas?

Who could have thought that my first home might be in Siam?

And indeed, I shall need to do everything differently from my Mama, I
cannot imagine her dealing with a native butler who has black teeth, (it is
something they chew, says Michael) or a lady's maid who crawls everywhere
— but who, I must say, is very skilled at fixing my hair, and takes it upon
herself to choose my clothes in the morning, always leaving out my stays as
she disapproves of corsets. She soaks some deliciously scented waxy white
blossoms in water for me to wash my face, and always has some ready to pin
in my chignon, so I start the day in a cloud of perfume.

I mentioned I need to start learning Siamese, and Michael has arranged
for me to take classes with a lady called Fanny Knox, whose mother was a
Siamese lady, and whose father was British consul to Siam some ten years ago.

Hers is a most romantic and tragic story; she married a noble from the court
here, but without beforehand securing the King's permission. The country
was still governed by a regent, as His Majesty was not yet of age, and the regent
was said to have wanted Miss Knox to marry his own son, her husband was
accused of rebellion and put to death. She lives in straightened circumstances
and is grateful for teaching opportunities. I shall tell you more when
I have met her.

Do you not have the feeling I am living a story from a novel? I do.

I am still awaiting news from Louis, but as they say, no news…

My dearest friend, I wish you were close to me to share my impressions
as I shared yours when your little Violaine was born.

My love to her, and to your dear husband, and of course, to you.

Julie put her pen down, and looked dreamily out of the
window.

She had become used to her room with its whitewashed
walls and spartan furniture, and at least Fie and she were
in agreement over the need to keep everything dusted and
clean. She had even grown to accept the little lizards that
climbed the walls and made a dry, coughing sound once

she had been told they ate the mosquitoes that managed to make their way through the screened windows and buzzed around her sleeping net at night.

But she was restless.

Her days so far were spent in writing letters, and waiting for them.

She had not ventured out of the house except once to walk up the *soi* to New Road, with Fie in tow, looking at everything with curiosity and interest.

She had peered inside cauldrons where glistening ham hocks bobbed in a cinnabar-coloured broth redolent of — what? she wondered as she sniffed the fragrant steam — ah, yes, star anise, and perhaps, cinnamon? how strange — and gazed at piles of pineapples and bananas tumbling from huge baskets, along with what must be some other fruit, small hairy scarlet or glossy purple pods and accepted one with a smile from the toothless vendor who cackled at her when she weighed it experimentally in her hand, surprised by its hardness.

With a laugh, Fie showed her how to split the rind to extract its sweet white juicy flesh that tasted of nothing else she had ever tasted before — flowers and lemon and perfume.

"This," Julie declared happily to herself as she grinned at the crowd that had formed around her, "is what fruit must taste of in heaven."

But Fie pulled her sharply aside to avoid being struck by a reeking barrow piled and festooned with dried cuttlefish and she yielded, dazed with the noise, the erratic traffic of carts and porters and the stares of the people milling around. Further on, she recoiled in horror at a makeshift dentist stall where a stoic looking young man was having a tooth pulled, watched by a laughing crowd as he gripped the arms of the chair he had been strapped to.

She leaned over a display of strange looking bundles wrapped in some sort of leaf being prepared by a wrinkled old crone. Fie picked one up, unwound the leaf to show her the filling of dark sticky rice studded with meat.

With some misgivings Julie tasted, and smiled her approval to the old woman who was peering at her with a worried expression. It was certainly tastier than anything served at Michael's table.

She tried to pick her way along the sidewalk but her skirt kept getting snagged on the baskets of the fruit vendors and after she had stepped into several muddy puddles so as to not be jostled, she decided it might be best to return to what she supposed should be called home.

But now that she had a friend, she would be able to see more of the city and to start, she would drop off her card at the French Consulate, which had been described to her as one of the most beautiful houses in Bangkok. Michael told her she could use his little buggy whenever she wanted, but she did not really know where to go on her own. Well, all this would change soon, she would go to Miss Knox's, and to visit Madame Malherbe, and perhaps explore one of the bazaars with her.

For there were surely things to see, and to do, were there not?

Michael smiled when she told him of her need to be more active.

"Ah, you have not yet turned into a lotus-eater, as so many of us do here.

"Enjoy your boredom, it means you are still one of the living, and not a dreamer as we are." And he reminded her of the land of the lotophagi in Odysseus, where life was spent in a delicious state of uncaring.

There was a scratching at her door, and Fie crawled in, refusing to walk normally despite Julie's many gestured entreaties. "It's a sign of respect," Michael explained, "an inferior cannot have his or her head above that of a superior. That is why servants bob their heads when they pass in front or behind you." Likewise, he had instructed her in doing the *wai*, the lovely formal salutation done by bringing hands together as if in prayer.

"To *wai* a superior, and that might be an elderly person, or a Prince or Princess, your hands must be at eye level, for equals at your lips or your heart. You bow more or less deeply, yes, like that, gracefully. Never, never *wai* a servant, it would embarrass them."

Fie flattened herself in front of Julie, and waved a flimsy piece of paper in one of her outstretched hands, clucking excitedly.

Could it be?

Yes, it was, it was a telegram, much folded over, and damp from having passed from sweaty hand to sweaty hand.

Julie swooped on it, and read, then read again, her eyes suddenly brimming with tears of joy.

Her real life was about to begin, for the telegram managed to convey the promise of happiness in all its unromantic wording: "Arrived Ayutthaya, two days away. Stop. Counting minutes. Stop. Louis."

Chapter III

Oh the blissful memories of the fortnight spent with Louis...

Julie felt they could sustain her for as long as his next absence would be. From the first delicious moments of his arrival until his departure, Bangkok had felt bathed in a golden light even when the monsoon lashed the roof and rattled the fretwork shutters, and they lazed in her bed, listening to the dripping leaves and coughing lizards and whoops of a bird who bellowed his love out at sunrise.

She had been quite shocked at seeing him at first, his face so thin and drawn with hard, leathery sunburnt patches on his cheeks and forehead.

He had grown a straggly beard, which scratched her cheeks when he gathered her up to him as if he never would let her go. "Pavie has one, so we all do the same," he admitted ruefully as he released her, and she ran her fingers along his face. "And you know, it is really not possible to shave every day."

He was Louis still, but a different Louis, less dreamy, more certain, a Louis whose eyes always seemed to see further than the quiet dusty rooms of the old house, who used strange and new words he said were Lao, and talked of building a nation where there was none.

He told her of Chinese tribes called the Black Flags and the Red Flags and of the war they waged on the defenceless Lao, and of malevolent Siamese officials who harassed the mission, and listening to him was just like one of the adventure stories she loved to read, but much more exciting than Allan Quartermain for the hero was her own beloved Louis.

He would jump out of bed naked and rummage through his portfolio of sketches to show her a drawing of the curling, furled leaves of a blue blossomed creeper called the butterfly pea — "I am still looking for the small silver grey orchid I shall christen the Julia Galletia"— and she would watch the sunlight dapple the muscles of his dear, poor, thin back, and bless her luck for having been granted a husband such as this, and not, say, Jean-Baptiste, husband of Amélie who was indeed a good man and was doctor to the insane at the Pitié Hospital, but always smelled of creosote and did not want to talk about his work "so as not to upset the ladies".

Then Louis would come back to bed and describe the pirogues pushing their way up the great Mekong river, when all the men, natives and French alike, had to heave hard on the oars to pull through rapids, or how they cooked the fish they had caught, threaded on a stick over the flames of a campfire. And travelling on elephants, those patient, intelligent and loyal animals, who carried great loads and bathed playfully with their carers in the evening.

"And the villages, Julie, you never saw such poverty and yet such happiness."

The children running naked, the maidens with their dark, liquid eyes, dressed only in a length of cloth, so elegant, the old men and women, so dignified. And Pavie, who was at home with all of them, and spoke their language, and loved them as they loved him.

"He is truly a great man."

Michael too listened with pleasure and interest to Louis' descriptions, and asked many questions. It was only the second or third evening, over an excellent bottle of wine — for if the food served at his house was still tasteless despite her efforts, his wine cellar was remarkable — that he ventured to comment on the purpose of the expedition. "Some believe that it aims at preparing a takeover of Laos by the French, what do you think?"

Louis put down his glass, and returned Michael's look. "If it were, would that be such a bad thing?"

Was Michael aware that the Siamese crown imposed an iniquitous rule on the poor Lao?

"Would French rule truly be preferable?" Michael asked equably. And ...was there not a treaty signed some thirty years ago which recognized Siamese traditional suzerainty over the Lao provinces and in any case over the west bank of the Mekong?

Louis shrugged with a self-deprecating smile. He was a botanist, not a diplomat and not the man one should ask about treaties, but from what he had been told, the one Michael referred to applied to Cambodia, not Laos.

"Well," Michael replied, "that's true to some extent, but again, the lands on the west bank and traditional suzerainty certainly extend to Laos."

Pavie thought the river was not the best demarcation, Louis countered, and that it made no sense. Furthermore, with the French presence in Annam, the balance of force in the region was changing and suzerainty could be changed as well.

So Michael was right, Julie thought uncomfortably, but decided as she had determined, to keep her own counsel. After all, who was she, a mere woman, to judge on the affairs of states?

Michael said no more, and filled their glasses.

He accompanied them to the East Asiatic Shipping office where Louis arranged for the first shipment of benzoin to his father in Paris: "I must keep my side of the bargain!" but of course, did not go with them to the French Consulate where Pavie himself was staying with Monsieur

Hardouin, the Consul. The great man kissed her hand, and complimented her on being so brave as to follow her husband to these "still savage, but very endearing lands", and Monsieur Hardouin congratulated her on her determination to learn Siamese.

He himself was a bit of a scholar, he admitted with a blush, and was at present compiling a Franco-Siamese dictionary.

"It is a difficult language, but I am sure you will find it rewarding. Your teacher, however, Madame Knox, well, Baroness Preecha as she calls herself, rightly, I suppose... after all, she was married....

"Please don't let yourself get embroiled in her... crusades, one might call them.

"She is so bitter still, against the Regent, Lord Srisuriwongse, and even against His Majesty who could not stop the execution of her husband, she has vowed to reform the judicial system singlehanded.

"But when she is not following her own obsession, she is really quite charming company. She speaks French as well, having spent quite a long time in Biarritz.

"In any case," he added pointedly, pushing his hands down into his pockets and rocking on his heels, looking down on her with a long measuring stare, "language would be no problem, you are half English through your mother are you not?

"Yes, of course, and you lodge with your relative, my colleague from the British Legation? But, I am certain," he finally added with clumsy and somewhat forced courtesy, "you are a most loyal Frenchwoman."

Julie raised her eyebrows in some surprise, and murmured, yes, of course she was, and on the subject of dictionaries, did Monsieur le Consul have any suggestions?

But he excused himself, and went off to whisper in Pavie's ear.

From that moment, Louis avoided discussing the Laos Mission with Michael.

They dined together at the Oriental Hotel, and drank champagne, and it was almost as grand as the Café de Paris. Louis ate as if he had been starved for months and kept looking around at the displays of purple orchids and the silver and the crystal as if he had never seen anything quite as beautiful, and Julie teasingly said he would no longer know how to behave at his aunt Boisenfray's table.

"Well, I cannot say I behaved that well before, stroking your cheek as I did. And what I really wanted was to kiss you, which I shall do now."

They hired a boat to go upriver to the Temple of Dawn, and hand in hand climbed the steep steps of the main *prang*, glittering and shimmering in the morning light with the encrusted shards of thousands of Chinese porcelain plates to stare at the city on the opposite side of the great river.

Bangkok was spread at their feet like a dream from a fairy tale, a folly, a riot of golden spires piercing the misty sky and Louis described the view of Luang Prabang from Mount Phousi.

"It is so much smaller than here, but oh, so beautiful. I shall take you there, God willing…"

Michael took them in his buggy to visit the royal area around the Palace, with its high white crenelated walls hiding what Michael described as a an enchanting haven of gardens and temples and palaces. He then guided them through the neighbouring Wat Pho and Louis knelt at her feet to help her remove her shoes. Together they explored the many quaint courtyards, marvelled at the immense reclining Buddha and to make merit dropped alms in the forty metal bowls lined along the wall. Julie gazed at the serene smile caught in bronze, thinking of tortured

Christs and weeping Madonnas while Michael explained the beauty of Nirvana.

"It is the realization that all suffering comes from craving, from need, and seeking release from them, no, not like the lotus-eaters I told you about, lotus-eaters are just sloths like me, enlightenment is a spiritual quest and it takes many life-times to achieve it."

Louis kissed her hard on the mouth. "My Julie is far from it, then. She has too much appetite for life."

And now, he had left, and she had spent a day bravely trying not to cry, and then moving listlessly around the house.

She discovered that if she herself wielded a duster, the servants would be ashamed and do the work themselves. "But sir," Pon told her, "Khun Mykin said touch no. So we touch no." And Michael confirmed that he had been afraid of their breaking his lovely celadon pieces, and truly, had not noticed or minded the dust.

"Fancy, my dear, these were made in Sukhothai, oh, it's a city to the North, I went there once last year, it is so, so beautiful, and was the capital long before Bangkok existed, so this bowl is over a thousand years old."

He caressed it lovingly, running his thumb on the greyish-green ceramic. She shrugged — the bowl was not particularly attractive to her, and promised she would see to the objects herself.

But once the house had been cleaned to her satisfaction, she seemed to have lost her restless energy, constantly postponing her first class with Mrs Knox.

She always felt tired, and sleepy, and when she was not napping under her mosquito net, spent long hours reading some of Michael's novels she pulled from the shelves. She could not even bring herself to fight with the cook, as food had lost any appeal. She only seemed to want the delicious mangosteens and bananas Fie peeled for her, and drank the herbal tea she prepared.

Michael was getting quite worried. He had become very fond of his lively and unconventional young cousin, and disliked seeing her so listless.

"It has been two months now since Louis left. Would you not like to surprise him with your ability to speak some Siamese when he comes back? He thought it might be sometime in October, remember?"

Yes, Michael was right, she should send a chit to Madame Knox.

But…next week, perhaps?

Surely, she would have more energy next week. It was this terrible heat, and the monsoon that tired her so. Or perhaps she had become a lotus-eater? she suggested with a laugh. Michael cocked his balding head at her, and said nothing.

Léonie Malherbe came to tell her of a house not too far away, to be vacated by friends who were moving soon. "It would be perfect for you, chérie. Close enough even to walk to your dear cousin's if you wanted to, and not too large. Furnished, naturally, but not badly."

Julie sighed. Of course, it was what she had wanted, and Louis had left it up to her to decide. But she had not the energy to even see the house, and the idea of hiring servants exhausted her.

Léonie drew her chair closer.

"Listen to me, you are pale, and growing thinner, and I fear you are going to turn into one of those sour, sallow Memsahibs who only pine for England. You are pining for your husband, that is normal.

"But show him he did not marry one of those useless girls!

"Unless… let me ask you. Do you feel unwell in the morning?

60

"No? Well, not all women do. But still ..." and she leaned forward, and whispered some indiscreet questions into Julie's ear, watched her blush, and sat back with a knowing smile.

"Ah. Only a bit of blood, you say. I have heard that it may happen.

"You should see a doctor, and I can recommend one, whom I absolutely trust, but I know what he will say. You, my dear, are going to become a mother."

"I was thunderstruck." Julie confided later that day to an exceedingly embarrassed Michael, in whose experience expectant mothers hid their condition under an artfully draped shawl, nine months later produced a baby, and certainly did not discuss it with any male within earshot.

"I thought that I was sick, with a tropical disease, or... well..." she blushed, "never mind what I thought. It just never occurred to me, which just shows you how little I have been told by Mama. And Amélie, my closest friend, said she knew when she began to be sick every morning even when she had not eaten oysters, and did not mention..." She gasped, covered her mouth, then laughed, her eyes dancing behind her hand.

"I am so sorry Michael, you will just have to blush with me, or get used to my telling you such things.

"I really do not see how I can be all maidenly and modest with you when we are sharing a house. It shall probably do you a world of good.

"But can you imagine Fie knew all along? Léonie called her in to give her instructions as to how to care for me — you are right, I really must start my lessons, I was so envious at the way she was chatting away in Siamese — and Fie said she had been feeding me this special tea, and bananas to keep my strength up for the past two months. And she never thought to tell me!"

Michael called for champagne, a bottle of which was

always kept on ice next to the staring fish. "The servants know everything, and are probably laughing their heads off at us right now. We must celebrate, my dear. Such delightful news!" Julie was bubbling on, her eyes brimming, they must send a cable to Louis, did Michael think that "care of the French Consulate in Luang Prabang" it would reach him? And oh! Her parents, but a letter would be better.

She grasped his hand. "I am so happy, Michael. And I shall not move house, at least not yet, later when the baby is born I shall need to, I don't think you will want to have a squalling infant around, I wonder if Léonie's friends' landlord might be willing to wait a few months?"

While her happiness and love for life seemed to have returned, Julie's energy did not. She started her classes with Fanny Knox, however, and came back exhausted the first day, barely able to summon the energy to climb the verandah steps. When Michael returned from the Legation in the evening monsoon downpour, he found her collapsed on the sofa with Fie busily fanning her. She was very pale, but delighted with her new friend.

"Such a charming woman, so knowledgeable, but oh, so sad. Her husband executed on trumped-up charges when her child was barely a few weeks old. Can you imagine? And she spent several years in Biarritz, it's surprising I never even had a glimpse of her, but she says she lived very quietly.

"And yes, before you ask, we did more than just chat, she started teaching me some useful phrases, and gave me a schoolbook to begin studying the alphabet... It seems difficult though."

Although Julie had been told of Fanny Knox's straightened circumstances, she recounted, she could not help but be astonished at the modest little wooden house set in a small garden with chickens scratching the dirt, and only one servant to show her in and serve tea.

Surely, a woman who had been married to an aristocrat, and whose own Siamese family, from what she had heard, was highborn and wealthy, would not live in such dismal surroundings?

But Fanny, after welcoming her effusively, gestured apologetically at the grim room with its cheap furniture and explained that all her money had been confiscated when her husband had been arrested. She maintained her household, her son and stepchildren by selling whatever jewels she had left and of course, by teaching Siamese to *farangs* — although, she added with a laugh, there were not that many who were prepared to make the effort.

She was still petitioning the King to have her late husband's estate returned to her, but... although the regent had been dead for several years now, his family remained the most powerful in the kingdom, two of the king's wives were his daughters, and the resentment generated by her marriage had not yet disappeared.

It was a huge scandal, she had been forced to flee the country only to return once the regent had died, and her father, who had been the British consul at the time even lost his position and was forced to retire in France where he lived until his death.

"But enough of my sad story," she said with a smile, "let us talk about you."

Julie had smiled in return, feeling drawn to this friendly woman with a lovely, serene face, and golden skin. She might have been Spanish, or Italian, for she hardly showed her Asian heritage, except perhaps in the shape of her clear, dark eyes and her ebony hair. She was taller even than most French ladies, and moved without that gliding sinuous grace Julie had come to associate with the Siamese, both women and men, impatiently hitching up her plain blue cotton sarong, as she rose to pour more tea.

They had chatted happily for over an hour, exchanging memories of Biarritz and Paris, before Fanny began to coach her in her first phrases in Siamese, patiently correcting her accent, and advising her to start learning how to decipher the alphabet.

"I have put my lesson to good use," she told Michael proudly with a yawn, "and asked Fie for lemon juice when I returned home, and she understood! And this evening, I told cook to prepare Siamese dishes, but —" she enunciated the following words carefully "*mai phet* — that means not too spicy!"

Then she closed her eyes, and, to Michael's astonishment, was instantly asleep.

The cable to the French consulate in Luang Prabang miraculously reached Louis, and his letter was delivered merely four weeks after the news had been sent.

"My darling lily-like wife,
I am always afraid when I receive a cable, and confess to have hesitated before opening it, fearing tragic news from my family. (And why? since to the best of my knowledge, there is no earthly reason to worry about them.)

But nothing could have made me happier, I believe, than to read that we shall truly be a family at the end of March. However, I now worry about you, and beseech you to take care of yourself and of the child you are carrying.

Have you seen a doctor? Pavie says that there is one attached to the French consulate, and that there is a laying-in hospital run by French nuns.

It is such a comfort to know that you are safe and well-looked after by Michael in Bangkok, here there are disturbing reports of cholera up-country, and I blush at how naïve and uninformed I was when — remember, my beloved? — I talked of having you by my side at the camp, and I bless your dear parents for absolutely forbidding it, which I am sure Pavie would have as well. Laos is no country for European women, and certainly not expecting mothers.

Please do not exert yourself overmuch, and remember that my happiness rests in your hands.

Ever since the day I met you, you have brought me nothing but delight, and I thank fate for having blessed me with your love."

Julie folded the letter and put in back in her pocket to read again and again. She felt too tired to reply immediately, although she had so much to tell, about her lessons, and about the doctor whom Léonie had recommended, a German man with kind eyes behind a pince-nez who had told her that her exhaustion would pass as she entered the fourth month of her pregnancy, and who had advised her to have the child at a Siamese hospital recently founded by the King. "The French nuns run a lying-in clinic, but it is for native women, and I do not think it would be appropriate for you. And you could, of course, decide to give birth at your home. But I shall attend you wherever you decide to go for your confinement."

She had not decided yet, the end of March seemed so far away still, nothing but a hazy future she could not begin to imagine. Surely, there must be things to do, to organize, but what?

Baby clothes to make, and ample dresses to order for herself?

She would ask Léonie, and Fanny also, because Mama would no doubt demand to be informed of every detail.

But before that, there was Louis' visit to look forward to, although she hoped her condition would not yet be too visible so as to be able to dine out and go on excursions with him as they had done during his first visit and that, as the doctor had promised, she would feel like doing more than drag herself from nap to nap.

She picked up the primer Fanny had given her, and

once more focussed her eyes on the lovely unfamiliar characters, mumbling their names, *Ko Kai, Kho Khai, Kho Kwai, Kho Rakhang, Ngo Ngu...* until she fell asleep.

The doctor had indeed been right, her energy did gradually return and she emerged from the dream-like state that seemed, as she laughingly told Michael over breakfast one morning, to have cast a Sleeping Beauty spell on her.

"Although," she confessed, helping herself to the eggs she had spurned for months, "I still find it hard to believe I shall become a mother. Imagine all I shall have to tell my friends when I return to Paris, when they talk about their experience of motherhood! Eating rice porridge with Fie's special herbs for instance, or the fresh coconut water she makes me drink, and green mango slices to suck on to stimulate my appetite..."

"Why don't you write it down so as not to forget?" he suggested. "Perhaps you could turn it into a book. It would certainly make for better reading than Mrs Leonowens' pious and bigoted observations."

She laughed. Not a book, surely, who would want to read about being *enceinte* in Siam? But yes, he was right, there was much she would not want to forget.

"*Bangkok, Kingdom of Siam, September 28th 1890.*

I am writing for you, my as yet unknown but already beloved child, so as to be able to tell you about life as it is lived in what is to be your country of birth, because you will have forgotten everything about it and we shall be back in France when you are old enough to understand these words.

Or perhaps we shall be elsewhere, living new adventures?

Your dear papa is soon to be here, within a very few weeks, coming all the way from a land called Laos on a boat going down a river named the

Mekong, then riding elephants and bullock carts to join another river called the Menam to embark on another boat.

Imagine my little prince or princess... I hope to take you to ride an elephant as well.

We live in a charming house in a big garden, with your Uncle Michael, who is very funny and kind, but who is terrified, although he will not show it, of having a baby around.

What he does not yet know is that he is to be your godfather as well. Your future godmothers are a French lady named Léonie and a half-British, half Siamese lady named Fanny, and your nurse is called Fie, she has short hair and black teeth, and she told me she is to care for you, as she has no children of her own. Are you not lucky to have such an unusual family?"

"*SEPTEMBER 29*[TH]

My first real soirée in Siam, at the Malherbe's splendid, splendid house and you were safely tucked away under my bodice. I think no one noticed that I am growing a bit plumper, and I wore one of my tea gowns, because Fie absolutely refused to do my stays. She says it will crush you. Never mind, many ladies were in flowing dresses, what with the heat, it is permissible.

It was a brilliant affair, Léonie played the piano — a concert grand, no less, which I begged off touching, and rightly so, for she is quite a musician herself, and you would not have wanted your mother to be humiliated before all these people, many English and French ladies and gentlemen, a few German. Monsieur Malherbe, whom I had met but once, is a gentle bear of a man, with even bigger mutton-chop whiskers than your Grandpapa. He must be a doting father, for he spoke to me of nothing but his two daughters whom he misses very much.

The dinner was exquisite, with both Siamese and French dishes, and beautifully served, none of the slapdash performances Pon gives us here, where the soup often overflows the dishes, and things get dropped on the cloth. I was so envious of the way Léonie manages her household, and begged her to give me advice, but she just says it comes with experience and that I should concentrate on resting for now. So I shall go and rest."

"*OCTOBER 3RD.*

I am so upset I do not know what to do. I cannot even tell Louis what occurred and must put words on paper if I cannot speak them out loud.

It was during naptime this afternoon, and for once, I could not sleep because of a burning, uncomfortable feeling in my stomach. Doctor Hertz had warned me that it might happen and said drinking cold water should help, so I went down to look for Fie, when I heard moans coming from Michael's room. Thinking he too was ill, I opened the door, and saw him on his bed naked with one of the younger servants, a boy called Chit. I must have gasped — I know I gasped, because he looked up, and oh, the look on his face before I ran away... Never shall I forget it. I rushed to the bathroom and vomited, again, and again, as if to get rid of the horror coming up my throat, and I am sure Michael heard.

How can I face him? What shall I do? He has now left for the Legation, but when he returns... what shall I say? I had heard, of course, of such men, but my own cousin, whom I thought I knew... and Chit... He always smiles so winningly, he is a beautiful youth, with eyes like a girl's, and I had indeed noticed — what? That he always speaks to Michael in a tender voice, that he did seem to be learning more English words than the others... Do the other servants know? Do they laugh at me behind my back, thinking me a fool? I want to flee, but where can I go?"

"*Later.*
Michael came back, and rapped at my door. He was as pale as I felt, and looked ashamed, and guilty, and so very sad.

He apologized for putting me in what he said was an unbearable position, but asked me not to inform Mama and Papa, so as not to embarrass his family."

She had never imagined anyone could look so distraught and heartbroken, when he sat on her bed. His round and earnest face had lost its usual genial expression and he ran his hand through his sparse sandy curls before taking her hands and pulling her down to sit next to him. He spoke in a low, gentle voice.

He was so sorry she had ... well, had discovered his secret and apologized for not being more discreet. It was really unforgiveable of him.

But he would not, could not, apologize for what she had caught him doing. He knew that the world saw it as evil and immoral, but it was not true.

He had always been this way, well before he knew there were boys such as he. Even in Biarritz, during that summer holiday, so long ago, he said with a rueful laugh, he played at war with Victor, but only because it was expected of him, and Victor was to him a completely foreign creature, as different, he felt, as she, Julie, had been at the time.

Throughout his childhood, he was puzzled, and frightened and did not know whom to turn to, somehow realizing that it was not to be discussed. And then, as he grew older, he met others like him, and oh, the relief to know he was abnormal yes, but was not alone.

"You know, there are far more of us than you suspect, I am sure you have met quite a few, and admired others without knowing. You must have heard of Oscar Wilde? Yes, indeed, and many others. In fact, if it were so uncommon, do you think there would have been laws against those who are as I am? We are born that way. In fact, one of my first..." he hesitated, "... friends... was a divinity student at Oxford, and said that he could only see it as God's plan for us. We seek love where we may, and love knows no rules.

"When you and Louis fell in love, you knew it went against everything you had been taught to want, but nonetheless, you followed your heart. I do the same, my dear."

His mother, although she did not know, could not know

for sure, must nonetheless realize it in her heart. Never, in any of her letters, had she mentioned the possibility of his finding a suitable girl.

"She loves me, you see, as I am." he said simply. "And I had hoped that someday, in time, I would explain it to you, and you might as well. Which is why I am so desperately sorry you will now want to leave this house."

Julie had listened in silence, tears running down her cheeks, her hands limp in his. And now, gazing at his downcast head, she tried to put herself in his place, and to express what she really felt rather than what she imagined her Mama, and most everybody would say, if they knew.

"Why?"

"Why? Because that is who I am, Julie."

She shook her head. No, why should she leave?

He was still Michael, she was still Julie, she did not see what had changed, except that he now could be more honest with her. He had become her dearest friend, and if she had indeed wanted to flee at first, it was because she was ashamed, because she had never thought, because she had never wondered, and because she did not understand. And now she did.

"Still," she offered in a tremulous voice, "it might be better, when Louis comes, if Chit and you were more discreet?"

"I am mortified that Michael left my room thanking me for understanding whereas I have been so uncaring to him up till now, never wondering why there seemed to be nobody in his life, not even the 'native girl on the side' that Charlotte Bowers said all the men have in the tropics.

It is I who should have asked for his forgiveness instead. I am truly a selfish person, and a very poor friend to someone who opened his home to me so generously.

I so much hope he did not see through me, and did not realize I am… well, not repelled, never that, but…. Well, yes, that.

I must be honest with myself if I cannot be truthful to him, and not just write that it makes me uneasy, or uncomfortable. But again no, I am NOT, I think, repelled by the act itself — but by the intimacy it implies. To me it is a parody of what Louis and I have, and Chit, for all his smiles and sweetness does not, I am sure, love Michael in the least.

Does he comply with his embraces because Michael is his master?

Surely not, I cannot imagine Michael being threatening.

And is it easier for Michael to engage in their — I suppose 'practices' is as good a word as any — because Chit is a native?

Is that what bothers me? Should I be as uncomfortable if Chit were a girl? Or is it because Chit is almost a girl, and behaves as one, in fact much as I do with Louis, the caressing voice and lowered eyes in public, promising so much in private?

How I wish I could talk to someone, but there is nobody, not even Louis, certainly not Amélie in Paris. In fact the only person I can imagine discussing this with is Michael.

Oh what a muddle...

I feel that I have aged ten years in a day."

Chapter IV

My dearest Mother,

We are all heartbroken here, as the day before yesterday we received word that Louis, Julie's husband, died somewhere near the border of Siam during his trip from Laos.

There is very little information about the circumstances, not even when it happened exactly, but it would seem he contracted a virulent case of malaria or cholera and the fever carried him off in three days. Julie received a telegram from Monsieur Pavie, the head of mission, who was in Luang Prabang and how long before he himself was informed, we do not know. Louis was travelling to Bangkok to spend some time with her before having to go off into the hinterlands for several months.

We do not even know where his body is buried.

She fainted when she opened the cable, and Pon, my head servant, ran to the Legation himself to bring me home. Since then, she has been almost catatonic, not crying or speaking, just sitting up in her bed, staring in space, and refusing all food and drink, and I really fear for her life and that of the child she is expecting. The doctor came and said we must get her to eat, but I do not know how, and it is useless to invoke the child as she does not seem to hear or care.

Although I knew him but briefly, I found Louis a very engaging young man, full of life, with a most appealing way of seeing everything as new and interesting, and who never appeared to view native people or cultures as being in any way inferior or less worthy than ours. He was full of extraordinary stories about his travels in Laos, and still seemed bemused at his good fortune in being sent there. And of course, he worshipped Julie.

If she lives, which I pray she does, I wonder if she ever will recover.

She has become very dear to me. I have never told you how she transformed my life here, making my house hospitable and sunny and airy, ensuring cook feeds us tasty meals instead of the swill he thought all Englishmen wanted, and filling our evenings with conversation and her constantly amusing and unconventional observations.

All the servants feel as I do, and Fie, her personal maid, has not left her bedside, crouching like a patient and loyal — I was about to write animal, but that would be demeaning to the love and devotion the woman shows-- her eyes full of tears but always fixed on Julie's face waiting for a sign that her spirit has not left us.

I have sent a cable to her parents, and asked them to notify Louis' family, as I do not think Monsieur Pavie has, and shall of course follow with a letter to Auntie Daphne in a few days in the hope that I shall be able to report some improvement in Julie.

Darling Mother, when you do write as well, please tell her as I shall, that she mustn't insist that Julie return to France immediately. The doctor strenuously advises against it for the moment, as she has not the strength for a long sea-journey.

Your loving and very sad son,
Michael Crawfurd.

BANGKOK, NOVEMBER 17*TH*, 1890

My dearest Mother,
Thank you for your very sweet letter, and for inquiring about Julie's health.

She is better in the sense that she now takes food and drink, but still will not leave her room, except for the All Saints Day Mass at Assumption Cathedral celebrated by the French Bishop, Monsignor Vey, when special prayers were said for Louis' soul. She had never seemed particularly devout — in fact, had been to the Cathedral only once before, and only at the insistence of the Bishop — but nonetheless it seems to have given her some form of solace, at least for a while.

She refuses all invitations, which is quite proper as she is in mourning, but I think that a quiet luncheon en tête-à-tête with her closest friend, the wife of a long-established French businessman, would do her good.

But she turns even that down, although she will see the lady in her room, as well as another, who gave her Siamese lessons. I can only wait, and hope, that time will help. Fie, her maid, never leaves her, and I think it is she who brings Julie the greatest comfort, although they can barely talk to each other.

Her parents have cabled that they want her to return to France, but she is in no state to travel.

So it seems the child will be born here.

Michael put down his pen, and sighed deeply.

His life, only six months ago, had been so pleasant, so predictable, despite of course the precautions and pretences to keep its less acceptable aspects from becoming known. But he was used to that, just as he had become accustomed to his hearty, and in his opinion, rather shallow and vulgar colleagues with their talk of women, and cricket, and tennis, and their supercilious manner towards his more bookish interests in the native language and culture — and after all, as they said patronizingly, he was related to John Crawfurd, linguist and diplomat, he of the famous diplomatic mission to Siam over fifty years ago. It must be in the blood.

And now... Louis' death had shattered them all, and transformed his vibrant and loving cousin into a mere shadow of herself, coming so soon after her discovery of his despicable weakness for Chit, Chit's body, his skilful hands and his unworthy heart.

Everything had changed when Julie had arrived. He did not blame her, how could he blame her?

But part of him, to his shame, longed for her to be well enough to board a ship, sail back to France, and relieve him of this dreadful responsibility he felt to her and the child.

What would happen should she not survive the birth?

He lay awake at night worrying, and during the day sought escape in his work, writing yet another report on what they were able to garner of the French push to foment unrest against Siamese control in the Khmer provinces of Battambang and Siem Reap .

Did the Foreign Office even read them, he wondered?

He signed the letter to Mother, and put it with the packet of dispatches to be sent under diplomatic seal.

This evening, he had to attend a dinner given by the Foreign Minister.

"We are all most sorry for your cousin's loss, but this is work, my boy," the Minister-Resident told him in his usual forthright way, when he called him to his office. "Of course, I am going meself, but that rat Hardouin is sure to be attending, you speak the lingo, I don't."

He sighed and fiddled with his paper knife. "Be a good lad, and try to get him to say something, anything we can report back to London, and let their Lordships see if they can make out the intentions of those Goddamn Frenchies.

"Of course, Whitehall don't give a damn about Cambodia and Laos. Written them off, you know... Their current obsession is whether Paris plans to build a railway to Yunnan, now that we've announced ours from Burmah.

"The Foreign Office won't get off my back about it, as if we somehow could read minds in both Paris and Saigon... it's all about the access to the coal mines in Yunnan, they say, as if that should make it easier to guess.

"Oh yes, thank you my Lord, oh, if it's about coal, then of course, I'll just check my crystal ball... Sometimes, I really wonder what they are thinking...

"Use your cousin's husband's death as an excuse to talk to Hardouin — well, yes, I know, not really done. Anyway, you'll think of something."

He would just have time to go home to change, and spend a few minutes in Julie's room. Lately, every evening, he had taken to reading aloud to her, and although she hardly reacted, he knew she listened, he even glimpsed a faint smile at the familiar opening words of "Pride and Prejudice", and he felt guilty at failing her tonight. Well, it just could not be helped.

She only nodded when he told her, sitting on her bed, with her pale, restless hands in his and when he asked: "Did you eat anything, my dear? You know you must eat," she turned to Fie, uncertainly. "Chicken soup, I think. I don't know. Nothing has any taste."

He got up from the bed, leaned over and kissed her forehead.

"Things will have a taste again someday. Believe me. I know."

And, goaded suddenly by the polite and yet dismissive way she raised her eyebrows in question, could not help asking with some heat, "Do you think you are the first to have ever lost someone dear?" then sat down again heavily, surprised at his own outburst.

"Forgive me. When you grieve, as I should have remembered, you are always the first to have known such pain. Good night, my dear."

Julie sat up against her pillows, needled into shame by his tone.

"No, don't go yet, tell me."

So he recounted the death of his first real love, his greatest love, his only love, in the Transvaal, during the Boer War, nine years ago.

"There is not a day that I do not think of James. He was... handsome, yes, but also gifted, sensitive — much too sensitive, you see, for military life, but it was the family tradition. After Oxford, he joined the King's Royal Rifle Corps, because it was expected of him, and Heaven forbid he go against his father's expectations."

He learned of his death in the papers, a list of casualties

of the battle of Ingogo. What a ridiculous name for a place to lose such a beautiful and promising life...

He could still feel the paper stiff in his frozen hands, the letters of James' name dancing before his eyes, and reading it again, and again, and again, and this helpless rage at having to find out with all of *The Times* readers. Nobody would have informed him of course... and there was nobody he could mourn with, so his grief was kept as secret as his love.

"But of course, it was easier in many ways. Pretending to others it never happened meant that I could pretend to myself." He sighed and appeared to blink back tears, then got up, and leaned over to kiss her forehead.

"Enough of my maudlin ramblings, I must get changed. Try to sleep, darling girl."

When the door closed behind him, Julie lay back. She did not need to try to sleep, in fact, she could barely stay awake most of the day. Fie no doubt added some of her special herbs to the soup she made her drink, and that was fine with her. The less time she spent awake, the less she needed to think about the endless future stretching ahead without Louis.

Returning to Paris, to that same old life she thought she had escaped. And with a child, to make sure she would never stray again.

At least Michael had only his love to mourn. She was also grieving for the life she and Louis had imagined, talked about during their lazy mornings when the sun splashed the bed and he had twined his fingers in her hair, planning other travels, South America, perhaps, teaching their children to feel at home with other cultures, to look at the world in wonderment and delight.

What would their child's life be now? She could see a little boy in a sailor's suit going on well-bred walks in the Parc Monceau, listlessly pulling a toy horse on a string along the orderly paths, escorted by a grim-faced nanny scolding him for dragging his feet in the dust. Or a little girl with a wistful look on her face watching her cousins play soldiers on the beach in Biarritz, and being chastised for getting her dolly covered in sand.

And herself, foist by Mama on increasingly aging and fat widowers, wearing black for three years, then grey, and then lavender forever... She closed her eyes and escaped in sleep.

With the dry, cooler season, it was easier to face an evening wearing tails, a starched collar, tie and waistcoat, but still, once they had drunk the obligatory champagne, wines and brandy, all the *farang* guests would begin to sweat like workhorses, Michael mused as he settled into the Legation boat to ride upriver to the Foreign Minister's palace. The Siamese diplomats, however, would remain very cool and suave, and gaze at them under lowered lids – except of course for some of the younger princes who still fancied themselves at Oxford or Heidelberg, and became rather boisterous as they matched the foreigners drink for drink.

Well, he should restrict himself to one glass, and make sure Hardouin had plenty.

In any case, he did need to express his condolences to his French colleague. Whatever one might think of the purpose of the Pavie Mission, it was known to produce excellent scientific material – the Royal Geographical Society never failed to quote it as an example when trying to raise funds for its own endeavours – and the loss of its botanist was sure to be keenly felt.

Wondering what could be the purpose of this hastily convened dinner, he hardly noticed or enjoyed the boat ride, usually such a pleasure with the people bathing, the thousands of houseboats open to the evening breeze and offering glimpses into the lives of ordinary people, floating markets in full swing, and the mingled smells of spices and incense reaching him over the smell of rotting vegetation and worse coming up from the depths.

On the landing deck, he was handed a glass even before he had quite regained his balance, and was ushered in to be met by the Minister, Prince Devawongse himself, an affable, portly, youngish man whose unfailing serene smile was often at odds with his watchful and harried expression. They both *wai*-ed deeply, but Michael bowed lower as befitted a half-brother of His Majesty.

"Ah, Khun Mykin," murmured the Minister in his erratic and perfectly serviceable English, "So happy you come. I hear you lose husband of Madame cousin. So sad. Please say."

Was there nothing the Siamese did not know? Michael wondered, not for the first time, as he expressed his thanks. He would convey His Highness' sympathy to his cousin.

"She teach French at Palace to girls, yes? Better than nuns, yes? She keep busy, no more cry."

Michael shook his head with a regretful smile. His cousin was not well, and...

"Yes, yes, baby no come not yet," cut the Prince impatiently. "But then, yes?"

Well, he didn't think that...

But the Minister had already turned away to greet the senior member of the diplomatic corps, the American Minister Resident, Jacob Child, who, wherever he was, always managed to look as if he wished to be elsewhere, particularly when he attended these strange glittering Siamese affairs, as if he couldn't face one more evening of incomprehensible protocol and slippery conversation.

Michael strolled away towards Hardouin, who was chatting uneasily with De Pina, the French Legation chancellor, and interrupted them with a smile.

Try as he might, he could not dislike the French diplomat, with whom he often felt he had more in common than with his own colleagues. Born in Penang to a coconut and nutmeg planter, Hardouin was an oddity compared with the average envoys from Paris, spoke fluent Malay and Siamese, and, Michael was certain, English, for how could he not, although he never admitted to it.

And if he ever was exasperated by the sometimes atrocious French his British or other colleagues spoke to him, he certainly did not show it.

"I wanted to express my condolences for the death of Louis Gallet. The sorrow my family feels at our own loss has not made us forget that it also is a loss for France." He offered with some diffidence, as both men turned to him expectantly.

Hardouin nodded. Indeed, he was a most promising scientist, was the guarded reply. And how was Madame Gallet? Madame Malherbe had recently given him rather alarming accounts of her spirits.

As Michael was beginning to answer, the Siamese Foreign Minister called them all to sit down.

"So informal tonight, but all friends," he said. "Welcome, welcome."

And then he dropped his genial and hazy demeanour to show himself as the accomplished diplomat he actually was, and his English became far clearer, confirming what Michael had always suspected.

He had an announcement to make: there were to be administrative changes in the eastern provinces.

His Majesty and his ministers were grateful to all the foreign friends of Siam, he confided in his best silky manner, particularly France, who had taught them so much about provincial administration, and such advice was helping them learn how to become a more modern and better governed state.

Therefore, His Majesty had ordered him to announce the appointment of three of his brothers as Khaluang Yai- — or permanent High Commissioners, he translated with a smile — to the border provinces of Nongkai, Champassak and Nakhon Ratchasima.

Now which brothers could they be, Michael mused — after all, King Chulalongkorn had at least eighty siblings — but quickly returned to the Prince's speech when he heard him say that such exalted royal nominations could only reinforce the authority of the Crown to the very edges of the Kingdom.

In parallel to the administrative reform, the garrison posts would also be strengthened, both in terms of troops, which would be doubled, as well as building improvements according to the latest military theories, — "for which we owe a great deal to the advice from England and France," His Royal Highness added with a little half-bow towards both heads of missions — "therefore ensuring a better and more effective Siamese rule over Laos, greater security for Laos itself, and Siam, of course."

"Clear message to France, what?" Captain Jones whisperedvery audibly, and Hardouin turned and glared at him.

"Good borders, strong borders—" the Foreign Minister continued, "are what ensure good relations between neighbours. You, friends of Siam, have taught us this."

He opened his hands with a self-deprecating look.

"We needed to learn such lesson, because our borders for so long have only been set in the minds of our people; an old man can say 'I am a Lao, but I am also a subject of

Siam.' But his son might say — How do you know this? Show me where Siam starts and ends. Show me where France begins. Now, we can show him and everybody, with stone forts, and soldiers with guns, lest anyone be tempted to make any mistake."

Hardouin went very pale, and Child, the American, was heard to whisper to Herr Kempermann, his German counterpart. "Well, that should just about cook the French goose."

Prince Devawongse just could not wipe that smug expression off his face; it was all his doing, rather than the King's, of course, Michael thought, with a twinge of sympathy towards Hardouin, who seemed to have lost that particular chess game.

Well, at least, Paris, Saigon's — and, more immediately, Pavie's — intentions would become clear.

Either the French abided by the Treaty they had signed almost thirty years ago recognizing Siam's possession of the west bank of the Mekong along with its traditional suzerainty over large swathes of the east bank or they employed force to gain control over those coveted provinces — and if they did use force... well that would be seen as an act of war, not only by Siam, but by the rest of the world as well.

In his mind, Michael began to draft the telegram the British Legation would need to send to London: were the French to decide to breach the Siamese borders in defiance of the Treaty and of all international laws, they would then control the whole of the Mekong basin.

Biting his lips, he wondered whether to add that it was unlikely, but that Pavie, supported by the Governor-General of Indochina was apt to behave recklessly — well, what was to stop them from pushing their luck all the way to Bangkok?

In which case the British would need to intervene to protect the neutrality of Siam. And what a mess that would be, Michael thought, as the other diplomats' eyes veered from the French to the British, and back again, trying to gauge their next move.

Captain Jones was too phlegmatic an old officer, and had weathered too many crises to fret before he needed to. He held out his glass to be refilled and admired the colour of the wine before drinking.

Their Lordships in London would just have to wait or find themselves other fortune-tellers: there was no point in trying to engage Hardouin tonight on the French railway to Yunnan project.

"He is going to scurry back to the Consulate like a bat out of hell to get word to Pavie," he muttered over the exquisite sour prawn soup that had just been served. "Mark my words, I give Pavie no more than two weeks before he appears here screaming Siamese interference in internal Lao affairs.

Might as well just enjoy the meal."

Chapter V

Julie arose from the dreamless slumber she loved because it enabled her to forget. But forget what? She could barely remember the sound of Louis' voice, the shape of his hands.

What remained ever present, and piercingly painful was the void where there once had been such happiness, a happiness that had died with him.

Her foggy, grey world was now circumscribed to the child she felt moving, kicking, invading her, but still, she could not imagine it as a living being.

She got up heavily, and moved to the bathroom. She unfastened her nightdress, let it drop to the floor, and looked at what had become of her body, hardly recognizing herself in the dull, sallow-faced creature with a swollen belly and sad eyes reflected in the mirror. And she did not care.

Fie had heard her stir, and appeared in the doorway. For some reason, she had stopped crawling about in her presence, and now walked normally, only crouching when she had to pass in front of her mistress. She smiled and gently passed a loving hand on Julie's belly, nodding approvingly as the child moved. "Very good" she cooed, and her eyes sought Julie's in the mirror, to encourage her to rejoice as well.

In fact, she and Michael seemed far more excited about the baby than its mother. Michael had engaged painters and workmen to prepare a nursery in the room next door, and tried to get his cousin to express a preference for light blue, or yellow or white walls.

"What for?" she had countered wearily. "It will be used only for a few months, until the child is old enough to travel back to France."

"Well, you don't need to return so soon, you know," he replied in a carefully offhand voice. "It might be better to wait a year or so. And don't ask me what you would do here, because I shall then ask you what you would do in Paris.

"Do you remember what you said?"

And she had blushed in recollecting that on Christmas Eve, she had broken down in tears and described to him the dismal and hopeless future she saw for herself and her child back in Paris. Also, he added, she mustn't forget the offer made by the Foreign Minister, to teach French to Royal Princesses at the Palace.

"We'll see." she finally sighed.

She let Fie wash her with cool scented water, braid and pin up her hair and dress her in the ample thin cotton gown her maid had somehow commissioned a dressmaker to produce, along with the swaddling-clothes that Fie submitted for her approval almost every day.

Blessing the Siamese custom to always be barefoot inside — her feet were so swollen, she could not imagine ever fitting into her shoes again — she descended the stairs, clinging to the rail, with Fie clucking and supporting her from behind.

Was this the Julie Lucas-Sauvain Louis had loved, the bright, impertinent, and fearless girl who had travelled to the other side of the earth seeking adventures? she asked herself despairingly. Her more recent adventures had been sitting at the table to take her meals instead of eating from a tray in bed, and taking a walk in the garden, her eyes dripping when she thought of Louis naming each shrub, plant and flower as if introducing her to very dear friends.

Michael was already seated, but sprang up to pull out her chair.

"A letter for you, my dear, from your Mama." he announced, flourishing the envelope, despite his inward misgivings. Who knew what entreaties and complaints it would contain this time, although how one could blame the poor woman who wanted nothing more than to have her daughter and future grandchild safely near her?

Julie opened it with her knife, unfolded the thin, closely written pages and looked up in surprise. "Augusta had just had a baby, a boy. I didn't even know she was expecting... He is called Edmond," she made a wry face. "Poor child. What a name...!

"Listen: A beautiful little boy, safely delivered last Sunday at home" she read, "*and who, thankfully, resembles his mother*"— What a typical remark for Mama, she remarked drily, and Michael's heart sang, she sounded like the old Julie — "*I had not wanted to tell you in my previous letters so as not to burden you with worries about your sister. He is to be baptized when you return as Augusta wants you to be godmother.*

"*Just think, a playmate for your own boy or girl, and whilst I grieve for you and with you, I rejoice at these new lives. The nurse is satisfactory.*" her voice trailed off, and suddenly, she sat upright, and resumed her reading aloud. "*I have finally become reconciled to your remaining in Siam until after the birth, although I cannot help but feel your doctor exaggerates the perils of the voyage in your condition, but I worry greatly about your traveling alone with an infant. Therefore, your Papa and I have arranged for Victor to come fetch you in Siam and escort you home. He will be arriving mid-March, in time for the birth, we hope...*"

She and Michael looked at each other, aghast, and she said "Oh, Michael, what shall we do?"

"BANGKOK, JANUARY 15TH *1891*

I have decided to resume writing this journal, although, heaven knows, I shall never be able to show it to Louis' son or daughter.

It seems to me that almost four months of my life were spent in some kind of dark night; I am now beginning to emerge from the awful nothingness, not that I have stopped grieving, indeed I feel I shall never stop, and that the knowledge that I shall never again see Louis, that he will never hold his child, will always be a part of me.

Mama writes that Victor is to arrive within a few weeks.

Glad as I am to see him soon, and grateful that he is willing to devote so many months of his life to come all this way to escort me home, I feel trapped."

She paused, and shifted heavily to find a more comfortable position on the hard chair, looking around at her plain, austere room, with the terrace doors open to the scents of flowers wafting up from the garden. She and Louis had shared breakfast at this table, had listened to the rain under the patched mosquito net. She had been so happy here.

She picked up her pen and continued to write: *"Trapped and resentful, that I am considered unable to fend for myself and the baby, and that I appear to have no choice in the matter.*

Michael says I should wait a year before returning to Paris, and I cannot, now, imagine leaving this life I have become so accustomed to. But I dare not write to Mama to tell her that Victor should defer his trip.

Perhaps when the child is born I shall feel differently."

"BANGKOK, JANUARY 31ST *1891*

Fanny has been to see me again, and I find I have so much in common with her, not least the fact that we both have parents from different countries who each considered that their own was far superior to the other.

I think I laughed for the first time in months listening to her describe her mother trying to sabotage a Christmas dinner because she disapproved of roasting a whole goose. Papa doesn't object to goose, but has nothing but disdain for Christmas pudding...

I find it easier to talk to her than to Léonie, probably because she too she lost her husband, although of course in far more dreadful circumstances. My husband has not been executed in a trumped-up trial, I did not need to flee for my life, have not lost all I own in this world.

But, as she said, my sorrow is no less than hers was, and fear for the future is unavoidable when your child has no father.

We have resumed our lessons — I need to do something to keep my brain busy and stop it from wandering in the same, desperate circles — and I realize that although I have forgotten most of the Siamese alphabet, I understand far more than I thought, from spending so much time with Fie.

I suppose it will be another memory for cold Paris winters, and something to talk about during dinner parties. I can just imagine those dinner parties I shall be invited to as charity — poor young widow, yes, her husband died in Laos... well, what <u>was</u> she thinking, marrying someone who was about to embark on this dangerous journey... Always been a bit headstrong, they say.

And my poor child, whom I realize I hate at times, because I cannot help seeing it as my punishment for flaunting the fate my family had designed for me. And I hate myself for feeling anything but the boundless love any worthwhile mother should have for this innocent life to be."

She heard the gate squeak open and Michael's buggy enter the garden.

He seemed to spend longer and longer hours at the Legation, and came back exhausted and exasperated when he joined her for dinner.

"You cannot imagine Pavie's latest ploy to claim Laos for France," he said with rueful admiration, spooning rice onto his plate, as Pon held the bowl at an awkward angle, beaming on approvingly.

"He is searching for something to prove that the Vietnamese Emperors had historical territorial rights over the East bank of the Mekong, which would make them de facto overlords of Laos, which rights, would, naturally, have now been passed on to France."

Rolling his eyes in mock tribute, he added: "He has scholars in just about every temple from Saigon to Haiphong going through manuscripts, the Imperial archives are full of students paid to scour the correspondence accumulated over centuries regarding Annam's relations with Luang Prabang, but so far, no luck, except from one or two ancient mentions in tax rolls for tiny, remote cantons along the cordillera.

"One really must award him points for being inventive. And persistent as well... You would think that he would be content with what he achieved last November, but no, he has to push on, and on, and on."

Captain Jones had been right in guessing Pavie would appear in Bangkok shortly after Prince Devawongse announced that military presence at the borders would be strengthened, and indeed, before November was up, he arrived, eyes flashing, beard bristling, demanding to be received by the His Majesty, or, failing that, the Foreign Minister at the very least.

How he managed was anyone's guess, but he was able to secure an informal agreement with Siam to freeze all military reinforcements on the east bank.

And, as London and its Legation in Bangkok watched on in scandalized yet powerless disbelief, a group of French businessmen, driven by the Colonial Party created a commercial venture, the "Syndicat du Haut Laos", to finance the development of shipping from the Upper Mekong all the way downriver to Saigon, ostensibly to exploit whatever riches Pavie had promised were to be found in the territories surveyed by the Mission, and incidentally to pre-empt any penetration by the British of the Shan states bordering both banks of the Mekong.

"Pushy little frogs, who do they think they are?" Captain Jones exploded when he found out. "When I pointed out that the Upper Mekong is our sphere of influence, Pavie just gave me that smug little smile of his. He claims it is a private commercial venture, no more, and that obviously, the area matters little to Britain. Why, he asked, had nothing then been done to exploit the Upper Mekong and its riches? And what, my lads, could I say to that?"

Michael could not help feel guilty in discussing Pavie's latest, brazen acts with Julie.

Not only was it a daily reminder of Louis's work, but also she was also a French citizen, and might feel divided loyalties.

There was nothing confidential, of course, in what he recounted at the table: the French press in Saigon was full of crowing, bombastic headlines about the recent achievements of the great man's exploits for the greater glory of *La République*.

Nonetheless, it was still a safer subject than to discuss her future, and she seemed to come alive when he brought back new information from the Legation, as if somehow, Louis were back among them for a few moments. She even smiled when he described the hunt for Imperial Annamese claims to Laos being desperately sought in dusty archives.

When he told her of the Syndicat du Haut Laos, she looked thoughtful.

"I believe Papa has invested in it, and Louis' father as well. Wait a moment..."

She left the table to fetch a letter from the desk in the drawing room, and came back out of breath to sit down.

"Really, I cannot wait for this child to be born, I feel as heavy as an elephant. Here it is... It's an old letter, actually, written before Louis died.."

She unfolded the paper and read: "*I have heard that Laos is the granary of Indochina, and has incalculable wealth. So, to support your husband's work, your father-in-law and I have become amongst the first investors in a commercial enterprise to develop trade between Laos and France. By getting in on the ground floor, so to speak, I hope to be awarded the procurement contracts to supply the engineering firms who will work on making the great river navigable, building locks, bridges and such. For let us not forget, my dearest little girl, that such countries hoping to join our civilized world need not only to sell, but also to buy.*"

"I suppose that Syndicat is what he is referring to?"

Michael nodded. "They have yet to find a way to bypass the falls so as to make shipping possible, before they tap into that 'incalculable wealth', though. But I hear a hydrographer has joined the Mission to find a solution. How do I know?

"Spies, my dear. Well spies is perhaps an excessive word, let us call them informers, everybody uses them and the Siamese more than any of us.

"How do you think Prince Devawongse knew you were expecting? "

She sighed. "I wonder what Louis would have made of this... Despite all his admiration for Pavie, I'm not sure he would have approved."

Michael felt a twinge. Much as he had liked Louis, enjoyed the man's conversation and admired his sense of adventure, it was certainly preferable for his standing at the Legation to share his house with the widow rather than the wife of a living and active member of a Mission headed by someone who seemed determined to wreak havoc in the delicate balance of forces in the Mekong Basin.

"I think Louis was an idealist," he replied carefully. "Shall I help you up to your room?"

For the following weeks, life seemed to entail nothing but waiting.

Waiting to hear about Pavie's next move, waiting for a telegram from Victor confirming the date of his arrival, and above all, waiting for Louis' child to be born.

And as usual, everyone was taken by surprise when it actually happened.

"BANGKOK, MARCH 7ᵀᴴ 1891,

Dearest Mother,
Three days ago, Julie was delivered of a son.

Both she and the child are safe and well, now, but the actual birth was somewhat dramatic and apparently a few weeks early, brought on by Julie falling headlong down the stairs. From what she remembers, she tripped on the edge of her gown and was unable to regain her balance.

The doctor arrived at the same time I did, and, I am thankful to say, sent me back to the Legation, where I awaited news.

She has bruises all over her body, sprained her ankle and is in pain, but claims it is bearable.

The baby, who of course is to be christened Louis, cries a great deal. He is rather small, but then, all babies are, to my inexperienced eye.

I have cabled the news to Julie's parents, although I must confess to having kept silent as to the circumstances of the event, I did not wish to add to their legitimate worries about their daughter's and grandson's well-being.

They replied expressing their delight and relief, and also saying that Victor, her brother, is en route, and is to send a telegram from Singapore to give us the date of his arrival.

Therefore my little house will be quite full. I hope the servants will be up to the task, as their number has been depleted. A young boy, named Chit, slipped away during the hullabaloo surrounding the birth, taking my gold watch and the cufflinks with rubies Father gave me for my twentieth birthday, along with a sizable amount of money, while all the others were busy fetching water, running to the Legation to keep me informed or whatever they needed to do."

Michael rested his head on his hand, willing himself to rejoice in being rid of the lithe, perverse, and desperately tempting creature who had turned these past months into a succession of bittersweet and guilt-laden moments.

Against his better judgement, he had let Pon hire him, feeling his blood thrill when he sensed the knowing, caressing look the young servant gave him as he wai-ed respectfully before lowering his gaze.

"Chit isn't really dishonest," he told Julie that morning as she awkwardly held her baby, trying to avoid resting him on her bruised upper arm. "It is just that… well… it was becoming impossible. He … I think he wanted to punish me."

"I know." She looked up at him in sympathy, managing for just a second to keep her eyes off her tightly swaddled child, although all that was visible was a tiny, red, wrinkled face, with screwed up eyes and a tuft of fine golden hair.

Fie was hovering, at the ready to catch the infant should his mother look as if she were about to tire, her outstretched hands almost visibly trembling with her need to hold him.

Relenting with a resigned smile, Julie surrendered the bundle and watched as the maid worshipfully placed the baby in the rattan cot next to his mother's bed, and rocked it softly, chanting a lullaby under her breath.

"Are you very sad?" she asked gently.

Michael shrugged. No. Yes.

"Is it possible to be heart-broken and relieved all at once?" he asked.

Julie took his hand and squeezed it. Probably. Tears spilled from her eyes and coursed down her drawn and pale cheeks, and she wiped them away with an apologetic look. She too was heart-broken, but also very happy, she whispered.

And very tired, he chided her, getting up from her bedside. She should not let him exhaust her by staying to chat, when she needed her rest.

She nodded, but caught his hand as he moved away. "Come back later, please. I feel as if I have months of conversation bottled up in me, waiting to get out."

"So, my darling Mother, what with the additions to my family here, and the ever increasing work at the Legation, I believe I shall be kept quite busy. But that shall not stop me from writing."

For Julie, the first days following the birth of her son passed in a strange haze of exhaustion, bliss and heartache, her delight at holding the tiny, mewling child and examining his every feature, engraving in her mind the lovely sucking motion of his lips, the cloudy stare of his grey-blue eyes and the insistent grasp of his delicate, flower-like hands.

"Louis, Louis," she murmured, tracing the soft cheeks with her finger. "If you only could see the miracle we wrought together, you would be so happy. And I swear he will grow up to be proud of his father."

But while she said the words, she felt she was only conforming to some image of herself as a character in a novel, and that the promise she made for her son's future was no more than a vague nod to convention.

Nothing seemed real to her except for this new life feeding at her breast, and the gnawing, bitter knowledge that she was both a mother and a widow.

She was absently aware of raised voices outside her bedroom, an argument between Fie and Doctor Hertz, with Fanny being involved as interpreter, as to the proper recovery of a new mother, as Fanny cheerfully recounted later while Fie fumed and muttered in the background.

"The custom here is to have the mother lie on heated planks for several days, increasing the heat until she is quite roasted. It is supposed to tighten the muscles, and my mother was a great believer in it. Having been through it myself, I can tell you, you are well out of it."

Julie laughed, because it seemed that it was expected, but could not drum up the energy to care.

Fanny took her hand, and continued brightly. "Fie is willing to admit that *farang* women are made differently, and don't need the treatment Siamese women do — although she says that from what she has seen, you don't seem that different to her, but she is adamant, however, that we must perform the ghost-child ceremony, to protect little Louis.

"Don't worry, you don't have to do a thing. It's going to be in the garden, but you can watch from your window."

And she leaned over to pick up the baby, put him in Fie's arms, and both disappeared.

Julie could not help a feeling of sudden panic — it was the first time the child was out of her sight, and she threw back her sheet, hobbled over to her terrace and opened the screen window. Leaning out, she saw that all the servants were assembled in the garden, and surrounded Fie and baby Louis, who was cooing happily.

Half hidden by the huge, waving leaves of a banana tree, Fie raised the infant to the skies, stamped her feet three times, and shouted out a threatening invocation, as all looked on. There was a moment of absolute silence before the cicadas resumed their metallic singing. Fie repeated the ritual stamping and yelling, followed by the others who seemed to try and outdo her. Fanny then chanted a response, and took Louis, who started to howl in fright at the loud and angry voices. An owl hooted, bats started to swoop above and the stray one-eyed cat with the misshapen tail who hunted the garden for frogs and mice was hovering curiously at the edge of the group.

Julie clasped her hands to her aching breasts, mesmerized by the scene below her. In the gathering twilight, with the dark shadows playing on their faces, those people, so familiar a moment ago, had become unknown participants in this foreign and pagan ceremony. She recognized none of the words she heard, and could interpret none of the gestures but she could read absolute belief in their expression.

Her rational brain was supercilious, telling her all this shouting and stomping about was a childish little bit of superstition, but another inner voice, seeming to come from deeper recesses of her being whispered that whatever they were doing was powerful and important, but also, inexplicably, reassuring and that somehow, it served to shield her son from harm.

Finally, with a satisfied smile, Fie made a final, determined announcement to the heavens, and the little group proceeded back into the house.

"What was that?" Julie asked tremulously when her child had been returned to her arms.

"The Siamese believe ghosts will threaten a cherished new-born and claim it for their own, so the purpose of the ceremony is to convince them that no one wants this baby, and that they shouldn't bother about it," Fanny explained in a matter-of-fact voice. "So Louis is now safe from ghosts, you see. Oh yes, of course, I too believe in them. They are everywhere, you know, and it is very necessary to keep them happy."

Monsignor Vey came as well, to inquire about the date chosen for the christening.

When told that Julie was waiting for her brother's

arrival, he tutted in disapproval, stroking his long grey beard.

So few infants lived beyond their first weeks or months in these unhealthy, unholy lands, he remonstrated, ignoring Julie's recoiling in horror. Did she want her son to die unbaptized, to be condemned to eternal limbo? Thankfully, he had come prepared.

He removed a small flask of holy water from the deep pocket of his dusty and faded cassock, and gently poured a few drops on the child's forehead before making the sign of the cross and blessing him. "You are now freed from sin, and a member of the Holy Church," he murmured. "I baptize you Louis, in the name of the Father, the Son, and the Holy Spirit. Amen."

"Well, he certainly has no bedside manner, but he meant no harm," Michael said tartly after seeing the bishop out, "and now it seems that you are covered on all sides. Although, I, personally, put my trust in Fie and the ghost ceremony."

By the time Victor arrived under a scorching, white, vibrating sky, Louis' wrinkled little face had filled out, and he was thriving on his mother's milk and the constant, loving attention of everyone in the household, from Michael to the coachman, who often stole up to the verandah just to gaze at the sleeping golden haired child in his little cot.

Seated by him in a rattan armchair, Julie was waiting for her brother with some trepidation. Her delight at seeing him was mixed in her mind with her fear of what life would be like back in Paris, and the memories of his disdain for the husband she had chosen. And she felt very uncertain about herself, as if, instead of Victor, it were her Mama who was about to enter the garden and look her over.

Although the bruises on her face had vanished, and she did her hair with greater care, she knew she would certainly no longer be taken for a Parisienne — not that clothes or toilette had ever been of great concern to her — but still...

She was gradually recovering her figure, thanks to Fie, who unbeknownst to Doctor Hertz, massaged her belly daily with a hot metal ball. It was rather painful, although it did seem to work. She had insisted that the maid cinch her in her loosest corset that morning, but the months of grieving had taken their toll, and her face appeared drawn and pale in the mirror. No amount of rouge would turn her back into the laughing girl she had once been.

None of that seemed to matter when Victor jumped out of the buggy and ran up the three steps to the verandah, sweeping her up in his arms.

He held her at arms length, looked her up and down, and declared "A Madonna, a veritable Madonna!", before hugging her again.

No, no, she protested, laughing, he, however, looked marvellous, so tanned and rested. He twirled his moustache and grinned.

"Well, almost a month on a ship... nothing to do but drink wine and chat up girls... who wouldn't look marvellous? And so this is my nephew?"

He leaned over, pushed aside the mosquito net, then lifted Louis out as if he had held babies all his life.

"Congratulations, kitten. The spitting image of Papa, poor child. And who is this creature who looks as if she would cook me up in a stew? Is this the wonderful Fie you wrote to us about?"

Yes, Julie answered with a giggle. She trusted nobody with Louis, and certainly not men.

Still holding the infant, Victor bowed ceremoniously before the maid, who could not repress a smile and clapped her hand over her mouth in embarrassment.

Watching the scene, Michael felt a sense of relief, along with some guilt, realizing that the Victor whose arrival he was so dreading, the aggressive and supercilious boy he had fought and disliked when they were both nine, existed only in his memory.

His fears of being made to feel inferior, that his house would be found wanting, or that Victor might somehow discover his secret life were nothing but shadows of his childhood. He was expecting, somehow — knowing all the while that he was being ridiculous — a dashing officer complete with golden epaulettes, a sophisticated drawl, and an imperious manner, instead of the friendly, sunburnt, sweaty young man with a panama hat and a rumpled suit he had collected at the Singapore steamer.

Julie would leave with her brother, or, as he had come to hope, she would stay.

But all would be well.

Chapter VI

It seems so long since I last wrote in this journal, my world has changed, I have changed, I am a mother.

Of course, when I married Louis, I thought I was transformed, that I had magically become a woman, but I now realize that it was but an illusion.

I wore the title and name of Madame Gallet just like I wore the gowns of my trousseau, pretending to be a grown-up, but inside, I was still the same Julie, a child playing at being a lady. No longer.

The girl I once was is as foreign to me now as is the heartbroken creature who thought her life was over when she lost Louis.

I read what I wrote in this journal merely a few months ago as if it were the diary of a stranger. How could I have felt hatred for my baby, for this innocent, golden child whom I now love so desperately, for whom I feel such fear, who is more to me than anyone ever was, than anyone can ever be?

Yes, more than his father...

I grieve still, oh yes, I grieve, but more for the unfairness of a life cut short so soon, as well as for a promise of happiness unfulfilled.

We had so little time together... married hardly a year and a half, and of those, we lived together barely more than two months...

I catch myself laughing, I sometimes spend whole hours without thinking of what Louis would have done, have said, have enjoyed.

I suppose I have decided to live.

Victor is very kind, and I truly am delighted to have him here with me, but I cannot help missing the easiness of the evenings spent alone with Michael, for naturally, he is more guarded in his conversation now.

Victor himself seems to have changed. He is still the charming, amusing and handsome brother I worshipped, but I feel his carefree manner is deliberate and put on.

He talks about reserving our passage on a ship to go home, but appears in no hurry to do so.

And in the meantime, I try to savour every moment and image of Siam, all the little things I hardly noticed when I arrived, so caught up was I by the excitement of waiting for Louis' arrival, and then the exhaustion and sorrow of the following months.

Showing Victor all the things I love here makes me discover them anew, the creamy, peachy flavour of the papayas we eat in the morning, the scent of the jasmine garlands the servants offer at the little spirit house in the garden, the bustle of the streets and the golden spires of the temples.

Victor is sometimes shocked at the dirt and the flies, which made me realize I no longer notice them, nor do I mind the little lizards on the walls or the overpowering smell of fish in the kitchen.

He has already managed to make some friends, two young French naval officers whom he met when he went to introduce himself at the Consulate, who are attached to the gunboat which is always moored on the river in front of the building.

He sometimes meets them for an evening on the town, such as it may be — probably a card game, billiards or drinks at the Oriental, and I welcome it, for I was afraid he might become bored with our company.

I have greater freedom to go sight-seeing with him, because I can no longer nurse Louis, I developed sores, and a fever, so Doctor Hertz found a young wet-nurse, named Mali, who has moved in with her own baby and shares her milk between both boys, whom all the Siamese of the house call Nhu (which means mouse, and is the usual term of endearment for little children). Louis is Nhu Thong, golden mouse, and little Somchai is Nhu Dam, black mouse. No one ever mentioned the father of her child, so neither do I, but I do wonder.

The house is now bursting, there are nappies drying everywhere, the babies cry, Fie shouts at Mali... Poor Michael, I believe he will be delighted to be rid of the whole lot of us.

I know I find it a relief to be away for a few hours when Victor and I take Michael's buggy to go explore the city, and I have absolutely no worries about leaving Louis to Fie, who is a veritable tigress, and lets no one near the cradle.

Last week was the Siamese new year, when people splash water at each other to wash away the sins of the past year and start, as it were, with a clean slate.

The servants did it to us with tremendous respect, first pouring water on our hands then heads. It is a lovely custom, and so refreshing because the heat is at its greatest this month.

Victor was invited to join the French Consulate members at a reception at the Grand Palace — he came back with amazed descriptions of the great painted giants, and the splendid frescoes and the overall glittering luxury of it all.

His Majesty made an appearance, along with several Princes, all dressed in silk and dripping with gems. I am really quite jealous, I should have loved to be invited to the Palace, and I guess I shall never get to see it. Michael attended as well, with the British Minister, and I had to stay home.

And last week as well, Baby Louis was officially christened at the Cathedral with Léonie and Fanny as his godmothers and Victor and Michael as godfathers. Many people came to pay their respects when we left the Cathedral, Monsieur Hardouin with his usual heavy courtesy, Captain Jones, the German Minister, and others whom I had never met.

The five of us had a quiet luncheon after the ceremony at the Oriental Hotel, with only the bishop as an extra guest. It was in a private dining room, as I am still in mourning, and cannot appear in public except to attend mass, and I was delighted to shed my dreary black dress as soon as I came home.

I hate it, it means nothing except to remind me that I am a widow, and never wear the thing when I go sightseeing with Victor, for there is very little chance of meeting anyone I know. Of course, Mama would be livid if she knew… I can just hear her accusing me of lacking respect for Louis' memory.

She actually had Victor bring me a hat of her choosing, because she feared I could find nothing appropriate here, and it is indescribably ugly, black (of course) straw, with satin facing, and the thickest, darkest, most impenetrable veil which is supposed to cover my face entirely. I can barely see through it.

I know that Louis would just say, "My Lily, I want you to be comfortable, and remember me with joy, not by wearing that hideous garment. And, while you are at it, burn the hat."

BANGKOK, MAY 1ST, 1891

I have been in Siam for almost a year now, and discover I have no desire to leave.

And as it turns out, neither does Victor, but he must. He was given six months leave, and what with the time spent on the journey, the end of his stay is rapidly approaching.

"Six months leave?" Michael asked in surprise. "Is that usual, even for family reasons?"

Victor sighed. No, it wasn't, he admitted sheepishly. The truth was, he made a fool of himself over a girl, the fiancée of a fellow officer. She was a flirt and a coquette, and he was not as cautious as he should have been; the affair became known, her betrothed was from a prominent family, and went to see their commanding officer clamouring for the right to challenge Victor to a duel.

"I told him not to be such an old fashioned idiot, he called me a low-class, nouveau-riche coward. Let's face it, kitten, maybe not low-class, but nouveau riche, we certainly are.

"But I shall let no one call me a coward. So I punched him in the face," he concluded. "And to spare everyone a scandal, I was told to disappear for a while, and to quietly request a transfer to another regiment when I return. So you see, coming here to fetch you was a perfect excuse — not that I wasn't delighted, of course."

"What did Papa say?" Julie asked, torn between horror and laughter.

"Oh, Papa was almost pleased. He thought I might be decommissioned, and would take over the business. Mama, of course, is mortified."

What about the young lady? Michael wanted to know.

"She... well, I imagined that I might be in love with her for two whole weeks. Then I became convinced I was.

And as soon as the ship left Marseille, I hardly gave her a thought. The last I heard before I left, she was married in white at the Madeleine wearing her mother-in-law's pearls, and a cardinal officiated."

Michael poured him more whisky and soda with a sympathetic smile, while Victor continued thoughtfully.

He had no desire to leave the army, knew nothing about and cared very little for the foundry business, except for the lavish lifestyle it provided him with. He was thinking that he might apply to be taken by the Naval Infantry regiment that was stationed in Saigon. Talking to his two officer friends, he had come to realize that life in the colonies might be for him.

"I enjoy what I have seen of this country, and was told that Indochina is very like it. So what do you think?"

Well, Michael answered drily, he was quite pleased that Victor's stay in Bangkok had proved so successful. But was it not somewhat drastic to make such a change in one's life based on six weeks in Siam?

Victor shrugged. The drastic change in his life occurred when he took that girl out on the terrace and kissed her. "In France, stupid as it is, this affair will always follow me, as will the hatred of that idiot and his very influential family. It seems to me that in Indochina, no one shall know, or, for that matter, care.

"So, kitten, I was planning to get us on a ship leaving from Saigon to Marseille, so I could have a look around. What do you say?"

Julie had been listening to the exchange without intervening, only thinking of her parents, and of their sorrow and disappointment when Victor would tell them his plans.

And hers.

"I'm not going with you," she said simply. "Listen to me: it just isn't possible. You know that Louis needs Mali's milk at least for another six months, at least. I can't just take her with me to France as if she were some sort of cow.

"Had I been able to breastfeed him myself, then perhaps — oh, stop looking so embarrassed, the two of you, it's ridiculous to pretend you don't understand what I am talking about. It's not as if I were going around flaunting my bare breasts at you."

Victor laughed, and raised his glass in a rueful toast.

"Ever the lady, I see, doing our Mama proud!

"Thank God for Augusta, then, her perfect boring baron, and her perfect boring child. Because you and I, kitten, are the black sheep…"

"I hadn't even consulted Michael before breaking my news, and felt quite contrite about it, although, after all, he had always said I should stay another year. I apologized to him over breakfast, and said that of course, I would move house to give him his privacy, but he looked so dismayed that I had to promise to reconsider.

'The truth is, my dear, you and Louis are as close to a family as I shall ever have,' he answered. 'I have become quite used to hearing both infants cry at night, and I believe that it shan't go on forever. So move if you feel you must, but not on my account.'

So I burst into tears, and was still mopping my eyes when Victor joined us. I expected him to tease me as he used to for being a cry baby — I shall never forget how he made fun of me finding me sobbing over David Copperfield, but he just gave my shoulder a little squeeze before sitting down.

I must say that much as I feel for him, having to give up his regiment and the high level career it promised, he is perhaps less the paragon I used to take him for, and I love him all the better for being more human, and prone to failings like the rest of us.

He will go by the shipping company today, and book a passage as soon as possible.

And I have asked Michael to inquire about the French classes at the Palace."

"*Bangkok, May 17ᵀᴴ 1891*

Victor left this morning on the Saigon-bound steamer, and the house feels empty, but somehow, all of us seem to have relaxed a little, as if lowering our guard. Michael no longer lives in fear that he will betray himself in some way, I am released from the role of the stubborn, bookish Julie I cannot help playing for my family, and all the servants have reverted to the slapdash service they consider suffices for just Michael and myself.

I sent a long and extravagantly expensive cable to Paris to explain why Victor is returning alone.

Surely, I cannot be blamed for putting my child's well being first?"

"*Bangkok, May 30ᵀᴴ, 1891*

Tomorrow, I start my classes at the Palace.

I was called in to be interviewed by the Foreign Minister at the Palace, and Michael escorted me there, but I was so nervous, I hardly noticed anything on my way in. Also, I was wearing my ridiculous mourning hat with its thick veil.

The Minister, whom Michael told me I was to call Your Royal Highness, was very kind and bustled up to help me to my feet when I curtsied.

I shall teach French conversation twice a week to two groups of princesses, and when I explained I had no teaching experience, the Minister replied that the princesses had no experience either, so we would all be beginners together.

Then he asked if I would wear my veil, and when I lifted it off my face and replied, feelingly, that I certainly hoped not, he said "Good, good. Princess want to see face, yes? Know you are lady, yes?"

I laughed and said that my mother never thought me much of a lady, which seemed to puzzle him, so I just agreed that I would certainly not let the princesses confuse me with anything else.

I shall be paid thirty ticals a month — paid, me! — And they will send a carriage to pick me up.

Michael showed me around the public areas of the Palace on our way out, and it is even more splendid than in Victor's bedazzled description. And, apparently, the classes are to be given in the inner court, reserved for women only. Michael says I am very lucky, no farang he knows of has ever been to that part of the Palace, except a couple of missionary women. I remember reading about it in Mrs Leonowens' book, how extraordinary that I should follow in her footsteps.

I do hope I shall not disgrace myself as a teacher."

Julie fidgeted nervously and pushed aside the lowered blinds of the carriage that had appeared early in the morning at the gate.

A sturdy lady with short hair and darkened teeth had alighted, wai-ed very low, then gestured that she should get in; she had been assigned to her as an escort, from what Julie gathered, and, beaming, put the blinds down as soon as Julie tried to raise them. Shaking her head, waving at the street, she explained by gestures that they were not to be seen. It was not appropriate.

The journey seemed to take forever in the hot, stuffy coach, and Julie was beginning to feel quite sick when they finally arrived at some gate, slowed briefly, continued for a short while over bumpy cobblestones and then finally came to a stop.

A soldier opened the door, and, sinking to his knees, unfolded the steps to let them out. Grasping her arm firmly, her escort took her down a busy alley, with throngs of people who all turned to stare at the *farang* lady with light brown hair under a pert straw hat. They approached a tall, forbidding wall, and Julie noticed that suddenly there were no men around, only women who all seemed to be headed the same way, inside an enormous half-opened wooden gate. Pushing through the crowd, her guide stopped just before entering, held her arm out and pointed to the threshold, which was decorated with gold leaf, then stepped clear over it, gesturing as she did, that the foreign visitor should do the same.

Julie nodded. "I understand, don't step on the wood."

Gathering up her skirt, she lifted her foot high and imitated the exaggerated movement, while onlookers cackled at her performance, and a little girl grabbed her hem to help.

And then, looking around, mopping her face and regretting she had no fan, she found herself in what appeared to be a world of fantasy.

There was a garden, with small, cleverly shaped trees, a low, jagged, rocky hill, a pond, a whole landscape in miniature. A bit further were an open-sided pavilion, with a group of ladies lounging and chatting, what appeared to be a theatre, and another garden full of roses. Birdcages hung from the branches of trees, filling the air with song and little girls with topknots ran around, giggling, and pointed at them.

And everywhere, tall, strong looking women in military-style uniform patrolled the area, holding thick rattan sticks. One of them stopped Julie's guide, obviously inquiring about the *farang's* business there, nodded at the explanations, and waved them on. They came to a group of buildings clustered around a small square, with narrow alleys leading from it, and doors open onto rooms where yet more women sat, sewing, threading flowers into garlands, or just enjoying the cool of the morning. The chattering conversations stopped as soon as they appeared, and Julie had the impression their passage created a wave of silence.

She wanted to slow down, to marvel at everything, but she was hurried towards a large building surrounded by a gallery with Italian-style columns and white marble steps. She should remove her shoes, she was told. An old wizened woman — a slave?— rushed to her on all fours and deftly unbuttoned her boots, hooting with glee at, Julie supposed, the foolishness of *farangs* for wearing such things.

This was her destination.

The Palace school.

When she recounted her first morning as a teacher, Julie could only describe it as entering a golden aviary, with marvellously coloured birds, perhaps thirty of them twittering away, who all suddenly froze, and bowed very low before her, their scarlet, pink, purple, saffron or azure garments gleaming in the cool shade.

From this enchanting frieze, an older woman with greying hair stepped forward, and *wai*-ed respectfully. Cursing herself for her clumsiness, Julie returned the greeting, and smiled, feeling very shy.

"Good day, Maem, I am Mom Ratchawong Keow, Princess Keow, in charge of the education of His Majesty's Royal Daughters and other princesses," the lady said in careful English.

"You are the lady from France, Maem Chouli, yes?"

Julie assented in a whisper, that indeed, she was.

"Welcome, Maem.

We have tea, and we talk."

She was shown a low stool, and she managed to sit, vowing to refrain from wearing her stays next time, as all settled on the floor and watched her in rapt attention. She looked back and gave them a smile, and giggles erupted.

Princess Keow merely raised her beautifully arched eyebrows, and they fell silent again.

A small red-lacquered table appeared, a servant in a yellow bodice and blue sarong crawled up with a tray bearing a golden teapot and tiny china cups, followed by another who offered a dish of minute sweetmeats shaped like pink, white and mauve fruit. "Eat, eat," urged her hostess firmly.

Julie obediently popped one in her mouth. Lovely, but tasteless.

"Shrimp in sugar?" asked Princess Keow, waving another servant up, and more still, with fruit carved to look like flowers, bits of chicken on skewers, and rolled up leaves stuffed with a sweetish paste and lime and chillies, everything presented more elaborately than even at the Oriental Hotel, with frangipani blossoms tucked in a corner of the napkin, or ginger cut in the shape of birds or rabbits, and pale green melon balls strung on a thread like a jade bead necklace.

Julie tasted, and sipped, smiled her pleasure, and tasted some more.

"Husband you die very young," the Princess announced.

Julie agreed. Sadly, it was so. "You have new baby. No good child without mother. Yes? You bring him to Palace next time, never mind."

Well, maybe not next time. He was still very small.

"You bring. Good. Now I name all Princesses here."

Then followed a delightful ballet of girls coming up when their names were called, smiling shyly as they wai-ed, and returned to sit in a row.

The youngest had topknots set off with a crown of flowers or a small diadem, the older wore their hair short as did Princess Keow, and all were arrayed in shiny, stiff silk cloth, wrapped around their waists and gathered between the legs to form a sort of pantaloons, with pleated bodices caught on their shoulder.

It seemed to Julie that they were all beautiful, or at least pretty, and never before had she seen such a grace of movement in the way they rose and sat down again, or fluttered their hands to adjust their clothes.

The names were a blur to her, she was just able to make out that each was preceded by "Mom Chao" or "Mom Ratchawong" or "Phra Ong Chao..." and she realized that these must be their titles. What did they correspond to? She didn't want to give offense by inadvertently giving precedence to one instead of another. Never mind, she would find out later,

Princess Keow looked at her intently, then sat back and arranged the pleats of her dark pink bodice cloth. She had enormous rubies in her ears, and bracelets with diamonds around each wrist, tinkling and catching the light as she moved. She might have been forty, or sixty, her brow was smooth, but she had lines of laughter around her eyes, and for all her imperiousness and the strict rule she seemed to impose upon her charges, she appeared a kind and fun-loving woman.

"Good," the Princess announced again. "Now you teach, I listen too, and maybe I speak French as well, yes?" She burst out laughing at the ridiculous idea.

"Yes, Your Highness," Julie countered firmly. "You speak French as well."

She had no idea how to start, she confessed to Michael that evening, everything she thought she had prepared for her first class — a lesson culled from the memories of her first day at school — simply vanished from her mind once she was faced with that extraordinary audience.

She had expected — well, something like a schoolhouse in Europe, cowed-looking children seated at desks, with improving pictures on the walls, maybe a few maps. Something grim.

"Grim? In the Palace of the King of Siam?" Michael snorted ironically.

"Life may be grim there, although not in any noticeable way. So what did you do?"

"I introduced myself, in French, pointing at my chest.

"Then I got each one to do the same, starting with Keow, repeating my words, giving their name. Everyone was laughing so hard, the guard-ladies — they are called "*khlon*", by the way — came to see what was happening, and stayed and laughed too. That's about all we achieved."

"And the day after tomorrow?"

She would do the same, suspecting the first lesson had already been forgotten, then move on to another simple phrase. Then, maybe, a song?

The song was a big success. The story of a monk who oversleeps, and forgets to ring the church bells, it seemed inordinately amusing to the giggling women of the Palace, and the "Ding Dang Dong" chorus delighted them. In fact, they must have sung it to others, because the following week when Julie entered the Inner Court and walked to the school pavilion, little impish girls trailed her bellowing "Ding Dang Dong" at the top of their voices.

She no longer needed an escort, and felt free to linger and admire the gardens, take a different turn and find yet unseen buildings in different styles, from elaborate Chinese-inspired pagodas to sprawling wooden houses on stilts.

After one of her classes, Princess Keow announced she was taking her to visit the Temple of the Emerald Buddha.

"I take also two English ladies, teachers of English to my girls," she sighed.

"Good women, but very sad looking."

"Sad, why?" Julie asked with empathy. "What happened?"

"I not know. Maybe no man but God?" Keow shook her head. "Wrinkled faces, hair like rice straw. Look old, but I think not old. Very sad.

"Ah, here they."

She rose from her cushion to greet the newcomers who

were striding up in a clatter of heavy shoes over the smooth paving stones.

The oldest one removed her hat and mopped her face before performing a perfunctory *wai* to the Princess then extended a firm hand to Julie.

"I am Miss Cole, and this is Miss Shakespeare." she added, indicating her younger companion who was gazing up shyly under her sunbonnet. "And you, I believe, must be the French lady who is trying as we are to drum some sense into the girls."

"Well ... only some French songs and conversation," Julie murmured, and she so enjoyed teaching the young ladies — they were all charming, were they not?

"Charming is as charming does," Miss Cole replied with a tolerant look, "though I'll grant you they make a pretty picture when they're all together." She then turned to Princess Keow and opened her parasol with a snap.

"Time's a wasting, my lady, if we are going to see the Temple before our class."

They were first guided through the many courtyards, as the Princess explained the vividly-coloured frescoes depicting the tale of the Ramakhien.

"Is well known like Bible," she said.

"Story of Gods, but not gods, yes? You understand? No? Never mind, complicated. Here is Rama — not God, but like God — going to war against bad bad — not God, I not know to say, to save his wife, with his army of monkeys."

"It's a pagan story, no better than a fairy tale," stated Miss Shakespeare, who seemed to have lost her initial shyness when faced with all the vibrant paintings of flying bird-women and winged monkeys.

She looked back up at the frescoes with distaste, then turned to Julie. "I suppose you're a Papist, and are not so bothered as we are by all this, although, of course, we are not allowed to say so in class."

Furthermore, she added with a grimace, the artists — well, if one could call them artists — were woefully ignorant of the laws of perspective.

"Just look at that mountain coming out of a roof!"

Julie shook her head. She found the wall paintings very attractive, actually.

Princess Keow beamed with benign good will and implacable eyes.

"Like fairy tale, yes. Like fairy tale, useful, yes? Teach good, evil.

"Instructive, is right word? Yes? Is instructive."

Miss Cole was looking confused, "I really have never understood.

"You pray to Buddha, but also to these idols? Which do you believe in?"

Keow was very firm. "We venerate Lord Buddha."

"So ..." Miss Cole persisted, "You think as we do, that worshipping these gods, making offerings ..." she pointed at a small altar in the corner of the courtyard where an elephant-headed statue was garlanded with jasmine.

"Surely, you must think all of this is idolatry?"

Keow frowned. "I not know idolatry. Making offerings is good. I think your class start now, yes? You see Emerald Buddha temple some other day."

And sweeping Julie behind her, she marched towards the next courtyard.

By then, Julie had asked Fie to shorten all her hems and had abandoned her proper buttoned boots for light leather sandals presented to her with great ceremony by Mom Sutthini, an earnest slip of a girl who always wove a garland of jasmine around her topknot.

If Mama should see me now, she thought as she kicked them off before entering the great hall of the Temple. No stays, no stockings, no shoes, and wearing a blue dress that shows my ankles when I am supposed to be in deep mourning. Black sheep of the family, indeed, and repressed a giggle before following Keow's lead and lighting incense in front of the dark green statue encased in robes of gold, the most venerated Buddha of the realm.

The two hours she was expected to devote to her classes soon became three, then the full morning.

Finally giving in to Keow's repeated demand, she brought Louis along, with Fie to watch over him... although the interest the golden haired baby gave rise to among the women of the Inner courts was such that she needn't have bothered. Everyone young and old, were vying for the privilege of dandling him on their knees, rocking him gently, spooning rice porridge into his pink, avid mouth and crooning to him while his nurse sat in awed silence.

"You should have seen Fie's face" Julie recounted to Michael after the maid's first visit to the Palace. "She was so frightened at just being there, she would have crawled on all fours from the great gate all the way to the school pavilion, and she kowtowed to Keow about fifteen times, which, I must say, Keow took perfectly in her stride. She just told me, as if it were absolutely normal, that the common people see the King as God, and that therefore all of the Royals have almost divine status. I just can't imagine that in England, and even less in France."

"Well, darling girl, in France, you chop king's heads off, so of course you can't. They have proper respect for the monarchy here," he replied teasingly.

In fact, the French didn't seem to respect anything much but the expansionist claims of La République, he continued more seriously. They certainly showed no respect for international law.

They were now asserting ownership — yes, ownership, on what legal basis one could only wonder — of all the territories on the East bank of the Upper Mekong above Luang Prabang, up to and including the river. The Legation had just received a report that the claim was made in the Chambre des Députés by the new French foreign minister, Ribot.

"We heard that Pavie, who couldn't find any Annamese source to bolster French demands, concluded nonetheless that there are too many trade routes in Upper Laos and the Shan states that lie between Tonkin and the coal mines of Yunnan to continue to accept neutral status of the area. He has advised the French government that a border should be drawn by force, if it appears it cannot be done by negotiation.

"You remember what Louis said, that Pavie considered that having the Mekong as border demarcation makes no sense?

"Well, he has obviously convinced France, and its Foreign Minister, who hates the English, jumped at the opportunity to defy us and publicly claim the lands."

"What will happen now?" Julie asked in concern, feeling, as always, torn between her national and family loyalties.

Papa, who had always despised colonial expansion for being costly and useless, had now changed his tune, with his stake in the Syndicat du Haut-Laos. Mama, however, for all her years in France, had remained staunchly English in her heart, and must be fuming at this new foreign minister who dared defy her beloved British Empire.

She sighed.

And there was also Siam to consider, Siam which had had

become her home now, and she was thinking of all her lovely butterfly women at the Palace, innocently befriending her while her own nation was trying to despoil theirs.

"What will happen?" Michael repeated wearily. "It's anyone's guess, really."
He had asked the same question when Captain Jones had convened everyone at the Legation to inform them of this recent development.

"My boy, who can tell...

"Do you want to know what I think and what I would actually recommend, if their Lordships were to ask me?

"Which, of course, they won't, as, in their high and mighty minds, being in Siam does not qualify us for any understanding of the situation.

"Well, I think we should just ignore the Frenchies, pretend it didn't happen, or that it is just too ridiculous to dignify with a reply. After all, between what is announced in the Chamber of Deputies and what is actually done...."

But surely, Michael had countered, was that not tantamount to hiding one's head in the sand?

Would it not be better to take a firm stand now, and make France understand that her attitude would not be tolerated?

"Perhaps it might have been better with Goblet, the former Foreign Minister. But Ribot is a hothead, and we are certainly not going to endanger our relations with France over Siam.

"You see, and although I don't always approve of it as you well know, I can understand London's way of thinking that those of us who are actually here sometimes become too involved. It makes us lose sight of the greater good, as it were.

"As you, young man, have just demonstrated."

Cowed at the public rebuke, Michael fell silent, as the Minister continued in a kinder tone: "Their Lordships may well decide to do as you recommend. I have no way of knowing as yet. Wait and see, my boy, wait and see. But remember, it is our interests we are here to defend.

"Not Siam's, whose only importance to Britain is as a buffer between Imperial India, British Malaya and France's colonies."

Julie had listened without interrupting, wondering, as she often did, if Louis would have understood, would have accepted how divided she felt.

He had loved her, yes. But he had worshipped Pavie.

Which love would have won?

Michael poured them both more wine. "No more long faces, my dear. Let us talk of something cheerful, like your parents' last letter. I saw that one came in the post today. What does your Mama berate you about now?"

Julie laughed ruefully. Where to start?

She was being blamed for Victor's applying to join the Naval Infantry Corps in Saigon — but Michael was blamed as well, so he needn't look so smug.

It seemed that Victor's request for a transfer would be approved, so he might be travelling east at the beginning of next year. How did she and Michael manage to convince this brilliant young man to turn his back on his family and everything dear?

"And of course, my refusal to return with him still rankles." She took the letter from her pocket. "Listen: *'Surely, a way might have been found to provide your son with milk throughout the journey, and I do not understand why you did not consider taking your wet-nurse, who could then have been put on the first ship back to Bangkok.*

'I say nothing of the disappointment your Papa and I feel at being

treated this way, and not yet knowing our grandson, because we are old now and do not count.

'But when I think of all the trouble and expense for darling Victor, just to escort you home safely. What could have possessed you to impose such a journey on your dear brother for nothing?'

"However, she is pleased to tell me that Augusta is expecting again, and, of course, that another Godmother needed to be found for little Edmond, which, apparently, was not a problem. *'Augusta's sister-in-law, who is a reliable (underlined twice) and loving aunt.'* Oh, and concerning my teaching at the Palace: *'I do not wonder that your head is turned at the exalted opportunity you have been given. But you must always remember the fate of poor Mrs Leonowens, and how shabbily she was treated. Royalty in heathen lands is not the same as royalty in the civilized world.'*

"And she wonders that I was reluctant to return to Paris?"

She should not be unfair, Michael remonstrated. Her mother was angry only out of love. And with her darling son about to leave for who knew how long, Julie really could not blame her.

"Oh, I don't, not really," she replied sadly. "And I know she blames herself more than anyone. If she had not agreed to my marrying Louis, if she had stood firm and insisted I wait for him in France, if, if..."

She seemed to shake herself, sat straighter in her chair, and forced a smile. "So long as she doesn't find out I threw away her black hat..."

Chapter VII

Julie woke before the first cries of the babies and stretched in the sunshine splashing her pillow. The house was still quiet, although the *soi* outside was already bustling with the street vendors hawking their fruit, she could smell the chicken skewers grilling at the stand of the old man who set up his cart just outside the gate, and she knew Fie would be standing at the gate, ready to make offerings of rice and stewed vegetables to the line of orange robed monks who were gliding by in silence, eyes downcast, their bronze bowls outstretched to receive their food for the day.

A bulbul was singing outside her window, and she rose to open the shutters. The heavy rain that had thundered most of the night on the roof had left sparkling drops of silver on the leaves of the banana tree and the scent of the frangipani blossoms seemed almost solid in the thick, humid air as she leaned out.

This evening was the festival of Loy Krathong, and she had been invited by Princess Keow to celebrate it at the Palace. All of her students had been excited for days, planning the lovely *krathong* they would weave, vying with each other to make the most elaborate bamboo basket decorated with flowers, candles and incense.

At nightfall, the fragile rafts would be set afloat on the roiling waters of the great river, with their candles and incense bravely lit, to carry away all sins and bitterness of the past year.

"Honour Lord Buddha, and Goddess of River. Siamese holy days often do both, for Buddha and old gods, yes?

"You come. Spend the night, yes? Cannot leave Palace at night. Bring baby and nurses, yes?"

No, Julie thought it best to leave Louis at home, but Keow would brook no contradiction. "Bring baby and nurses. Have room, never mind."

Well, certainly, there was room, she could not help thinking drily.

In the five months she had been visiting the Palace twice a week, she still had not been able to explore every courtyard, and frequently got lost when she wandered away from the school pavilion towards Sivalai gardens and the Emerald Buddha temple. But there always seemed to be someone, a guard, a court lady or a soldier who knew the *farang* woman and took her safely back to the gate of the Inner Court, or steered her away from the Royal Residence where, she had been told, were the Yellow, Green and Blue Rooms, the Royal dining and bedrooms.

After all, she assented, why not?

Fie had made friends amongst the serving women, and poor downtrodden Mali was terribly envious at having to hear her tales of the perfection that was life at the Palace. It was only fair to let her have a glimpse as well.

Keow had informed her that she was to be given a bed in the Princess' own apartments, a suite of cool, airy chambers above a sitting room where she had been given luncheon or tea several times. The floor was smooth polished tiles, with silk cushions and triangular bolsters strewn about, and at the clap of Keow's beringged hands, low ornate tables laden with refreshments always appeared in a few minutes.

Glass-fronted cabinets displayed all manner of objects, from the sublime to the ridiculous, Julie reflected with a smile, gazing at what even she could recognize as priceless porcelain cheek by jowl with a set of cheap china dogs and a pair of chipped Toby jugs.

The walls were hung with English hunting prints and a calendar several years out of date advertising Prudential Insurance, along with an intricate hanging of knotted silk. In a corner, a huge Chinese bed of fretted, carved and gilt wood draped with muslin mosquito nets — "Family me Chinese, a little," explained Keow, — and there were generally some elderly princesses seated on cushions gambling over a mah-jong game and cackling as they shared gossip and nibbled sweetmeats.

All in all, she thought, a delightful room.

Had Julie been asked, she would have admitted, to her immense surprise, that although she still grieved for Louis, she had never been happier.

This life, for which nothing had prepared her and so foreign from the future so carefully charted by her family, suited her perfectly.

She needn't bother with most conventions, she had companionship with Michael and her new friends at the Palace, who also fulfilled her curiosity for anything unusual or exotic.

"In fact, she wrote to her friend Amélie, *it is as if I were living in a novel by Monsieur Loti, a explorer in a new world discovering something unexpected wherever he looks.*

You would certainly find it very limited — there is no theatre or concerts — or only amateur productions, which I cannot attend anyway, being in mourning — no books, except for an unofficial lending library operated by several British ladies — no elegant shops, no tea-rooms...

But there are bazaars, which are great fun now that I can haggle in Siamese and have learned to ignore the dust and flies. I assume it might be possible to be served hot chocolate at the Oriental Hotel — but in this weather, all one wants is lime juice, and, as far as theatre goes, I have my twice weekly sessions at the Palace, which are more entertaining than anything ever seen on stage at the Opéra Comique.

I have several friends, whom I have already mentioned, Leonie who is invaluable in giving me advice about child rearing and house management and fashion and dressmakers, and Fanny, with whom I continue to take classes in Siamese, which I then put into practice when I go teach at the Palace.

Yesterday, I was invited to attend the festival of Loy Krathong, where you float a votive offering on the river, and as it was after nightfall, I spent the night at the Inner Court.

The ceremony was beautiful, His Majesty the King appeared on the Royal barge with the nine-headed serpent, all of us went down on our knees, and, although I had been told not to, I raised my head to watch him light a torch on an extraordinary raft bearing an image of the Buddha.

Never have I seen such a sight: the King was garbed in ceremonial attire, crusted with gold and gems and his crown was a pointed tiara similar to those worn by the fantastical creatures painted on the Palace walls, and for all that he is a rather small man, he seemed more divine than human.

"His expression was remote and indeed, it must be a strange feeling to be adored as a god.

"All of us then trooped down to the river's edge at the water gate of the Palace to release our own little crafts carrying away all of our sins, and the river was alight with all these thousands and thousands of candles bobbing downstream, with the full moon casting a lovely silver light on the flowers bedecking the krathong, *as the little floating baskets are called.*

The royal orchestra was playing shrill tunes meanwhile, and one cannot imagine anything as colourful and impressive as the crowds massed on the banks, the fireworks and my friends the Palace ladies in all their finery and jewels.

I, too, had been dressed for the occasion — don't tell my Mama if you see her — in pink and yellow silk, with the attendants giggling at my clutching of the traditional skirt and bodice for fear of losing them and finding myself suddenly naked.

In fact, I was entrusted to the masseuse when I arrived in early afternoon, and was rubbed, kneaded, and scrubbed with turmeric — a yellow root that is supposed to be good for your skin — to within an inch of my life, my hair was washed in some sweet, thick powder and I was anointed all over with fragrant oils. My hair was coiled and braided with flowers, my eyes painted with something dark and mysterious — and you would not have recognized the old Julie you knew.

My cousin Michael certainly didn't when we crossed paths by the river gate.

Michael was not the only *farang* diplomat she encountered that evening under the full moon.

As she went up to him laughing to show herself off dressed as a Siamese court lady, she saw his eyes were fixed elsewhere, on a tall, massive silhouette. He started when she came before him, pirouetting like a ballerina, and smiled. "I never would have recognized you, dear girl. If your Mama could only see you now!"

But his gaiety appeared forced, and his eyes went straying back to the cluster of men where she recognized Monsieur Hardouin and Monsieur de Pina, the French diplomats. The tall man with them turned and she gasped, with memories of the last time she had seen him, at the French Consulate, when he complimented her for following her husband.

"Pavie?" she whispered. Michael nodded, a somber look on his face.

"He has just been appointed Consul-General in Bangkok.

"I know Louis admired him, but think what you will, my dear, this spells trouble."

He was not alone in his views, he told Julie over dinner a month later.

On His Majesty's instructions, the Foreign Minister, Prince Devawongse, had called in the British, American and German envoys to ask their opinion on the latest demand of France, couched as a diplomatic request, but containing an implicit threat: to negotiate the border separating Siam from Laos — or face the resolution by force...

"What will Siam do? Well, it's really more a matter of what Siam *can* do. Negotiate, of course.

"But who can do so on Siam's behalf, who is also a French speaker, a lawyer, an expert on international law, and who is emphatically not French?

"I doubt such a man exists..."

Weeks and months went by, and nothing appeared to change in the lives of *farangs* in Bangkok despite the misgivings and mistrust simmering beneath the surface: the French and the British still encountered each other at the Oriental Hotel, danced at the Christmas balls, some played billiards or tennis together, Captain Jones still attended mass in French at Assumption Cathedral, where Monsieur Pavie greeted Julie one Sunday shortly before Easter and spoke feelingly of Louis, his dedication and the tragedy of his untimely death.

"But," he said searchingly, holding her hand in both his huge, calloused paws, "I had no idea I would find you living in Bangkok. Did you not want to return to the bosom of your family?"

Yes, well, Julie replied in a diffident voice, her health at first, then that of her son prevented a long sea voyage. And now, she felt most comfortable living in Siam, and taught French at the Palace, so...

"You teach the beauties of our language here? I did not know. But that is remarkable, and a very worthwhile endeavour! Through your lessons, you are the very embodiment of France's mission to civilize.

"Anything which might extend and strengthen the influence of France at the Court is of great use to your country, as of course you realize..."

Julie stifled an inner giggle behind the veil of her hat, picturing the lessons where they sang, dressed each other's hair, played at being shop holders to teach numbers, or, as last week, when she had been shown how to perfume her clothes by enclosing them in earthenware jars with a scented candle smouldering under the lid. No, it would not damage the garments, she had been assured, and in fact protected them from moths.

She nodded gravely.

Yes, she had no doubt her lessons were creating a great love for France among the Princesses.

"I should be most honoured if you were to come to dinner at the Consulate," Pavie continued. "I realize you are in mourning still, but surely, an intimate dinner... This very evening?"

"What could I do but accept?
"France's mission to civilize, indeed!
"I wanted to say that the Siamese are very civilized already, thank you very much!" she complained to Michael after coming home and kicking off the new soft leather slippers she had commissioned a gentle Indian shoemaker with dark and soulful eyes to produce in several colours from her own design, with neither straps nor buttons so as to be able to remove them easily whenever she entered the Palace school, or a temple or the house.

"Although I want to be able to talk about Louis with someone who knew him, I can't help but feel this dinner has nothing to do with him; Monsieur Pavie only came up with the invitation once I mentioned teaching at the Palace."

"What else could it be?" Michael objected with a laugh. "I know he is a bachelor and has no experience of women, but even he cannot imagine that you spend your time at the Inner Court talking politics. Maybe he wants to offer you marriage, now that he knows you can withstand life in this country. Don't wear black, though, wear that lovely grey gown from your trousseau. It's dark enough to be seemly, but you look enchanting in it.

"What does it matter that it is an afternoon dress?

"Do you honestly believe Monsieur Pavie can tell the difference?"

Julie shrugged. It was still a bit tight about the waist, but she would try to get Fie to pull very hard on her corset laces. And Michael was not to go all embarrassed when she spoke of her undergarments, had he rather pretend she wore none?

Whatever it was Monsieur Pavie wanted of her, she was not looking forward to getting back into her stays for this event.

When she alighted from the buggy in front of the Consulate, and smoothed her long gloves after arranging the silk of her skirts about her, she stifled a feeling of panic. She could not help but feel that this dinner was a harbinger of soirées to come in Paris, when she would be asked to brighten the evening of a grey-bearded widower with a paunch.

The major-domo offered his hand to help her ascend the steep steps leading to the verandah, and Monsieur Pavie bustled up, smiling with delight.

"Ah, Madame. You make me the happiest man in Siam tonight."

Julie bit her lips, with the incongruous feeling that perhaps Michael's ridiculous jest would turn out to come true. The man could be her father...

But Pavie continued, she knew Monsieur Hardouin, of course, and Monsieur de Pina?

Both men bowed, and she let out a deep, relieved breath, reassured that had he wanted to propose to her, he would not do it with his staff in attendance.

"Shall we go in to dinner immediately?" he proposed, as there were just the four of them, and offering Julie his arm guided her into the long wood-panelled dining room, where the major-domo and two footmen waited with covered salvers. One he was seated, Pavie unfolded his damask napkin over his beard, pausing to carefully smooth the embroidered RF, for République Française, of the monogram. He ran his thick thumb over the engraved silver spoon with sensuous pleasure, and Julie was reminded of what Louis had told her with admiration, and Michael with some disdain: Auguste Pavie was of humble beginnings, and was by training a telegraph operator.

Never would he have imagined representing his country, and in such luxurious style.

A five-course dinner was served, with wines and champagne, far more food than was usual at Michael's erratic and abstemious table, and while Pavie ate with what seemed to her rather unseemly greediness she could feel herself becoming giddy and uncomfortable.

She fumbled in her reticule to find a handkerchief to dab at her forehead, and became aware that all three men had fallen silent and were considering her carefully, "as if I were a strange and unknown species of insect in a museum" was the way she described it later to Michael.

Finally, Monsieur Pavie cleared his throat.

"We are all very interested to hear that you teach the ladies at the Palace.

"In fact, it might please you to know that I saw His Excellency the Foreign Minister this very afternoon, and your name came up."

"Oh, did it?" Julie murmured demurely, while she wondered how long it had taken the Frenchman to bring up the conversation with Prince Devawongse, and more importantly, why.

"Yes indeed. He expressed some incomprehension, however, at how you can be both French and English."

Many people did, particularly the French and the English, Julie stated with feeling, as Pavie ignored her aside, and continued: "His Royal Highness expressed the great delight of His Majesty in hearing that his noble ladies are now learning about France."

She nodded with what she hoped was a gratified smile, while De Pina smoothed his little Garibaldi-like moustache and goatee, and stared at her with what Julie was quite certain was dislike.

"And so, we were thinking..." Pavie seemed to be seeking the right words, when Monsieur Hardouin interrupted him, his face flushed and his sweaty greying hair plastered to his skull.

"It appeared to us that you might perhaps include in your teaching something about our — by our, we mean France's, naturally — role in the world, our defence of liberty and fraternity, particularly as it pertains to the rights of the Kingdom of Laos."

Stunned, Julie put down her spoon. "Surely not", she blurted, before giving herself time to think, and bit her tongue for being so impulsive.

Pavie frowned, his enormous hands crossed over his starched napkin, now stained with dribbles of dark sauce. "Why not? Do you not agree?

"Your husband was a great believer in the rightful freedom of Laos and of the special role History has entrusted us with — you notice I do not say God gave us this mission, and I often take task with our good missionaries who try to force their religion on the poor people here."

She swallowed, as if she were six years old and being chided by her father, and desperately tried to frame an acceptable answer.

With a forced, and to her ears, artificial laugh, she

explained that the level of proficiency in French of her delightful students certainly did not make them able to understand anything beyond the basics of everyday life.

"My name is Chuttarat, I like to eat mango, you are wearing a red dress...." she expounded brightly. "We sing. We count. I very much fear that we are nowhere near freedom or fraternity ... and of course, we have no maps, and even if we did, I very much doubt any of the ladies could place Laos on it."

Pavie nodded, reluctantly.

"But," Julie continued in an encouraging voice, "perhaps, after a few years?

"If, of course, I am still here to continue teaching?"

De Pina was still looking unconvinced, while Hardouin crumbled bread between his fingers.

"You still live with your cousin, I believe?" he asked as if genuinely interested.

"Yes? Another way you could serve your country, of course, would be to inform us..."

"No, no, no," Pavie cut in, glaring at Hardouin. "Not inform — merely, how shall we say, advise us, yes, 'advise' is surely the word you were looking for, Charles?"

Hardouin made a face, but quenched, continued "*Advise* us, then, if you happen to hear anything from your cousin that might be of interest to us?"

Seething inside, her breath taken away at the insult to either her family loyalties or her intelligence, Julie summoned her memories of all the silly, mindless girls she had ever despised in Paris, and favoured him with her most obliging and innocent look, her voice sheer syrup.

"Interest? Interest such as what? Things he talks about with his colleagues? Well... There is to be a performance of the Mikado organized by the amateur theatrical society. Michael is very much looking forward to it. Is it such things you wanted to know?"

Pavie gave her an indulgent smile.

Not quite, perhaps titbits from the British Legation. Although he was himself quite fond of Gilbert and Sullivan, and should be delighted to attend.

"I know," she cried triumphantly, and lowered her voice.

"Colonel Boyd, the American Minister, has arrested a Mr Collins, a foreman at the Bangkok Docks for living with a Chinese woman, although he has a wife in America... and..." She looked around as if to ensure greater secrecy... "she is with child."

De Pina threw down his napkin in disgust and glared at his colleagues, as if he knew asking any thing of such a woman were hopeless.

"Everybody knows that. It is even in the papers." he muttered. "Boyd claims he wants to 'Americanize' society here," he added with contempt.

Then... Julie opened her eyes guilelessly and looked at each man in turn. If they already knew that, she really did not know what they expected of her....

But it did not seem fair either to the wife left behind, or to the Chinese lady, who will have no one to look after her or her baby.

She prattled on, collecting her reticule, and fan, and finally took her leave, remembering her upbringing enough to thank her host for the first soirée she had attended since — she dabbed her eyes as convincingly as she could... since...and went down the stairs, cursing Pavie, Hardouin, and de Pina with every step.

"Can you imagine? CAN you imagine?" she repeated, pacing the floor of the drawing room in her anger, tearing off her gloves.

Sprawled on the couch, instead of being as incensed as she was, Michael was convulsed with laughter.

"You actually told them I was looking forward to the Mikado?" he chortled.

"I hate Gilbert and Sullivan. Oh, God, I wish I had been a fly on the wall...

"Bravo, my dear, a sterling bit of acting. But don't lose any sleep over it. I can't say that, if the tables were turned, we wouldn't have tried the same thing."

Then sitting up, he continued more soberly that what this had revealed was the extent of the Pavie's worries, and how far he was prepared to go. And another weapon the French had decided to use was public opinion. They were backing that rag of a newspaper, the *Siam Free Press*.

Had she ever read it?

"I glanced through it once or twice at the Oriental" Julie replied. "I never found it terribly interesting. And as you don't take it here, I really never read it."

Well, it had the worst sort of editor, a venal, bitter, rabble-rousing Irishman called Lillie. He seemed to now endorse the French position, lock, stock and barrel. "I wonder how much Pavie pays him. You may not find it terribly interesting, but it is widely read here in the business community."

That was all very well, Julie retorted in a weary voice, but there was a more urgent matter. She needed to move house. Now.

She did not want such unsavoury, unacceptable, insulting proposals ever to be made again, and if they were no longer sharing a house, it would occur to no one to try. "No, don't object, you know I'm right.

"Oh... and when I imagined for a moment that Pavie was going to propose to me... You beast, you put that in my mind, and I was thinking of ways of letting him down gently..." She collapsed in an armchair, now laughing as hard as Michael was, tears streaming down her face.

"Well, I don't think Pavie is going to suddenly offer you his name", Michael snorted. "Your performance tonight will have done nothing to change his mind about women being helpmeets. And I suppose you are right about moving. Let's see what we can find for you nearby. But I will sorely miss you and Louis."

She was in luck. Nearby, in the next *soi*, there was a grey wooden house, surrounded by a lush garden, with enough rooms for herself, the nursery, Victor when he might want to visit and Fie, Mali and little Nhu Dam, plus the servants she needed to hire.

"I find good servants for you," Princess Keow announced. "We send real cook, yes? Good. No thanks, never mind. Easy."

The furniture was plain, but serviceable and both Fanny and Léonie took her to buy whatever they thought was necessary.

"Rattan furniture for the verandah, of course," Léonie said firmly. "I know just the place." Or "Don't bother buying pots and pans. Give the cook some money. He will take his cut, but it will still be cheaper that way." Fanny advised.

But the first evening after Julie had moved in, despite the clatter of the servants coming from the outdoor kitchen, Mali's soft singing in the nursery, and the knowledge that she needed but walk to the next *soi* to have Michael's company, never had she felt so forsaken.

"BANGKOK, JUNE 17TH 1892

My new address is Bangrak, Soi Mahesak 3, and I have done everything required by Siamese custom: Fie and Fanny — and indeed Keow, who seems to pull innumerable strings from her courtyard in the Palace — all insisted that I have a spirit house installed before I moved in, and Brahman monks came to determine the right place and perform the ceremony that serves, from what I gather, to ensure the spirits residing in this place take us under their protection.

My house is as nice as possible, its grey wood exterior was blistered and peeling, so I had it repainted with white trims and fretwork and shutters. I had some very simple white linen curtains made for all the rooms, most of the furniture is cheap bamboo. After all, I shall not live here forever, and I find the copies made of English settees and tables and sideboards so dark and depressing...

There is a smell of paint and varnish and soap which I find very pleasant. Princess Keow had the servants she despatched bring baskets of flowers from the Palace. These servants... they seem very good, and respectful, but I cannot help miss Pon and his motley crew.

When I think that, as I remember telling Michael, I was looking forward to being mistress of my own household... Of course, in my mind then, I was to make a home for Louis when he came.

Well, now, I am making a home for another Louis, whom I love more than words can express, and his father is a lovely, but shadowy memory.

I cannot stop crying."

Why shouldn't Michael take all his meals with her? she asked after their first dinner in the cool of her dining room, while the rains shook the fretwork of the shutters, and the punkah made a refreshing breeze over their heads. Her cook was so much better. Did he not enjoy the fish?

Michael leaned back in his armchair, and took a sip of the brandy her head servant had just poured.

"Indeed, the food is very good, my dear. And I promise, I shall come very often. But.... But..." He tilted his head at her, then smiled and blushed all at once.

"Oh, you have met someone!" she cried with forced delight, and inner misgivings. If Michael were no longer so available to her, she would truly be alone..."Do tell!"

He shook his head and pursed his lips to contain his air of excitement. "Too soon, really.... A boy... His name is Somboon. He... well, he appeared at the gate, looking for work. His father gambled away whatever little money they had, and he must provide for his mother. No, don't ask me more, I promise I will tell you more when there is more to tell.

"Now, without being a cad like Pavie and asking you to play the spy, have you heard anything at the Palace about relations with the French?"

She rolled her eyes at him. Did he seriously think that her students would be informed? Or for that matter, that they would be interested?

Although, she reflected, Princess Keow, perhaps, might have learned something.

"But I would be the last person she would discuss it with. Why?"

Pavie was putting a great deal of pressure on Siam, because he himself was subject to unrelenting pressure from the Colonial Party in the French Parliament.

"Well, Pavie claims it is justified."

A French Vietnamese detachment had been captured by the Siamese, in retaliation the Lao stronghold of Ailao had been seized, and the status quo he had been able to achieve last year was only a distant memory; in other words, the Kingdom's resistance to French military incursions on the East bank of the Mekong seemed to goad Paris away from the negotiating table and towards the use of force. "So you see, it should be best if talks could start very soon, before something irreparable happens."

The monsoon dragged on, the air was thick with hot, cloying mists and violent storms filled each night with electricity. Everyone's tempers seemed frayed. Even at the Palace, to Julie that haven of harmony and delight, Princess Keow was overheard chiding her royal charges with unusual asperity, and the little princesses spoke in whispers and exchanged frightened glances.

Seated on her cushions, she mopped her forehead and sighed, sharing morning tea with Julie. Her serene, lineless face was troubled, and she munched on the sweetmeats with no appetite, even spurning her favourite shrimp in sugar.

"His Majesty very tired and worried, Queens very tired and worried, so we very tired and worried. I know not why, never mind. No pleasure in nothing.

"His Majesty sick very sometimes. Need change.

"When rainy season over, we go to Ayutthaya. You come, never mind."

A few days later, she was about to climb in the carriage amidst the bustle and noise of the Outer Court, and trying to keep hold of Louis who, now that he could walk, refused to be carried, and ran ahead into the crowd.

Fie was burdened with the baskets of fruit Keow always insisted they take back home, and the little blond toddler was revelling in the attention and delight that always accompanied him wherever he went. Extracting him with an apologetic smile from the loving grasp of a soldier who was showing the child the hilt of his sword, she heard her name called, and was stopped and greeted by Joseph Caulfield James, the Crown Prince's tutor.

"I had heard you were teaching here as well," he exclaimed with a grin, "and I was hoping to meet you. Well, it seems French is about to become more useful at Court, don't you think? Oh, haven't you heard?

"There is to be new Special Royal Advisor, for the

border issues. A Belgian gentleman – well, you couldn't expect them to employ a Frenchman to do that job!" he ended with a laugh, fanning himself with his straw hat.

Julie laughed with him, then fended off his many suggestions as to how they might spend an evening together.

No, she really could not dine at the Oriental, or dance at the Club after tennis. And no, she entertained no guests at her new home, only her cousin. She was in mourning still, she explained soberly.

Joseph took in her red dress, and the flowers Mom Chao Chuttarat had woven into her chignon.

"Don't look terribly mournful to me," he commented with a hurt sneer.

She handed Louis up to Fie who was already seated in the carriage, and turned back to the young Englishman who could not keep the wounded expression off his face.

"You wear mourning on the inside, so as not to evoke pity from those you meet," she said gently. "I hope you never need to discover this for yourself.

"Good-bye, Joseph, I am sorry, truly, but I know there are many young ladies who would love to go dancing with you."

Yes, it was true, Michael confirmed that very evening, a Belgian international lawyer had been found in Cairo, of all places. A Monsieur Rolin-Jaequemyns, who had arrived earlier in the week.

"And not a day too soon, if you ask me.

"The stock of two traders of your Papa's Syndicat du Haut Laos have been confiscated a couple of months ago at Outhen, and Pavie is livid with rage – at least he pretends to be.

"I think he is secretly delighted, because it gives him more grist for his mill in claiming Siamese aggression. In fact, we hear – yes from one of our spies at the Consulate, don't try to guess who, dear girl — he is drawing up a catalogue of what he claims are the many cases of unwarranted acts of aggression and bad faith by Siam. And Prince Devawongse is refusing to back down and return the confiscated goods, which is, to say the least, unhelpful.

"Meanwhile, His Majesty is ill, Princess Keow was right, and he has gone to recover at his summer Palace on Koh Si Chang Island, so there is no one to arbitrate at the Royal cabinet.

"I don't envy Monsieur Rolin-Jaequemyns the task he has taken on, and wish him luck."

Chapter VIII

"*Saigon, November 15ᵀᴴ, 1892*

Dear Kitten — and dear Michael, because I know you will read this letter to him,

Who ever said life was easy in the colonies?
Ever since I arrived in August, I have been swept up in a frenzy of work, which explains that I did not write.

We have been on manoeuvres for the past three months, preparing for action on the Lao border, in case you didn't know. I was assigned to the Regiment of Tirailleurs Annamites, and I command one hundred and twenty of these tough, fearless, sun hardened little men, whom I am pleased to have on my side rather then the reverse.

It was all march up, march down, march around, in the heat, in the rain — and by the way, can I really hope that the rainy season is over now? — in the jungle, with plants dripping over your heads, uniforms sticking to your backs, sweat running into your eyes and strange animal noises from the tangle of plants you need to push through. Some plants can slake your thirst, some plants can be used to clean wounds, and some cut like the sharpest knife and are extremely poisonous; I think I can now tell which is which. My hardy soldiers have taught me far more, I fear, than I taught them.

Between operations, each lasting two or three weeks, when I return to Saigon, I am so tired that I fall into bed and sleep for days.

I lodge with three fellow officers in a villa belonging to a Chinese landlord, a wispy little man with an enormous and forbidding wife. They live in Cholon, where most of their countrymen congregate, and the area is a world apart, a maze of shops, alleys, temples, noise and smells.

He is happy just to take my money when I go to his house to pay rent, she however, has taken it upon herself to find me a spouse — well, she says 'spouse' when she and I know both well it means what is here called a 'little wife' or 'mousmé' — and occasionally she invites me to meet one of her many nieces. Although, of course, they are not nieces, at least, I do not think so.

Imagine the look on Mama's face if I were to return to Paris with one of those delightful little creatures in tow, with their tiny hands, shrill voices and cool, evaluating eyes.

Of course, when we are in town, and when I finally wake up, there are all the obligatory amusements, cafés, billiards, balls, the Club Sportif where you go to read the latest papers and to be seen rather than to take exercise — did you understand from the above than I do not feel in need of more exercise? — and an officer's mess where the most delicious food is served, and has as many waiters as Maxim's. And probably as many cocottes, though here they are called differently.

Dare I say it, my dearest sister?

I am, if not happy, at least very satisfied with my life.

Shall you come visit me, to remind yourself of what life in a real city is like, with countrymen and women who dress elegantly, chat, gossip, sit and flirt at café terraces?

And in the meantime, may I spend New Year with you in Bangkok? We are told that the early months of next year are to be very busy for us. I leave you to imagine what plans they have made for us poor soldiers.

I long to see you and little Louis, who, I hear, is walking now.

All the love of your brother,

Victor Lucas-Sauvain"

"Well, well," Michael said reflectively, handing Julie back the letter.

"*Preparing for action on the Lao border...Pleased to have them on his side rather than the reverse...* And *'the first months of next year are to be very busy...'* Do you think that just slipped out? Or did he mean to write it?"

Julie closed her eyes and shook her head. She didn't know.

Although... Victor enjoyed playing the part of the thoughtless, dashing, devil-may-care officer, but he was really rather deliberate.

"He probably meant to write it," she finally said, and

angrily slapped down the paper. "His mail might have been read by censors, he might have been accused of spying for the English.

"How could he have been so mad!"

"Or," Michael said in a careful voice, "he may have been told to write it."

Her eyes flashing, she rose in challenge. What did he mean?

Michael sighed. What he meant was that Victor was an officer, and did as he was told. Had he received an order to include this information in a letter to his sister — a sister who taught at the Siamese court— could he have refused?

No, of course not.

He joined her at the window where she was standing with her back to him, and clasped her rigid shoulders in an awkward embrace.

"I'm sorry, I suppose that I have become ridiculously suspicious, but that's what working at the Legation does to you these days.

"Don't give it any more thought. Please."

Yes, Victor assured them both cheerfully when he arrived on the steamer from Saigon, he had deliberately written all this information this as a warning to Michael.

He put down his glass, and ran his hands though his hair with a rueful smile.

The idea that his letters might be read by military censors had occurred to him only much later.

Julie swatted his shoulder with an annoyed look, and left the room to give Louis his bath.

Despite himself, Michael was still not convinced, but forced himself not to care and returned Victor's genial look. What did it matter, really, if his cousin had been ordered to dole out these bits of information? It certainly did not reveal anything they didn't already suspect.

What was the mood in Saigon, he asked. Was it bellicose?

Victor stretched his long legs, and shrugged.

"What do you expect? With the papers full of the border incidents, trade in Laos threatened, and the hysterical speeches of Deloncle in Parliament echoed by Lanessan, the Governor-General of Indochina?

"And you English are not really in favour, I can tell you. What with your occupation of Egypt, you can expect a call for retaliating on the Mekong to trump your influence.

"At least that is what I hear from Papa, who, by the way, seems to have turned his coat and becomes more of a colonialist by the day.

"Of course, the Siamese are not helping by digging their heels in, you know.

"Seen from Saigon, and bearing in mind I have no opinion whatever on the border dispute, even I think they should be more conciliatory."

"What would *you* have them do?" Michael asked impatiently. "Just give in to French demands?"

Victor shrugged again.

He was no diplomat, only a mere captain, and knew only of the military aspects. And if it came to using force, well, really...

His voice became very dry and disparaging, and he stood to pace the room, ticking off his points on his fingers as his voice rose.

Siamese troops on elephants?

With outdated and often defective canons, and no modern command as the French had?

How many of the Siamese troops were actually soldiers and not mere conscripts who had been handed an obsolete weapon?

Did Michael know? No?

Well, he could tell him: the Siamese army counted four thousand men, of whom only two thousand were usable.

Granted, most of the military instructors were Danes,

but the majority of the troops were ill-trained Laos or Khmers, known to be somewhat… "apathetic is the kindest word to describe them…" he sneered. The ammunition reserves were low, weaponry in poor condition. Which just about left the elephants.

What he would have the Siamese do is be realistic, he concluded, and picked up his glass, with a challenging look.

"You seem to know a great deal about Siamese combat readiness," Michael stated in as flat a tone as he could muster.

"I am paid to," Victor replied coldly as he sat down again. "I am, first, foremost, and only, an officer in the French army."

Julie strode into the drawing room, carrying Louis to say good night, her bare feet slapping the floor in exasperation, and glared at them, her face flushed and her dress wet from having been splashed by her son playing in his bath, her hair sticking to her cheeks.

"Enough! Both of you! I could hear you from upstairs!

"We are here to celebrate the New Year, not argue about matters of state!"

She buried her face in the boy's sweet-smelling blond curls to hide her disquiet.

Might her own brother be called upon to wage war against Siam?

How then could she face Princess Keow, and all her friends at the Palace? How had their own lives become embroiled in this ridiculous border dispute?

She set the child down in his long nightdress, and he took a few steps with his lovely tottering gait towards Michael showing off the painted wooden horse he had been given for Christmas.

Michael gathered him up in his arms, and kissed his soft damp hair.

"Your Mama is right, old chap. We should be spending the evening enjoying ourselves, and not talking about things we cannot change.."

Victor took him from his cousin, and dandled him on his knees.

"And also, complimenting your Mama on her new house."

He looked around at the uncluttered, serene room glowing softly with the oil lamps and candles.

"I very much like your house.

"It is as different from the villa I live in in Saigon as you can imagine, mine is full of lamps with coloured glass shades, red velvet sofas with the springs sticking out, dusty tasselled curtains and pictures of shepherdesses with frilly petticoats...

"And I really envy you this painting. Where did you get it?"

Julie smiled in relief at his change in tone, following his eyes to the canvas wall hanging, a delicately painted scene from the Ramakhien with muted gold highlights.

It was a gift from her friend Fanny when she moved in.

"It comes from her Siamese family, as she could not afford a gift, she actually gave me this. I think it's rather valuable... I was very embarrassed, and didn't want to accept at first, but she looked so hurt that I finally did.

"I have never met anyone quite so generous," she continued. "When I took her along on my shopping expeditions to furnish the house, I could not detect the slightest trace of envy."

She waved her hand at the low bamboo tables, teak armchairs and plain, glass-fronted cabinets. "Although, of course, most of what I bought was rather inexpensive, what would have been the point of spending masses of money on a house I shall not live in for more than a few years?"

Victor considered her last words with a nod, while Louis squealed as he tugged his uncle's moustache with shrieks of delight.

"No, don't pull, little mouse, it hurts. So I take it you have made plans to return to Paris, then, in time?"

In time, Julie sighed.

At least that was she wrote to Mama and Papa, and Victor was not to tell them otherwise. But she really did not know. She was happy, here, she concluded simply, and could not imagine living anywhere else.

"Off to bed, now!" she told the child, as, protesting, he let himself be picked up by Fie who had just crouched in with polite bobs to Michael and Victor.

"Is it not now time for dinner and champagne? Just let me get changed."

"BANGKOK, 4ᵀᴴ OF JANUARY 1893

I have decided that the time has come to throw off my deep mourning, and start going out in the world once more. Not that I have missed it thus far, I was content with my work — although, can my two mornings at the Palace really be called work? — and with my life at home with Michael and my son for company.

But I believe Louis would not have wanted me to become a drab and boring housebound woman.

So I selected the more conservative dresses of my trousseau, had Fie cinch me in my stays and accompanied Victor and Michael to the round of parties held to celebrate the New Year. No one seemed shocked at seeing me out so soon, and I was welcomed very kindly, even by Mrs Jones.

I cannot say I chose my moment well though, and thinking back on it, I would have rather stayed home. There is a definite feeling of unease, whenever the French, the English and the Siamese are gathered together.

Victor and I went to the Consulate to offer our season wishes to Monsieur Pavie, and he was most effusive on meeting my brother.

'I did not know that our charming Madame Gallet had a brother gallantly serving La République,' he cried. 'With men such as you, our Empire is well protected.'

To me, of course, he behaves as if I were a silly little woman. I realize now how much I dislike him, and always have; it did not start only when he asked me to spy on Michael and thought me stupid enough not to realize it.

Do I blame him for Louis' death or was I jealous of the sway he had over him?

There was a ball organized by the British Legation at Customs House, and Joseph flaunted an excited, newly-arrived, red-haired little Miss Mitchell, the daughter of a barrister, all the while giving me sidelong glances, as if he expected me to be jealous. She is quite charming, really, but treated me like an old lady, and actually tried to speak her boarding school French to me.

I danced with Doctor McFarland, who impressed everyone when he kicked up his feet in a reel, and with Admiral de Richelieu, who commands the Royal Siamese Navy, and who despite his name so famous in French history is actually Danish.

His eyes twinkled when he introduced himself, and said 'Yes, Madame, Richelieu, just like in the Three Mousqueteers!' I wonder how that came about.

I chatted about Paris with Prince Damrong, a former Minister of Education, and now the delightfully titled 'Minister for the North', who has recently arrived from a long journey to Europe and the Levant. I was quite dazzled by his wit and culture. He saw all the plays and exhibitions, heard all the concerts, strolled in all the museums, and made me feel rather provincial. He is also quite the dandy, and made all other men there seem dowdy.

It is he who met Monsieur Rolin-Jaequemyns in Cairo and convinced him to come advise His Majesty.

And so, last, but not least, I met the famous Monsieur Rolin-Jaequemyns, who was followed by every eye and each time he spoke to someone, there were whispered speculations on what might have been said, and why.

He has a big walrus-like moustache, and hair he parts down the middle, and he looks very wise but very friendly, determined to like everyone he was introduced to, and complimented everything he saw.

He is accompanied by his wife Emilie, a very pleasant and vivacious lady.

She asked my advice as to living in Bangkok, setting up house, and servants, as they are still at the Oriental Hotel.

'I shall have someone to speak French with,' she said very warmly, 'and I know we shall be friends.'

They have two daughters at school in France whom they both miss very much, and I suddenly felt rather guilty, thinking of Mama and Papa, who probably miss me as well, and have never met their grandson.

Signor Antonio, who owns a studio on New Road, had been commissioned to take photographs, and Victor and I sat for one, me in all my splendour with my dark blue gown, orchids in my hair and Victor in his uniform. I shall take Louis to have his portrait taken as well before I cut his curls, and send both to Paris."

She put down her pen and frowned. Why had she never thought of sending them a portrait of the child before? And one for Monsieur and Madame Gallet, Louis' diffident and unassuming parents, who had sent their first and only grandson a picture album for Christmas, and done it so early, no doubt fearing shipping delays, the parcel was delivered in October.

Her mind went back to that evening, when she was speaking with Emilie and spotted from the corner of her eye Michael huddled in a little group with Captain Jones, Prince Devawongse and Monsieur Rolin-Jaequemyns while Victor had been pulled into conversation with Monsieur Pavie, Hardouin, and another officer from Saigon.

When she had later asked him in her most casual voice what they were talking about, he airily replied nothing, just Saigon military gossip.

"Of course military gossip," Michael had commented with a somber look once they were back at the house and Victor had left them to end the evening over brandy and music at the nearby Trocadero Hotel with his fellow officer. "Such as French combat readiness.

"I am truly very concerned, dear girl.

"What we have been able to piece together from Court gossip is that the Royal Cabinet is now torn between factions.

"With His Majesty ill and away, Prince Devawongse and his brother Prince Svasti, who, I think, is a bit of a hothead, are dominating at present, and the voices of moderation that we are advocating along with the Germans and Americans, are simply not heard.

"Do you know what Prince Devawongse replied this evening when Captain Jones was advising conciliation?

"He said that Siam has no more to lose by fighting than by not fighting, and resistance would attract the world's attention to their rights, so then perhaps something might be done to prevent Siam being eaten up by the French. Obviously, it was a message to be communicated back to London, and my Minister took it as such.

"Yes, you understood me: Prince Devawongse believes – or at least we think he believes – that this claim to the East bank is but a ploy to attempt to takeover all of Siam up to the border with Burmah.

"In other words, that Pavie fabricated this dispute to then use it as an excuse to overrun the Kingdom. Do I agree with Prince Devawongse's views?"

Michael paused, ran his hand through his hair and sighed.

"Well, I'm not sure he is wrong...

"All I can say is, thank God for Monsieur Rolin-Jaequemyns."

He shook his head in despair, untied his white cravat, flinging it aside.

He sank into an armchair, and looked up at Julie with a bleak smile. "And incidentally, you can be sure Victor's mail will be read in the future now that his family ties in Bangkok are known. He had best be careful what he writes."

And now, Victor has left. He received Michael's warnings about censorship with his usual carefree grin, saying he too had realized that. In the future, he promised, he would write only about his landlady's, Madame Liang's, nieces.

I miss him, but am happy to have my tranquil house to myself once more, though it can barely be called so, with two boys crying, fighting over Fie's and Mali's attention, the one-eyed cat who followed us here and meows loudly and incessantly, a rooster who crows at sunset as well as sunrise, three hens to give us eggs, a gifted cook who sings as much and as badly as the cat and four squabbling servants.

Speaking of servants, I asked Michael about his young man, Somboon. He blushed. 'I am happy' he confessed. 'Is it bad of me?'

Of course not, I reassured him. Happiness is precious, and should be grasped when one can, not when others say one should.

I feel I have become very wise.

When Mama sees my portrait in a ball gown with my shoulders bared, albeit ever so little, and Louis dead only these two years she will surely disagree."

Michael was appearing daily more careworn and tense, and could manage only the occasional dinner, busy at writing reports and accompanying his Minister to hurriedly convened meetings, to preach moderation to the French, conciliation to the Siamese and attempt to garner support for negotiations from everyone else.

But in the first days of March, Monsieur Pavie with a grave look that did little to conceal his overall air of triumph informed all the foreign Legations in Siam that French parliamentary credits had been voted to undertake, if need be, a military operation on the Mekong.

He had formally presented to the Palace his country's claim to the entire East bank of the Mekong, and stated that France's demands would be backed by force, if, and only if, he stressed, Siam were to prove itself so unreasonable as to refuse this simple realignment of the border and withdraw all garrisons on the East bank.

"It seems to have had a sobering effect on the Royal Cabinet," Captain Jones informed Michael a week later, running his hand through his straggling hair. He looked even more dishevelled than usual, his collar rumpled with sweat and sleepless nights.

"His Excellency Prince Devawongse, on the advice, one can only assume, of Monsieur Rolin-Jaequemyns has proposed that the matter be settled by international arbitration, and has offered a standstill agreement pending the arbitration's outcome. The ball is in the French court.

"Let's wait and see."

"It's not a bad test of their intentions," Michael offered diffidently, "If they refuse, we'll know that Devawongse is probably right in thinking them dishonest."

"I'll tell you, my boy," the grizzled old officer stated with a somber look, "I don't know if Prince Devawongse is right, but for my part, I certainly think them dishonest.

"Just can't abide Pavie. Never could."

"What is an international arbitration?" Julie wanted to know as they lingered over dinner that evening.

It was a way of solving disputes, Michael explained, by submitting them to neutral and impartial third parties who were expected to be knowledgeable about the rules governing the case in question, in this instance, international treaty law.

"And, I suppose" he added with a sigh, "the geography and history of Laos and Annam as well. The problem is, nobody in the world knows more about the geography of Laos than Pavie."

"A standstill?
Pending international arbitration?" Pavie gasped in utter dismay, waving his arms and pacing the reception chambers of Prince Devawongse's palace as the Foreign Minister and the Belgian adviser watched his theatricals with horrified fascination. "Involving third nations and lawyers who have no idea of what they would be arbitrating about?

"It could take months, nay, years before a settlement might be reached.

"With the unfortunate Lao people suffering under the yoke of the Siamese crown and the border area a veritable powder keg?"

"Monsieur, Monsieur," Rolin-Jaequemyns attempted to interject, "The border area is a powder keg only because France's military incursions make it so, and..."

But Pavie swatted his objections aside, and sank his massive body in an armchair as if felled by the sheer enormity of the Siamese request.

"Well," he finally sighed, "it is up to the Government of the République Française to decide whether to submit the border dispute to arbitration, although I would advise most strenuously against it given the urgency of the matter, and," he added preening himself and stroking his beard, "my opinion on these matters is certainly valued by the Quai d'Orsay."

But he could already tell His Excellency the Foreign Minister of Siam that there was no question of a standstill agreement.

No.
None. None whatsoever.

A week later, he invited all of the French community in

Bangkok to a reception in honour of Captain de Coüy, the commander of the Far Eastern Naval division who had arrived on the *Lutin,* a gunboat stationed in Saigon that had just steamed up the river and moored at the Consulate's dock, while two others, the *Comète* and the *Inconstant* stayed at anchor before Paknam, the mouth of the great river.

To her great surprise, Julie received an invitation to attend, and prepared herself with misgivings to wear a deep violet dress made from glossy *satin duchesse* her mother had sent last Christmas with an attached note stating that the colour was appropriate for "*demi-deuil*".

Half-mourning colour, perhaps, Julie thought, although it was too beautiful not to use, and she instructed the seamstress to cut the bodice as low as she decently could.

"Aha," exclaimed Michael when he saw her come down the stairs. "I can just imagine what all these proper ladies shall say when you enter the Consulate. Not only a widow, but a merry widow at that!"

She had fretted, and pulled at the bodice ruffles this way and that, but whatever she did, it was more appropriate for a ball than for an early evening party, and she finally draped a lace shawl over herself to attempt to cover her exposed arms and cleavage.

She grimaced. "I know. It's all wrong, isn't it? I'll go up and change."

"Don't, that violet colour does something to your eyes, you look absolutely lovely. Give them something else to talk about than extending their colonial empire."

To her relief, Pavie and the other diplomats ignored her, and to sidestep the attention of the young naval officers who considered all the unattached females their rightful due, she scanned the assembly searching for a friendly face while she tugged on her shawl to expose less skin.

She spotted Mother Marguerite, the superior of the Sisters of Saint Paul of Chartres, who was standing in a corner, looking very small and shy and moved towards her with a smile.

The nun greeted her with a small sigh of relief — if only, Julie thought wryly, to have something to do with her hands other than finger her beads nervously — and a compliment on looking so well, with such a beautiful dress.

"Such a becoming colour. And I so envy you being able to have bare arms... Can you imagine how hot this robe is?"

She looked down with distaste at her plain grey linen habit. "Is it sinful of me to miss lovely clothes, and colours, do you think? Well, if it is, the Lord should see my regrets as the sacrifice I make daily for his sake." She smiled, as if remembering lovely dresses she had worn.

"I believe he understands, though I am quite sure Monsignor wouldn't, and therefore shall not confess to such worldly desires.

"Now enough about my weakness, I hear you teach at the Palace?

"That makes us colleagues of a sort, you know we have a little school attached to the lying-in hospital we operate for native women?"

They only taught proper care for newborns and attempted to put an end to all those unhealthy and superstitious practices such as having the women resting on heated planks once they had given birth, "but I can tell you, it's not easy to contend with their mothers — so we certainly don't even try to teach them French," she explained, laughing at Julie's descriptions of her frivolous and endearing students, and the classes spent singing songs or playing at being shop keepers.

"I'm sure that your games are as close to a shopkeeper as most of them will get," Mother Marguerite said, refusing a glass of champagne with a wistful look. She looked about, taking in the many waiters in white uniforms, the splendid, airy room with its sculpted wall panels.

"I do not usually attend such gatherings. Do you?"

Julie smiled. No, not often, as a widow, she added, she was hardly ever invited.

Monsignor Vey, the Bishop, who was hovering nearby, overheard and turned to them, extending his hand to have his ring kissed.

The nun obliged, bending so low it was almost a genuflection but Julie contented herself with the merest bob of a curtsy so as not to embarrass the prelate with a plunging view of her bosom, challenging him with her eyes: he was either to raise his hand higher, or do without the homage, and he let in drop in defeat.

"Just so, just so, it is right and fitting neither of you ladies go out, but you are here to pay tribute to the steadfastness and glory of la République," he warbled in a rather overloud voice, pitched to be heard throughout the room, and added sotto voce in a biting mutter "Particularly in these days when our loyalty is questioned, in our own country of France which was considered in better times to be the Eldest child of our Mother the Church."

"We must all assure those who speak in the name of our beloved France of our unfailing support in their endeavours," he concluded before trotting off to fawn over Captain de Coüy and Pavie who were holding court on the verandah.

Mother Marguerite rolled her eyes.

"Men!" she dropped in a disparaging voice.

"Steadfastness and glory? Really! Misery and bloodshed, more like.

"If it were not for my faith, I should truly despair of them."

And, gathering her robes, she swept away, her plain, careworn face troubled under her wimple.

On the fourth of April, shortly before the beginning of celebrations for Songkran, the Siamese New Year, the Foreign Minister made another attempt to contain the looming crisis.

It also happened to be the day after the French overran Stung Treng, a fort on the Mekong, as Captain Jones pointed out the following morning.

"This time, now he sees the French really mean business, he has offered to withdraw all Siamese garrisons but two from the East bank.

"Pavie turned him down again — all the garrisons must decamp forthwith — and is crowing about it all over Bangkok.

"Bloody arrogant, trouble-mongering man!

"His Majesty is returning from Koh Si Chang in a couple of days.

"Don't know what he will decide, not much of a decision, really... After Stung Treng, the frogs are about to take Kong Island, which is about as close to Siam as you can get without actually *being* in Siam. He'll have to fold.

"But at least, Paris is accepting the principle of arbitration."

"So, what does it mean for us, sir?" Michael asked diffidently.

"The hell I know, boy," Jones growled. "Depends on the mood of our Lords and masters, doesn't it?

"Possession of the East bank entails control of the Shan States, and if the Shan territories are still as important to London as they were last year, we'll take a stand, and try to have our interests included in the arbitration, if it actually occurs.

"If we don't succeed... well, your guess is as good as mine.

"At least, they've got rid of Ribot, probably thought

him as much a liability as we do, although Develle, the new Foreign Minister is weak, and easily swayed by the Colonial Party, who hates Britain's guts...

"Do we placate the French, do we tell them to be damned? I truly don't know."

At the Palace, all of Princess Keow's charges were rejoicing. His Majesty, their Lord of Life was returning from Koh Si Chang. Surely, that meant he was cured of his illness.

"I let them talk, never mind," she told Julie, with a worried smile. "But Queen Saovabha, she say he worried very. Not better."

Julie looked down at the mangosteen she was squeezing in her hand, trying to hide her feelings of guilt.

It was removed it from her fingers with a reproving cluck.

"Stain dress," she was chided. "Mangosteen colour no go away. You no worry, never mind. Teacher Chuli friend of Siam, yes? So good, yes?"

Julie raised her brimming eyes to the older woman's understanding face.

"You are very kind, Your Highness."

Keow sniffed, and hitched her bodice cloth back over her ample shoulder, the rubies on her hands catching the sun.

"Not kind, never mind. Not easy be woman, not easy be half child.

"Teacher Chuli half-child, no?

"Half mother country, half father country, two countries, one heart only, one head. No sad face, no tears. Eat, eat."

"BANGKOK, APRIL 15ᵀᴴ 1893,

Yesterday, I met His Majesty the King, and two of his Queens for the first time.

I had been invited to take part in the Songkran celebrations, and I was standing in the Outer Court watching a military parade go by, with shrill fifes and throbbing drums and suddenly, all the ladies around me fell down to their knees with their heads to the ground, and when I looked up, he was standing before me. I sank into my deepest curtsy, and thank heavens I was wearing a proper dress, and not Siamese pantaloons or, even worse, a sarong.

Princess Keow rose on her elbows to introduce me, and His Majesty thanked me with a very kind look for teaching French to his ladies.

Both Queens smiled graciously before moving along, stopping to exchange a few words with various Princesses while I tried to catch my breath, dazzled by their jewels.

As I so often do, I wish I could paint so as to render my memory of that enchanting scene, the military band with their uniforms just like toy soldiers, the golden and green and red roofs of the Palace, the orange of the monks' robes and the multi-coloured royal ladies, who swayed and glittered in the sunshine of late afternoon, resembling a huge bouquet of the most exotic and delightful flowers. And finally the King with his medals, and sash, and royal insignia, and the Queens, one dressed in soft carmine and pink silk, and the other one in the deepest purple and the tender green of rice shoots.

I find that His Majesty seems tired and alone, and indeed, how can he not?

He has decided that if France wants war, then France shall have war, or so Michael tells me.

I partook of a special Songkran meal today, Khao Chae, which is cold rice soaked in iced jasmine water, with many savoury side dishes that must have required at least twenty cooks to prepare, so delicate and intricate are they, such as little balls made of dried anchovies in a lacy coating of egg yolk, tiny stuffed peppers and strands of caramelized beef. Quite delicious.

There is to be a ball at the Ministry of Foreign affairs this evening regardless of this tense situation. I wonder why they have decided not to cancel it.

I shall wear my new violet dress again.

Meanwhile, true to his word, Victor writes about this little Mademoiselle he takes to balls at the Club Sportif, and this other little "niece" whom he takes back home, and nothing, nothing, of what is about to happen at the border."

"We really cannot tell what the Cabinet wants to do." Jones sighed at the morning Legation meeting. "Do they truly believe they can kick the French out of the East bank?

"Crawfurd, your officer cousin was right, of course, the Siamese have inadequate weapons, inexperienced soldiers, not to mention the probably useless conscripts they are levying in the provinces.

"Meanwhile, they are barring the river and building three new forts to prevent incursions upriver. Well, for 'preventing incursions', read French gunboats from reaching Bangkok. Did you know," he mused, "that the main fort, the one next to Wat Arun, was built by the French two hundred years ago?

"Somehow, history always manages to come back to bite us in the rear.

"All right, everybody get back to whatever you were doing. Everybody but Crawfurd."

Sitting behind his desk, he rubbed his forehead, and spoke in a low voice, after checking the terrace door — if the British had an informer at the French consulate, it stood to reason that the French had one here.

"Devawongse believes, and I don't know how London will react, that we will come to their aid... I am honestly not sure we will antagonize France over Siam, but that's not what worries me most, it's out of my hands.

"You know what *does* worry me most, my boy?

"That upstart little telegraph-operator Pavie met with Eaton, you know, the preacher who is standing in for that prig Boyd who is on sick leave to the States? God, why, why, why don't the States have a real diplomat for once?

"Anyway, Pavie told him that the French Far Eastern naval division is at the ready in Saigon, ready to back up the gunboats at Paknam.

"Of course he held him to secrecy, and of course, bless his honest Baptist heart, the Yank told me.

"Which means they could seize the islands in the gulf, or, if they felt like it, just steam up the river and fire at the Palace. No one actually believes these forts being built would stop those gunboats for more than a minute.

"I've sent a telegram to London, of course, and also to Singapore. If they want to back Siam, the time is now. Why can't London say 'Hands off Siam, or else?'

"Well," Michael mused, "it's the 'or else' that matters, isn't it? They have to mean it."

Jones sighed. "And what you are saying is that they won't mean it. Of course not. They can't."

He rested his head on both hands, staring at a map without appearing to see it.

"Get some rest before the ball this evening, sir," Michael advised him gently.

"As you said, it is out of our hands."

To try and dispel his misgivings, Michael decided to walk back home to change for the ball, planning to stop at a Chinese merchant of antiquities and curios, an old man with a wispy beard who kept treasures in silk-lined boxes and unwrapped them caressingly under a flickering oil lamp. He had long had his eye on a small bronze Bodhisattva from Cambodia and was hoping to haggle the price down.

Sidestepping the vendors seated on the sidewalk and the food hawkers, he made his way through the crowded street, stopping to buy roasted peanuts from an old woman, and munched on them as he continued towards the shop on New Road, remembering the lovely serene expression on the four-armed idol, but was suddenly struck by the change in people's attitude: the normal good humoured banter was replaced by sullen, downwards faces as he passed by instead of the wide smiles and jests a *farang* usually elicited, and he found himself deliberately jostled by a group of young truculent-looking men who glared at him as he recovered his balance.

The crowd's mood was nervous, volatile, different from the usual elation of Songkran, as if somehow the tension of the Court had been communicated to the common people.

Abandoning the Bodhisattva for today and deciding to make directly for home, he was relieved to finally reach his front door and be fussed over by Somboon, who bustled around proffering a cool towel to mop his face and an iced lemon juice, muttering all the while that Khun Mykin should not have sent the buggy ahead, they had all been so worried when it came back without him, he should not have walked, it was dangerous.

"Dangerous?" Michael asked with a smile. He walked home often.

"Dangerous." Somboon repeated firmly, easing off his sweat-drenched shirt, and massaging away the knots of tension in his shoulders. Standing in the doorway, Pon nodded to confirm.

Did Khun Mykin not hear? The French boat was coming to make war, and there were other boats at Paknam. When the boats attacked the palace, the Chinese population would riot, and loot, and kill them all.

Starting with *farangs*.

Where did they hear this? Michael asked, amazed as always, at the speed at which news, whether real or not, spread in Bangkok.

"Old Granny Khop. The one who sells grilled fish, at the entrance of the *soi*? She has a son whose wife's niece knows a man who has friend who is a guard at the Palace. *He* was told by a servant who overheard a conversation..."

Michael raised his hand with a laugh. "And you believe something that has passed from — how many? Ten? Twelve other persons?"

Trying to sound more confident than he actually felt, he spoke in a slow and serious voice.

"There is no threat. Really, all of you, you mustn't listen to these rumours.

"Because these are nothing but rumours, and not true."

Somboon brightened visibly as he started to prepare his master's starched shirt and dress coat, but Pon still appeared unconvinced.

"I tell coachman be ready," he muttered, and left the room with a serious face.

"Will you save me a dance?" he asked Julie when he collected her from her house. "Seeing how beautiful you look, I thought it better to put in my claim now, before you get overwhelmed with invitations from all the dashing men in uniforms, vying for the chance to hold hands with the Merry Widow herself."

She settled back against the cushions, and fanned herself, the feathers in her hair bobbing with each lurch of the buggy.

"I'll see," she replied in an arch voice. "It all depends on the uniform."

She smoothed her long gloves up to her elbows, and continued with a thoughtful look. "I know you are just teasing me when you call me that, but I cannot help but wonder if that is what others think, and that I have forgotten Louis... How could I forget him?

"Mama writes that if I stay in Bangkok, she calls it 'that

backwater', it is just because I live more freely and need not worry about behaving properly or following conventions. And of course she is right."

The reason she stayed in Bangkok was because she was happy here, Michael countered gently. And that is what Louis would have wanted for her.

She played with the ostrich plumes of her fan, combing them with her fingers, and said nothing. He tried again.

"Do you think that going back to the sad, proper life in Paris that you know you will hate will make you feel less guilty about being happy without Louis?"

She sighed, and turned to him, blinking back her tears to not spoil her artfully blackened lashes. "That's just it, you see. I feel guilty that I don't feel guilty. Or is that too twisted for you?"

He gave her a mirthless laugh.

"Not too twisted at all. That is a description of my daily life.

"Come, let us dance until we forget what we were talking about, and spit in the eye of those who disapprove!"

"Bangkok, April 17th 1893

If Michael were at all interested in women, I would probably marry him.

We danced the first waltz together, and then — of course — he ended up huddled in a corner with Captain Jones and several other diplomats.

Prince Devawongse complimented me absent-mindedly on my dress, and also on my work at the Palace, saying Princess Keow relied greatly on me, but he seemed to be thinking of other, graver matters and soon left me to join Monsieur Rolin-Jaequemyns and his wife who were doing the rounds of the guests.

I was very impressed with the ballroom, which was decorated in enormous swags of dark pink and violet orchids, and an ice sculpture representing the Temple of Dawn had been commissioned from the Oriental

Hotel and was gradually melting into a huge puddle and dripping on to the floor.

None of the French had arrived yet, which all of us found a bit strange.

That Monsieur Pavie should want to assert his great importance by arriving late was to be expected, but the others are usually much more courteous, particularly as we were invited by His Royal Highness, and to slight a brother of the King is to slight His Majesty himself.

The band was playing fashionable tunes, from Strauss to Lehar's Merry Widow, and I saw Michael give me a knowing smile from his end of the room, when Léonie and her husband arrived, somewhat upset.

She promptly dragged me aside from where I was chatting with Doctor McFarland's wife and whispered that they, along with the most prominent members of the French community, had been called to the Consulate.

'Monsieur Pavie has received an anonymous letter containing a death threat and two Frenchmen were molested this afternoon on New Road.

We were being warned about possible unrest, and actually advised to go to Saigon for our own safety. My husband won't even think of it, and I shall stay with him, naturally. You live so close to New Road, chérie, should you not consider moving in with us?'

Nobody knew which Frenchmen, she admitted, or what had actually been done to them.

As I was telling her I should not move before I feel there is a need, and in which case, I shall return to Michael's, there was a hush, just like at the beginning of a play when the curtain goes up, and Monsieur Pavie appeared, followed by his staff. He paused at the door, looking for all the world as if he expected us to break out in applause just for condescending to attend the evening.

Lord, how I detest this man.

The Foreign Minister rushed up to him, and both conferred in low voices.

I expect Monsieur Pavie was telling him about the attacks, and I expect Prince Devawongse had already known about it, for he was shaking his head in a soothing way, and replying most earnestly.

Whatever was said, Monsieur Pavie appeared satisfied, and after speaking with Monsieur Rolin-Jaequemyns and his wife, he came up to me, *looking me up and down and making me feel I was showing too much bosom and not enough French loyalty.*

'Our delightful Madame Gallet,' he hissed. 'So decorative as always, and such a lovely member of our foreign community.'

He kissed my hand, then murmured that I had perhaps heard about the loathsome, craven attack on our fellow countrymen.

'I would urge you to show caution,' he dropped with contempt, 'except of course that you have placed yourself outside our group, and prefer to see yourself as more British than French.'

I did my best to look offended and surprised.

'How so, Monsieur le Consul?' I inquired. 'Was it not you yourself who were congratulating me on fostering a love of France among the ladies I teach at the Palace? Need I remind you that I do not teach them English?

'Did my husband not die, whilst serving France, under your orders?'

He had the decency to look flustered at my reply.

I fought off the attentions of an odious fellow countryman, a journalist named Lucien Fournereau. He brags about having taken a photograph of His Majesty, and also of the Queen, and crowed about his trip upcountry, to these 'poor, miserable provinces where unfortunate farmers live under the rule of lazy, uneducated potentates.'

Upon hearing that I teach at the Palace he asked whether I did not agree that the 'firm hand of a benevolent, enlightened rule was necessary to guide the vacillating throne, and should not that rule by necessity be that of France?'

It was all I could do to remain civil and say that I did not really know enough about France's benevolent rule elsewhere.

I realize I must be careful in what I say, and to whom.

When he complimented me on my dress with a sly, patronizing smile, I realized it was a veiled insult, and that I looked somehow wrong, provincial, overly ruffled and generally not fashionable. Oh well...

He, however, is a most dandified, affected man, but I must admit that his evening habit was beautifully cut and that paired with a green and pink silk damask waistcoat, he was the most elegant person there, and that we all must have looked like bumpkins in his eyes.

There was great excitement around eleven o'clock, when suddenly, the band struck up the royal anthem, and His Majesty appeared.

We all froze, then bowed and curtsied, and the King came by to exchange words with all of us. He remembered meeting me yesterday at the Palace, and repeated his words of thanks in a very diffident way. I honestly believe he is shy. He stayed for about half an hour, which he spent mainly with Monsieur Rolin-Jaequemyns and Pavie, and of course, he did not dance.

I, however, had the misfortune of being claimed for a waltz by the famous — or rather infamous — Mr Lillie, the editor of the Siam Free Press *and who, according to Michael, is in the pay of the French to spread lies about M. Rolin-Jaequemyns or Britain or whatever France does not approve of this week.*

Of course, I could not refuse.

He is an Irishman, tall, with rust-coloured hair and a truculent reddish face, and also very damp hands that I could feel kneading the back of my bodice. I am sure he left dark stains.

He speaks in an insinuating voice, and pressed me with questions, about Michael — 'does your dear cousin not have a fiancée languishing in England? Or is he pining for his French relative?' — whereas he knows — I am convinced he knows — what Michael's real life is and were he able to get proof, he would expose him in a heartbeat."

"I realize that, dear girl." Michael said with a fatalistic shrug. "But I really do not think he would even imagine looking for someone as insignificant as Somboon to tar me with. Let us just be thankful he does not accuse us of improper relations, as he seemed to imply.

"Meanwhile, he has bigger and better fish to fry than us. He has just written the most libellous and vicious attack against Rolin-Jaequemyns in his paper, accusing him of being a bankrupt businessman and a fraud.

"That's not going to go down well at court.

"Rolin-Jaequemyns is considering suing him for libel, and has published an article in the *Bangkok Times* to dispel the rumours of an imminent French attack, because many people, and not just *farangs*, but Chinese as well, are preparing to rush off to Singapore or Saigon, or Penang.

"So your Mr Lillie will probably forget about us for the time being."

Two days later, at the Legation, Jones was veering between relief and fury.

"A gunboat!" he exclaimed, waving a telegram at Michael. "An actual gunboat, to arrive within the day from Singapore. I didn't ask them for a gunboat, for goodness sake, I asked them to take a stand on whether or not they will stand by Siam! What they do is send a goddam gunboat to...." he squinted at the telegram, "...to protect and reassure the British population."

"I grant you, it will be a popular move among our Union-Jack-waving Brits here. Afraid of their shadows, they are.

"You have no idea how many have come to see me, asking me what I will do if the crisis comes to a head. Well, now I can tell those asses to get on the gunboat." He shook his head. "Have *you* ever felt threatened or frightened, boy, tell me? Have you?"

Michael considered him with sympathy.

"Of course, Sir, what matters is how the French perceive the presence of a British gunboat before our Legation. It might just encourage them to show some restraint."

Jones sighed and sat down heavily.

"Yes, it might. And it might also lead the Siamese to think we will back them no matter what, and do their best to resist the French.

"These are not easy times, let me tell you, and I am getting too old for this."

He seemed to shake himself out of his despondency, and smiled.

"Now, let me give you rather amusing news: the

Siamese held an inquest about the molestation of the two Frenchmen on New Road, and invited the French to participate.

"It appears that the event took place elsewhere, maybe another road.

"And maybe they were not really Frenchmen, only French 'protégés' that is to say Laos or Khmers. I ask you, if the crowd attacked them, how on earth did they know they were French protégés? They look just like every one else here. And maybe they were not molested, only thought they might be.

"So basically, we can take it that in fact nothing actually happened.

"And it also appears that the 'anonymous death threat' was perhaps written by Lillie, or so RJ thinks.

"I shall call him RJ in the future, can't abide those double-barrelled names, and foreign ones at that. ...

"So it seems Pavie is playing dirty. How dirty, that is the question."

Michael did not smile in return, and got up to return to his office.

"As dirty as he thinks he can, I suppose. Then he will wait for Siam to make a serious move, so he can take action.

"He's playing chess.

"He won't accept the negotiations we are all advocating, but he won't say so. He'll string us all along, claim his good faith, and of course the best intentions of France, but he will wait until anything, any incident he can blow up, any shot the Siamese return from across the border, and he'll kill any possibility of a peaceful solution, saying that Siam provoked France."

Jones nodded.

"You have a good political mind, you know. Better than

mine, but then I've never claimed to be a real diplomat, I'm just an old soldier.

"Anyway, I'll put your theory in the telegram I'm sending to London.

"But in this case, I very much hope you are wrong."

The following weeks, it seemed to Captain Jones' relief that indeed, Michael had been wrong.

Rolin-Jaequemyns was continuing to put his faith in international law and preparing Siam's case for arbitration, although he told Jones he was somewhat discouraged by a message from Lord Rosebery in London stating that England was backing away from any participation in the arbitral proceedings and expressing his belief in a fair settlement with Paris.

"Nothing to get dismayed about, Monsieur," the British Minister replied in his hearty manner. "If the settlement were not fair, he will take a stand, believe me. He won't let Britain be pushed around by Deloncle and the Colonial Party. We just don't want to appear prejudiced and accused of having too much influence in Siam."

There were reports of many border incidents, exchanges of gunfire, but no one was harmed, and after each one, Pavie visited the Foreign Ministry to protest, but nothing more.

"He's waiting for something more important. Just like a cat watching a mouse" was how Michael described it to Julie.

"He's more like a spider, spinning his web," she retorted. He laughed.

His Minister was beginning to think he had misjudged Pavie and French intentions, he said, and, despite Pavie's mournful and almost daily visits to Prince Devawongse, every one had started to believe the worse had passed, and that the crisis had been averted.

"But you do not." Julie stated flatly, knowing the look on his face.

No, he did not, he agreed.

But, just like his Minister, he hoped he was wrong.

"BANGKOK, MAY 9TH 1893

Michael has just been, and when I saw the look on his face, I began to fear the worse.

There had been a battle on the Mekong, at the Island of Khone. The Tirailleurs Annamites regiment attacked, and there were casualties on both sides. Three French officers had been killed, and their commander made prisoner.

'We know nothing yet,' he repeated, 'no names, truly, I would tell you if I knew. Believe me.'

So I sit here and watch Louis play with the toy soldiers Victor brought him at New Year, and curse men's need to make war, starting when they can barely walk or talk.

And I, who never believed in prayer, find myself imploring God to spare my brother... What else can I do?"

"MAY 12TH 1893

Victor is safe!

He was not involved in the battle at Khone, and the prisoner is a Captain Thoreux.

In fact, no French officer was killed, contrary to the first, confused reports, as was gleefully stated in the Siam Free Press, *extolling the superior training and quality of the Annamite soldiers over the Siamese forces.*

Mr Lillie describes the capture of Captain Thoreux as a shameful and loathsome deed, but of course, nowhere does he say that crossing a nation's border and attacking unprovoked a garrison of twenty-five men with over one hundred and fifty soldiers would be seen elsewhere as an act of war.

I now read all the papers I can get my hands on, including the French press from Saigon that I have sent to me here, but of course, they take two weeks.

Michael has seen a telegram sent from the British Embassy in Paris saying that that Deloncle and his Party want to seize all the islands in the Gulf of Siam in retaliation.

Will this folly never stop?"

Aside from her evenings playing with Louis, Julie's only respite was to be found at the Palace.

In the Inner Court, it seemed no news transpired that was not happy, or amusing, and certainly nothing connected to a threat on the Kingdom.

One of the younger Princesses, Mom Chao Piam, had decided to teach Julie the art of Siamese cooking, and all of them, starting with Princess Keow, followed suit with glee.

"They all have been taught to cook," Julie marvelled, in recounting the sessions to Michael when she returned, her hands reeking of garlic and stained yellow from peeling and pounding turmeric.

"My friends and I were well educated, but I believe not a single one of us has any idea what to do in a kitchen. Of, of course, we all learned to instruct our cooks, choose menus, and check the housekeeper's accounts, but no more.

"Keow suggested I show them how to prepare some French dishes, but I would not know where to start."

Michael raised his eyebrows in disbelief. "Was it not you who offered to teach my cook all that time ago?"

She shrugged, embarrassed. "Well, I thought I could just tell him to do better, as Mama did when she complained to the kitchen. ... But I really had no idea how to go about it, except asking him to prepare Siamese food.

"All the girls are amazed no one ever saw fit to teach me, and Keow is rather disapproving and sniffy.

"But now... If I ever go back to Paris, I can open a restaurant." she concluded with a laugh.

"What a good idea," he replied with a forced smirk. Just the type of endeavour her Mama was sure to approve of. "Have you prepared something for us this evening?" he inquired.

Something in his careful and detached tone made her look up.

"What is it? No, don't say there is nothing, I can tell. I know you far better than your Mother ever did. So tell me. Bad news?"

Michael made a face.

It was not good news, and he really shouldn't tell her.

"You shouldn't tell me because I am French, and you fear you are passing information to the other side, or you shouldn't tell me so as not to worry me?"

He sighed in response. Both.

The Siamese had somehow managed to get a copy of a letter Pavie had written to Lanessan, the Governor General of Indochina, saying that he if he were to engage a naval action to blockade Bangkok from the river, then it should be used as an opportunity to impose a protectorate over the Kingdom, to "round off" as he put it, the French Indochinese Colonial Empire.

Julie stopped rubbing her hands to attempt to remove the turmeric stains and looked down at them.

"I see. So Prince Devawongse was right."

He could not see her face in the shadows of the early evening.

It was only "if", Michael insisted, and we do not know what Lanessan replied, if at all, or if France were to agree to the idea.

He would certainly need the approval of Paris, one cannot just seize a country, and he did not think London would permit it.

"But you don't know? If London would let the French take over Siam?" she asked quietly.

No.

It all came down to the value Britain gave to Siam and the trade routes towards China versus good relations with the French, he answered.

But, he hastened to add, it was not all that easy to impose a protectorate on a country that did not want it, and the French were spread rather thin over Annam and Tonkin.

So they would probably think twice before embarking upon Pavie's scheme.

"Don't worry overmuch, my dear. We are all working very hard to prevent this happening.

"And if it does... well, you would probably make a fortune by opening the first Siamese restaurant in Paris."

Chapter IX

The rains had come with a vengeance, as if the dark, rolling clouds and the thunder and lightning that streaked the horizon almost every evening were to be seen as a metaphor for the unsettled, tense mood prevailing in the Kingdom.

Seated at a table in her room, head in hand, as she prepared to host a small party to celebrate her third year in Bangkok, Julie allowed herself a moment of nostalgia for Paris, for her parents and for the life she might have had.

If... if she had not been seated next to Louis at that dinner party, if she had not been so headstrong and listened to her Mama's objections, if...

What would her life have been?

She would have finally married, accepting a suitable banker, or doctor, or lawyer, who perhaps might not have been as boring as she feared.

She would have a townhouse near the Bois, perhaps, with summers spent in Biarritz, the obligatory concerts and evenings at the theatre, two children, a perfect nanny, a temperamental cook.

Her days would be devoted to doing... what?

Conferring with her housekeeper, meeting Amélie for tea, taking her children to see their grandmother and listening to Mama's advice, seeing her dressmaker, her corset-maker, ensuring her husband found a well-ordered household when he returned home for a well-prepared dinner.

And here, instead, she spent her time between the Palace, chatting and giggling with her delightful, exasperating and ever entertaining students and her home with the son she adored, her beloved and trusted Fie, the precious affection of her cousin and the easy, undemanding friendship of Fanny and Léonie.

But she had to admit that at times she was lonely, and longed for a presence by her side when she woke up in the night, a man to hold her and to cherish her, and reassure her when she felt beset by the constant, always present worries. About the crisis looming between Siam, France and Britain, about Victor's safety, about her future, and Louis'.

She wanted someone to help her make the decisions that often kept her from sleeping.

She sighed.

To advise her, reassure her... and above all, to hold and cherish her.

But would she be willing to share her life with a man again?

She was mistress of her own household, every year Papa's bank in Paris transferred money to the Bangkok branch of the Hong Kong and Shanghai Banking Corporation and she answered to no one as to how she spent it.

If she were to marry again, she would lose this precious independence...

Victor, who had arrived the evening before on two weeks leave had led her to wallow in − no, not regrets, she would never regret marrying Louis − but a certain melancholy.

"When I am marching in the jungle, and hear the screech of a wildcat, and everything seems so strange, and foreign and unlike what I expected my life would become," he had confided over brandy on the verandah, as they watched the display of lightning illuminating the spire of a nearby temple, "I often ask myself where I would be now, had I not been idiotic enough to let that girl get under my skin. Don't you?"

Ask herself where she might be now if she hadn't let Louis get under her skin? she replied playfully. Never.

And she hadn't. Until now.

"The real question," Victor continued, still staring at the sky, "is what is to become of Louis if you stay here. Where will he go to school? What future will he have?"

And that, if she were to be honest, was the most important thing, more important than her own happiness.

Stung, Julie inquired if he was passing this message along from their parents.

"Because if you don't think Mama writes exactly that in every single letter, you misjudge her gravely."

Well, Mama was right. And what about her own life?

Did she not want to marry again? She was only twenty-eight. She did not seriously believe she could go on living this life, so cut off from every civilized pastime, music, books, friends.

"I have friends. And of course, when Pavie makes Siam a French colony," she replied tartly, "then all your 'civilized pastimes' would be brought to my door."

Victor sat up.

"You know about that?"

Julie snorted. Everyone knew about that. Pavie was not exactly discreet in his ambitions. It was all over the French press, and the English press in Siam as well.

"Well, well, my little sister, all grown up... neglecting her adventure novels for political dispatches. So? What do you think?"

She rose from her rattan armchair to put an end to the conversation, fearing that she might reveal some of Michael's confidences if she allowed it to go any further, and also afraid Victor might judge her as did Pavie, think her a disloyal Frenchwoman.

"If that happens, I think I shall marry a teak-wallah from Borneo, and become queen of the head-hunters."

But of course, in many respects, Mama and Victor were right.

Although weighing her life against the one she imagined she might have had gave her no cause for regret, she realized that sometime, not very soon perhaps, but sometime, she would need to decide about Louis' future, and thus her own.

But not now.

She got up, and called Fie to help her dress for her party.

If her life in Bangkok were finite, then she was determined to make the most of it.

Victor was enchanted with Fanny, her wit, her exotic beauty and, Julie assumed, her heavy-lidded way of considering him with a cynical and knowing smile.

"So you *do* have women in Bangkok who are not just simpering memsahibs or straight-laced wives," he exclaimed to Michael.

"We do, old chap, we do, including your sister, who is the foremost of them. We just don't have that many. But I should watch myself with this one, she's too old and too wise for you. Do go and flirt with Henriette Rolin-Jaequemyns, that's a much better idea."

Victor gazed in appraisal at the plump blonde in pink who was chatting with Léonie Malherbe.

"No, I think not. She's the kind of girl who wants marriage, and what I want is an affair. A safe affair, I might add. "

Michael shook his head with a laugh. "Fanny would not be safe under any circumstances. In that case, better stick to your Chinese nieces in Saigon."

He went up to Julie who was overseeing her servants pouring champagne and passing trays of canapés and pastries.

"A success, don't you think? The Oriental's bakery did you proud, everything is delicious. And your dress is lovely."

Julie looked down critically at the coral-coloured confection she had made by a new Italian dressmaker who had opened a shop on New Road.

"Do you like it? I'm not sure about these leg o' mutton sleeves. I know they're all the rage in Paris, but I find them rather vulgar... Oh!" she gasped, her hand on her mouth. "Just listen to me; I sound just like my mother."

She looked around at her guests.

"Yes, they do seem to be enjoying themselves.

"Why is it then that I have the feeling we're all dancing on a volcano?"

Michael leaned over to kiss her scented, powdered cheek.

"Because we are, my dear. That's exactly what we are doing."

Her feeling of unease was prescient, Julie realized.

The very next morning a telegram arrived for Victor cancelling his leave, and Michael rushed from the Legation with news that a French official, an inspector of the Garde Civile named Grosgurin had been ambushed and killed by a Siamese detachment in Kieng Kiek.

He dropped his voice in dismay. "They say he was murdered in his bed."

Victor, who was busy slinging books and clothes in his bag, looked up at the news.

"Well," he said as he tightened a strap buckle, "that explains why my leave was cancelled. I have been told to report to the Consulate who will find a way to get me back to my regiment."

He straightened, and smiled. "I suppose they don't want me hanging around on the loose in Bangkok at the mercy of the first British diplomat who might come by."

At the door, Julie was silently twisting a pleat in her skirt.

"My buggy can take you," Michael offered.

"That is just what I need to ensure they see me as an English agent," Victor laughed. "No thanks, old man, I think I'll take a box-gharry, if the servants could get me one."

Michael clasped his hand, revealing deeper worry in his eyes than he would have liked.

"You'll take care, won't you?"

Victor nodded. "And you, you'll take care of them?" with a tilt of his head he showed Julie frozen in the hall and Louis chasing the rooster in the garden with shrieks of delight.

"I promise."

With a quick kiss on his sister's cheek, he was on his way.

And that, Michael thought as he saw him enter the box-gharry, so elegant, so enviably and effortlessly the image of a dashing officer, is what a real man looks like when he's off to war.

"BANGKOK, MAY 19TH 1893

Michael was needed back at the Legation, and although he didn't like to leave me, I told him I am fine. And I am, I suppose.

Victor is in no immediate danger, as Michael was at pains to repeat, and may not even arrive in Saigon before this whole fracas is over.

But I worry for him, and I think of Mama, who mercifully does not yet know of these more recent events, and imagine my feelings if my baby Louis were off to war.

Pray God he never is.

If it were possible to find a land that no powers fight over, where people are kind to each other, where you can bring up your child without fearing someday he will wear a uniform and carry a gun, I would move there immediately.

I thought that I had found this in Siam, 'that back water' as Mama calls it.

I was mistaken.

So perhaps no such land exists."

For a country poised on the brink of war and the loss of its independence, Siam was remarkably calm, Michael mused on his way to the Legation.

Since Grosgurin had been murdered — and it truly could be called nothing else, loathe as he was to use the same term as Lillie in his almost apocalyptic article, the man was lying in bed, delirious with malaria — and despite the expected pressing protests by Pavie, life appeared to continue, although it was not life as usual.

People were tense and frightened, and it showed.

Beneath the apparent quiet, lurked the feeling that a keg of explosives was smouldering and about to blow up.

The British Embassy in Paris reported the hysterical reactions to Grosgurin's death and the mounting pressure and demands from the Colonial Party.

"Revenge! Revenge!" shrieked all the French press headlines, and announced in bold inky triumph that the Governor-General of Indochina was about to order the annexation of the islands in the Gulf of Siam, as well as the takeover of the Lao capital, Luang Prabang, of such historic and spiritual importance for Siam.

Lord Dufferin, the Ambassador to Paris, also informed them that although Foreign Minister Develle had grave misgivings about embarking his country on yet another colonial adventure, he had told him personally that he had no other choice but to approve such a bellicose stance, trapped as he was between the recently-appointed French Minister for the Colonies, Monsieur Delcassé, and the ugly prevailing mood in the country.

"From what Lord Dufferin writes of Develle, one gathers that he cannot be relied upon even at the best of times," Captain Jones stated at a morning meeting, "and that he's a wavering follower of whoever speaks loudest.

"But nonetheless, Lord Dufferin says he was hoping for something better from him. Meanwhile, Delcassé is making political hay out of the situation, and besides the islands and Luang Prabang, he also is clamouring for action at Battambang."

"So," Edward French, the Consul, summarized in a cool, emotionless voice, "an attack on all fronts along the Mekong, from northern Laos to Cambodia?

"Is Britain going to stand by and watch, sir?"

Jones rubbed his red-rimmed eyes, and spoke without looking up, as if to himself. "Not if I can help it.

"I have finally managed to make London aware of the seriousness of the situation, and stressed that if Siam goes to France, then we shall be facing the frogs all along the Burmese border. Everybody's worst nightmare."

He straightened up and stretched his spine.

"Ugh, too many sleepless nights. I wish the Court would do its business in the daytime like the rest of us, and not start work at midnight.

"So. Next thing. There's this trip to Koh Si Chang in a week's time. For those of you who didn't know, His Majesty is inviting the foreign community — and yes, French, that does include the ever-stimulating Monsieur Pavie — to a trip to Koh Si Chang on his yacht. The idea is to inspect the works on the forts in Paknam, then spend two nights on the island.

"Obviously, I will be cut off from telegrams, and I need

someone to stay here and be in touch with Whitehall in case of any emergency.

"That's you, French, as my second in command."

French nodded his thanks, and rose from his chair. Preening himself, he stroked the ends of his moustache, trying not to turn and see how Michael, the Minister's favourite, was taking this slight.

"And I want you, Crawfurd, to come with me and be my note taker. You have the best political mind of us all, and I'm going to need your advice."

Chastened, French looked at his shoes and left the room.

"Can't stand the man," Jones confided after the door closed behind him.

"Always have the feeling he thinks he could do a better job here than me. And his name! Why doesn't he call himself something else, these days? Oh, for heaven's sake, Crawfurd, you needn't look so disapproving; I know he can't help his name.

"So, now. This trip.

"It's to be some sort of celebration, I've no idea of what and I've no idea why the Palace hasn't cancelled it, but there you are, it's going ahead.

"I don't expect anything momentous to happen, but what with the French attitude these days, I wouldn't put it past them to attack the island when we're on it.

"No, actually, I don't think so, but you can never tell.

"Your cousin going?"

Michael nodded.

Yes, Julie had been invited. She was very excited, and honoured to have been invited.

"Good, good. At least, there'll be a pretty face to look at. My lady wife was asked, but she gets seasick just by looking at a boat. Can't tell you how much she dreads our return journey, when we do finally go home.

"What I want you to do more than anything is to keep your ears and eyes open. Anything interesting, you make a note.

"Think your cousin would as well? Sometimes ladies drop things as shouldn't."

Michael smiled in regret. "She felt insulted when Pavie asked. So I really do not see myself ..."

The Minister nodded his understanding.

"Can't be very comfortable, being both French and British these days, not knowing which side to cheer along."

Michael got up, and collected his papers.

"No sir, it's not. And she is cheering the only side she can."

Which side was that? Jones asked.

Michael smiled again. "The Siamese side, sir."

Julie sat on her bed, surrounded by a mound of dresses, petticoats, and tea-gowns.

What would she need?

Princess Keow, who had issued the invitation just said;

"Two dress, never mind. And white. *Farang* ladies wear white only." But did that apply to evening dress?

A parasol, a hat, two hats?

And they would be going by train to Paknam, and if she wore white on the train, she would need to change afterwards, her dress would be filthy from the smoke and steam. So more than two dresses.

Part of her was apprehensive at leaving Louis behind, although she knew he would hardly notice, and part was elated and excited at seeing the countryside outside of Bangkok.

"Can you imagine? In three years I have never been further than Koh Kret Island, and that is a short boat ride upriver." she exclaimed when she heard the details of the journey.

"And the sea... to walk on the beach... it will be heavenly."

The Royal yacht was rather heavenly as well, Michael told her.

"Oh, I shan't be on the Royal yacht, at least not the one the King will be travelling on. I will follow on another with the ladies. But I shall attend the banquet, of course. And I still do not know what to pack."

"BANGKOK, JUNE 4ᵀᴴ 1893

I hardly know where to begin, so filled were the past three days.

We were told to get to the station very early, as once His Majesty had left the Palace, it would be impossible for us to get through.

It was like a festival, and one had the impression that everyone there, Siamese and farang, was determined to leave behind their worries or cares and enjoy themselves.

I was whisked off to a curtained area, where ladies could enjoy a cool drink 'in the private' as a Scottish station master told me, and then with the sound of the fifes and drums that seem to escort the King wherever he goes, he arrived, shook hands and greeted us behind our curtain, and we were assigned our open-sided wooden cars. Then we were off!

Thank goodness, it did not rain as it can even mornings in this season. The train dawdled through the suburbs, with dwellings often sheltering below tarpaulin, or dried banana leaves. How do people live there, and how can they always manage to look so clean, and so happy?

Crowds were gathered on both sides of the tracks and cheered or kowtowed as their sovereign went by, and little brown naked children jumped up and down in excitement.

We stopped at Paknam after a four hours journey, and H.M. inspected the works on the three forts. We were even treated to a demonstration of a canon that appears from the top of a mound, shoots at whatever is at the mouth of the river, and vanishes down again.

Very noisy and impressive, and I hope Monsieur Pavie, for whom this display presumably was organized has taken note.

And then we ladies were discretely shepherded onto the second best yacht, where I joined up with Keow and some of her friends and relatives. My little students were not included in the outing.

'Young.' Keow just said sadly, as if it explained it all.

'Young.' I repeated with a laugh. 'So I am glad I'm not so young, then.'

One of the other, older, princesses I sometimes see at the palace chortled. 'Not always good be young. Be old good too, never mind.'

When the boat pulled away beyond the silty, churning waters of the bar, we could see gunboats, French and English recognizable by their flags, at anchor and immobile under the hot white sun, the rigging of their masts looking like lace and the cannons shining like dull silver.

I could make out sailors busying themselves, ready... for what?

I turned away and sat next to Keow, and looked at the horizon, admired the beautiful glimpses of many small islands with nodding palms and china-white beaches, and felt at peace, for the first time in many weeks.

We arrived at the Royal residence of Koh Si Chang at sunset, a beautiful stain of orange spreading over the skies, with grey-violet streaks of cloud reaching out to the dark.

Next to me, Keow looked preoccupied.

'What are you thinking, Your Highness?' I asked. Without looking at me, she replied that those two colours would be good for a phasin.

I know she was lying, and I know she was thinking about the crisis with France, but the extraordinary sight of the Island Palace wiped everything else from our minds. It is a huge building of golden wood, with rotundas, balconies and verandahs, a whimsical folly jutting on a low cliff top with a covered jetty leading to the sea.

'No nails in wood. Not one.' Keow said with pride. I found that difficult to believe, but I am assured it is so.

I shared a huge room with all the Siamese ladies and their maids. Of course the other European women were with their husbands so, being single, I was the only farang *in the wing reserved for women, and also, I suppose, because I am familiar with the Inner Court.*

I don't know what the rooms for the Europeans were like, but I was delighted with where I was: a vast area, with wide polished teak planks that were cool and smooth under my bare feet, and windows open upon the sea, with split bamboo curtains that roll up and the beds, like those at the Palace, were just low, wide tables, with quilted silk mattresses and triangular cushions to rest one's head. And women seated on the floor, women lounging on these beds, maids fanning them, and laughter, laughter, everywhere.

They were overjoyed that I could speak enough Siamese to be understood, although they teased me because I know so few of the special words one must use with royalty, and proceeded to teach me.

I can now converse properly with His Majesty about his shoes, his bed and his dinner, although I cannot imagine the circumstances in which I might be called upon to do so.

It was like being back at the convent with Amélie, laughing, trying on each other's jewellery, they picking up every one of my clothes and gasping in horror at my corset.

But, of course, they could not attend the banquet though they helped me prepare for it. Keow's closest friend loaned me her emerald and diamond earrings because I had chosen to wear an old dress from my trousseau, my sea-green one. It looks a bit dated, but who here can tell?

Everyone made a tremendous show of pulling on my stay laces and I could barely breathe when they were finished with me.

I was almost sorry I was not to share their dinner, lounging in the comfort of a cool cotton phasin, but Keow whispered they would wait for me before going to bathe in the sea.

Have I become so jaded that I can write that the banquet was like every banquet, with delicious Siamese food, indifferent western food and too much wine?

I could hardly wait to get back to the ladies wing, to shed my clothes and join them to splash in the waves clad in nothing but a length of cloth, with the woman guards keeping watch.

How different the sea was here from the rough Atlantic,

Julie reflected as she wrote, with its cold, harsh surf and the stinging wind that blew sand into the eyes and hair.

The soft warm water off Koh Si Chang was like silk on her bare skin and the exact temperature of the perfumed night air, while a strange phosphorescence lit the gentle lapping waves to the colour of dark sapphires.

She could have remained in the water for hours.

It was the best moment of the trip.

The most exciting moment, however, came the following morning.

I was walking with Michael and Emilie along the jetty, following the King who was explaining something to Captain Jones, Monsieur RJ (Michael told me Captain Jones has dubbed him thus, and it makes it much easier to write about him) with Pavie and Eaton, the American minister in tow, when great excitement broke out.

'A warship,' someone cried out, 'a warship has been spotted and is approaching!'

His personal guard immediately moved to surround the king, who blanched.

Jones was heard exclaiming. 'I knew it, I knew it!' and Monsieur Pavie just gloated, his smile going from ear to ear.

There was no time to get His Majesty to safety on his boat, and in any case, the yacht would be no match for a warship.

I was not afraid, I think no one really was, the main feeling was disbelief and outrage. How dare they?

Another cry from the watching post, the ship was steaming up very fast, and suddenly, it came into view, with the Union Jack floating prettily and snapping in the breeze.

I imagine the relief the King must have felt, but my eyes were fixed on Monsieur Pavie, who was pale with rage. I almost laughed out loud, so comical was it.

On reflection, I think that was the best moment of those three days.

The commander of the British gunboat *Pallas* from

Singapore had received orders to come moor at Paknam and reinforce the reassuring presence of the *Swift*, he told Captain Jones after disembarking and saluting His Majesty, and Paknam had signalled their presence at Koh Si Chang. So there he was.

"You could not have timed your arrival better," the Minister told him, tears of repressed laughter in his eyes. "I would not have missed that scene for the world."

Monsieur Pavie was reported to be furious, and France was considering protesting formally to London at the presence of another British gunboat at the Bar of Siam was what Michael gleaned from the first, hurried meeting once they had returned to Bangkok.

"But how can they?" Jones kept on laughing. "They have one of their own right next to ours, and the third one has just left for Saigon!"

More seriously, he told his staff that the King, seeing Pavie's face at Koh Si Chang, had remarked that the British gunboat's arrival was no doubt linked to the presence of the three French ones at anchor before Bangkok.

Pavie, still smarting and humiliated from the scene, replied that there were only two gunboats at present, which were there solely to protect the French community from the risk of riots and disorders that everybody knew were brewing in the city.

"HM just said that the French boats were the cause of the risk, and if they went on their way, the situation would return to normal immediately.

"And Pavie found nothing to counter that!"

So, he continued, what was the news he missed while they were away?

Edward French shuffled through a sheaf of papers; yes, from the latest telegram received this morning the French press was protesting what was called a bellicose move to send a British warship to Siam.

"They say we intend to declare a British protectorate over Siam, sir."

"And of course, they want to beat us to it," Jones sneered, as French continued, "Lord Rosebery is following the situation very closely and keeping Her Majesty the Queen and the Viceroy of India apprised of it daily, and finally, in Bangkok, the commander of the detachment who is accused of killing Grosgurin, one" — the Consul looked down at his papers — "one Phra Yoth, shall be tried to determine whether he acted unlawfully. The Siamese are suggesting that an international court be set up so as to avoid any feeling of partiality."

"That's nice of them," Jones remarked. "Not sure we would have gone as far."

"Oh, and yes, received yesterday," the Consul added, "A Monsieur Le Myre de Vilers, he who was formerly Governor-General of Cochinchina and is now member of the French Parliament for the Asian colonies, is standing for re-election and due to arrive in Bangkok later this summer en route to Saigon to defend his seat."

"Well, well, well..." Michael murmured. "Le Myre de Vilers... Do you remember him, Sir?"

Jones shook his head. "Aside from the name sounding familiar, can't say I do. So?"

The former Governor-general of Cochinchina knew the region well, Michael said. His were the mind and the authority behind the protectorate imposed upon Annam and Tonkin, the pushing of the Khmer-Siamese border westwards, and, it was he who had appointed Jules Harmand consul here, oh, maybe ten or twelve years ago. He always feared the growing British presence in Asia, and saw it as a direct threat to France.

"His avowed and very public reasoning was that Harmand should, and could, counter our influence in Siam.

"Harmand tried to do so, not very successfully, I might add, by cultivating the old regent's faction against the young king's.

"His theory, which he tried to get the regent to endorse, was that all His Majesty's endeavours to modernize the Kingdom were bound to bankrupt the nation, and that he would be forced to borrow huge amounts from Britain which Siam would never be able to repay, giving us an excuse to cash in on his debts and seize the country.

"We all know how that ended, with the regent eventually being forced to retire from public life, and the King emerging stronger even than his father."

Jones shook his head ruefully. "Obviously, this man Le Myre doesn't like us much. So you think his arrival is bad news?"

Michael sighed.

He may just be stopping through before going off to campaign in Saigon. But...given Le Myre de Vilers' experience and knowing his views of Siam... When one added that to what they had just heard of the French public opinion's view of the arrival of another British gunboat, the death of Grosgurin, and everything that had already occurred on the Mekong...

It could certainly not be good news.

It was not.

Two days later, Pavie demanded a meeting with Prince Devawongse and Monsieur Rolin-Jaequemyns to inform them that Monsieur Le Myre de Vilers had been entrusted by his government with an "extraordinary mission" and plenipotentiary powers to demand reparation amounting to a million francs for all the incidents which had occurred since 1891 and during which French lives and property had been lost.

Furthermore, he, Pavie, was presenting them with an ultimatum: either the border dispute along the Mekong was resolved to France's satisfaction, or the French military push forward would continue.

"How," the Foreign Minister inquired, his voice trembling with contained rage, "were they to settle a border dispute when the French demands had not been made clear?

"Was that not the subject of the international arbitration Siam had requested? Should not all countries respectful of international law await the deliberations of the arbitration body?"

Pavie handed him the letter of the ultimatum with a bow.

"The fair and legitimate demands of France have always been clear. All of the East bank of the Mekong, with the river as a border, and may I say, I find my country is showing considerable restraint, as I have always considered that the Lao provinces straddling both banks should not be split asunder.

"If you were to refuse, the French Navy shall blockade Bangkok."

And with another bow, he left.

"And what Pavie did not tell Devawongse and Monsieur RJ," Jones read to Michael and Edward French from a coded, top-secret telegram that had just been put in his hands, "is that France suspects Britain of wanting to use the blockade threat as a pretext to disembark troops and declare a protectorate and claiming it is at the request of Siam itself — I tell you, it's absolute madness.

"But in which case, France shall land her own troops, which are held ready in advance, in even greater numbers.

They are sending a detachment of the Foreign Legion from Oran, in Algeria, for that purpose.

"So whatever happens, France sends troops, whether we protect Siam, and whether we don't."

He slammed the flimsy paper down on his desk.

His hair was standing on end from being raked through with his fingers, his white suit was rumpled, and his regimental tie was askew.

"And there you have it gentlemen, war, between France and Britain, in the city and outskirts of Bangkok, while the poor Siamese sit and watch us as at a tennis game, wondering whether they shall have to teach their children French or English."

"What do you think, Sir?" the Consul asked diffidently. Michael noticed that Edward French seemed far less sure of himself these days, and gossip had it that he was considering sending his wife and children to the safety of Singapore.

"What I think? I goddam don't know what to think! What about you, Crawfurd?"

"That we should avoid playing into their hands, Sir. In any case, we had no plans to impose a protectorate. It's just fear-mongering for French public opinion."

"So?"

"So we do nothing to encourage the Siamese in the belief that we will fight in their place, distasteful as it is to both you and me. But stand by them in pushing and demanding negotiations. And wait."

Each day brought news of a further advance by the French, in Kemarat, Kham Muon, Muang Nim...

"At this rate, they'll get to the border with Burmah, and we'll all go home." Jones remarked at a lunch he gave for the captains of the two gunboats.

"In that case, not to worry, sir," Captain McLeod, the senior of the two replied. "We'll take you there on the ships."

As the clouds of the rainy season rolled over the dark skies, the city seemed to wait, poised in tense expectation of a conflagration. Rumours were rife, and Somboon and Pon apprised Michael of them each morning with his tea.

The Chinese were rioting in their quarter of Yaowarat, encouraged to do so by the French priests.

The French had invented flying ships to make their way over the rapids in the Mekong, and would soon be here.

They were planning to take His Majesty captive off to France.

There were French warships arriving in the river and the Siamese navy was sinking boats full of stones to bar the way.

And this latter rumour, Michael told Julie after reaching her house in relief after yet another day at the Legation reading and writing dispatches, was true.

He stretched his hand out to take the cold whiskey and soda Noi, her manservant, had just poured.

"Admiral Humann, the Commander-in-Chief of the French Asian fleet is due to arrive before Paknam within a few days, and Pavie is demanding that a pilot be given him to steer the ship upriver. Of course, it goes against the treaty clause that applies to all foreign powers in Siam and restricts us to one, and only one, gunboat beyond Paknam.

"Admiral de Richelieu has obtained approval to block the passage with those sunken boats Pon was so excited about, and also with drums of dynamite and underwater mines, reserving only a very narrow channel to allow commercial shipping through.

"Sounds tricky to navigate, and I wouldn't want to be on the Singapore packet these days."

He drank, his eyes closed, then looked at Julie, sitting at the edge of her armchair, her fingers twisting nervously, obviously fearful of asking; nonetheless, she spoke up, as casually as she could. "Do you know which regiments were involved in the advance on the Mekong?"

He shook his head.

"It makes sense to assume Victor is involved somewhere, though," he replied.

Had she not heard from him?

Nothing.

However, she had received a long letter from her mother, with, unusually, one from her Papa. "They are worried at what they read in the press, and want me to come home. Listen."

She went to her desk, and picked up a thick sheaf of closely written pages.

"You are behaving with utmost recklessness, and endangering the life of your son. We have read in the Indépendant *that even the wife of the Belgian counsellor to the king has fled the country, and your Papa and I may only conclude that the insalubrious climate you live in has somehow affected your reasoning. We beg you to heed those who know best and to book the first passage back to France.*

You no longer have the excuse of your son's health, as, by Victor's account, he is thriving, and fail to see what else might be preventing you from returning to your home."

She looked at him with a frown.

"It was not very wise of Emilie to leave when she did. I know her mother was ill, but still. Now, from Papa: *"My darling little girl.*

We worry so much about both of you, and our fears are made greater by distance and the contradictions between your letters where you only

mention parties and Louis' progress and the improvements to your house,
with what we read in the newspapers.

I understand that you enjoy the existence you have carved out for
yourself, but am afraid you are unaware of the danger of your situation.
Quite often, when one is too close, one cannot see properly.

And I, along with your Mama, long to see our grandson and to have you
near us, and safe."

She closed her eyes and a tear trickled along her cheek.

To cheer her up, Michael recounted the rumour of the
flying gunboats.

"You, know, it's not entirely untrue, and I wonder how
that one ever reached Granny Khop, who seems to be the
main source of news on the *soi*.

"The French have developed portable gunboats to
sidestep, as it were, the Khon rapids and waterfalls."

Julie gave a half-hearted laugh. Surely, he was joking.

"No, not at all. And actually, it is no joking matter, if
it works.

"They have ordered small light gunboats that will
go up the Mekong to Khon, then — and that's the
extraordinary and worrying bit — be hauled off the water
and on a light railway that will bring them up river above
the falls.

"And then, back on the water. Where they will impose a
greater military presence and patrol what they see as their
border, whilst having the capacity to reach the Upper
Mekong, where we obviously don't want them.

"So, not flying exactly... but certainly unwelcome,
although it's probably over a year before it happens."

He stretched his legs before him.

"Do tell me some amusing anecdote from the Inner
Court, just to get my mind away from all this. Because
if it weren't enough to have conflicts between the French

and the Siamese, the French and the British, there is now fighting between French and the Minister."

Julie raised her eyebrows. Between the French and his Minister? Between Monsieur Pavie and Captain Jones? What was new about that?

No, no, Michael laughed. Between Edward French, the Consul, and Captain Jones. But he could see how she was confused. The minister may have had a point when he said he should change his name.

What was the matter between them?

Well, French — *Edward*, he emphasized — was now taking it upon himself to go behind Jones' back in communicating with Whitehall, and had informed a very highly-placed advisor to Lord Rosebery that Her Majesty's Minister Resident was as good as promising military support against the French — the *nation* of France.

"It's all right, I'd understood," Julie said, annoyed.

"You needn't spell it out for me. So does he? Promise military support?"

Michael made a face.

He was afraid so. Perhaps not promise exactly, but imply it would be forthcoming, certainly. And Captain Jones had been reprimanded by London, and told to wind down Siamese expectations. Which he resented personally, of course, but also because he thought the Siamese were being treated shabbily.

"Are we eating soon?" he asked. "I'm sorry, dear girl, but I am truly exhausted, and should like to get to bed early."

Julie cocked her head, and looked at him slyly.

"Get home to Somboon, you mean. Lek is about to serve, let's sit down at the table. And since you asked, there is nothing amusing to report from the Palace. In fact, it's rather sad."

When she had arrived at the Palace this morning, one of the younger girls, Mom Luang Angkanit, had refused to attend her class, saying "France people bad people."

The others were playing with their bracelets, looking at the floor, the ceiling, at anything except Julie.

"So what did you do?"

Julie shook her head. She just stood there, at a loss for words, whether in Siamese or in French, feeling tears coming to her eyes.

Princess Keow was incensed.

She grabbed a switch from somewhere, and slammed it on the little table her teapot and cup were on, upsetting the lot.

The pot broke, tea was streaming everywhere, and they faced each other, Keow and Angkanit, eyes flashing. Meanwhile, one of the younger girls started to sob, and the others froze, their heads down, barely seeming to breathe.

Finally, Angkanit lowered her eyes, and Keow ordered her to come and clean the mess.

Maids were hovering nearby, their hands twitching from the urge to mop up before the royal lady could, but nobody moved.

Finally, Angkanit took a step, and Keow snapped: "Crawl. Crawl like the unworthy creature you have shown yourself to be."

The girl inched forwards, on her knees and elbows, picked up the broken china, and handed it to a maid.

"Now kowtow to Teacher Chouli, to beg her forgiveness."

Julie stepped forward to protest, but Keow raised her hand to stop her.

"Kowtow!" she repeated, lifting her switch and Angkanit prostrated herself in front of Julie, her hands, face and knees in the hot tea.

"I cannot expect you to forgive this silly girl," the Princess said later. "But I hope you will forgive me."

"For what?" Julie asked, at a loss. Her Highness was no more responsible for what Angkanit had said than Julie herself was for the French attitude towards Siam.

"I lost my *chai yen*, my cool heart," Keow replied. "You should never have seen that. And also, I hoped I had trained my girls better."

For the rest of the morning, Angkanit sat sniffling in a corner, the other girls were sullen, and no one laughed.

Michael spooned more curry on his rice, and looked at her. "Was all of this in Siamese?"

Flustered, Julie made a fluttering movement with her hands. "I was so upset, I don't really remember. Yes, actually, I suppose it was. How could you tell?"

From the way she was recounting it, without throwing in Keow's idiosyncratic expressions in English. "You didn't have her say 'never mind' once.

"Well, congratulations then, my dear. That is quite an achievement."

When he kissed her goodbye on the verandah, she put her hands on his shoulders, and looked up at him with a smile.

"Somboon is a lucky man."

Michael could feel himself blushing. "I treat him well, you mean?"

What she meant was that Somboon was lucky to have Michael's love.

"I have an idea," she exclaimed lightly, her eyes dancing, "let's get married.

"I won't interfere with your life, you won't with mine, and we'll be happy as tinkers."

He kissed her cheek again, and gazed at her face, incapable of telling whether she was serious or not.

"Now wouldn't that get them talking, starting with Mr Lillie."

"Two things," Jones ticked off on his fingers after calling Michael and French into his office early on the 9th of July.

"First, Whitehall tells me that Lord Rosebery managed to extract a promise from Develle that, if the French send their ships to Bangkok, he shall inform Britain beforehand.

"Second, the French are steaming here from Saigon, it won't take them more than another two days to reach Bangkok, and Develle did not inform Whitehall.

"What does that tell you?"

Given the seriousness of the situation, the full British staff was in attendance, eying each other nervously, unwilling to speak first.

"That they're up to no good, Sir," Stringer finally suggested with his schoolboy's snigger. "Develle's a devil."

"Thank you, Stringer." the Minister replied patiently. "Delighted to have your input."

Michael cleared his throat. "Sir? If I may?"

What struck him was this promise Develle made.

"A promise the French Foreign Minister did not keep." The Consul reminded him in a pointed voice.

Yes, precisely. What if... "And it's only a theory, here, what if the Minister *had* kept his promise?"

Jones patience was wearing thin.

"But he did not," he snapped. "Which is what we were talking about, damn you."

Michael took a deep breath. He was not used to being taken to task, and allowed himself a brief moment of

198

sympathy for French, who was the usual butt of their Minister's anger.

"What if Develle had never given the order?" he ventured. "Or gave it, and rescinded it? Or what if it were Lanessan and Pavie who took the initiative?"

Jones stopped his pacing and spun on his heel.

"What do you mean? Pavie and Lanessan between them pre-empted an instruction to be given only by their Minister, putting said Minister in an impossible situation, and risking war? That's unthinkable."

Michael shrugged.

Not really, if they had not been informed of Develle's promise to Lord Rosebery; why would Develle have informed them?

And if they expected to win a new colony for France, well... could Develle then blame them afterwards? He'd probably give them a medal.

Captain Jones sat down, and gave Michael a long shrewd look. He was beginning to be interested in the younger man's theory.

"So what does that tell *you*?" he repeated.

Michael made a face. That they expected from Britain words and bluster, but nothing else.

"And that is probably what they will get." he ended apologetically. "Of course, this is nothing but guesswork.

"But it came to me when I was thinking about Le Myre's arrival and the fact he is given plenipotentiary powers. It appears... well it might be that Develle doesn't trust Pavie to handle this affair with Siam.

"And Pavie, in a miff at having the crisis taken out of his hands and outranked by the arrival of an envoy with plenipotentiary powers, decided to jump the gun."

Jones scratched his head.

All this did make sense in a strange way, and no one could blame Develle for not trusting Pavie.

"But I certainly can't put your theory in my telegram to London. I don't think they take kindly to guesses.

"So... let's summarize the situation for Whitehall:

"The French gunboat *Lutin* is moored before the Consulate. Fine, they are allowed that one warship, as are we, according to Treaty terms.

"There is also the gunboat *Comète* now at anchor close to our own *Pallas*; no legal problem there, so long as it does not go upriver.

"However, I hear from McLeod that the crew seems to be preparing for combat.

"Captain Kirby from the Swift reports the same about the *Lutin*. He actually called it a 'shockingly warlike state'.

"Moreover, we are informed that the sloop, the *Inconstant,* which seems to go back and forth between Saigon and the mouth of the river, is arriving before Paknam, with or without the Admiral on board, and demands a pilot for passage to Paknam.

"Why it needs to be there, no one knows, but the French state they are authorized to anchor at Paknam by article 15 of the Treaty. Which is the case. Devawongse, however, has refused and declared that if the French ships pass the bar, they shall be fired at and stopped by force.

"Pavie asked him to confirm his refusal and threat in writing, which, RJ tells me, was done.

"What we *also* know is that other French warships are cruising the Gulf, standing by, as it were, to blockade Bangkok if the Siamese do not give in to their demands.

"Meanwhile, the whole of the Siamese fleet, such as it is, is massed immediately above Paknam to block the mouth of the river, commercial shipping can hardly pass the sunken barriers so Chinese merchants can't export their rice, ditto for all imports to the city from the south, and the Chinese population is rumoured to be about to riot citywide.

"Is that it?"

Except, as Consul French dropped in a disparaging tone, Crawfurd's reading of entrails and tea-leaves, that was it, they confirmed.

"And it's quite enough," Jones summarized with a sigh. "It's a keg of dynamite begging for a match."

Chapter X

"*Bangkok, July 11ᵀᴴ 1893*

Such a strange atmosphere prevails.

There is complete quiet in the soi *and also on New Road.*

No vendors, no housewives out to buy fish, no fruit stalls, no portable kitchens frying bananas or chicken, just the blind beggar who probably has nowhere else to go, a few dogs nosing in the stinking detritus and crows swooping down on the fruit peel and worse littering the sidewalks. The street sweepers have not been by, thankfully the evening rains will wash away most of the filth, but the gutters will get clogged and the stench will worsen.

I received a visit in the morning from a lady-in-waiting of the Inner Court who was sent by Princess Keow with a message.

"Do not come to the Palace until you are asked back, do not leave your house," she said, refusing even to enter and have a cool drink, and getting back into the carriage after a quick look around to be sure nobody had seen her in conversation with a French woman.

I do not feel unsafe in the least, and so have been to walk around the neighbourhood with Fie, stopping to empty a handful of small coins into the beggar's tin cup then going all the way to Fanny's at her little house off Windmill Road.

She too is nervous, but, as she said, she knew not about what, when every rumour is immediately contradicted by another.

Some say the Palace is under attack by the French. No, it is the Chinese who have looted the Royal Treasury.

And as far as we can tell, nothing has happened at all.

We sat chatting of other things, and she told me for the first time about her youth in Bangkok, before the bitterness of the later years when she fought against the Regent and his family to marry her beloved Phra Preecha.

Such a carefree time she described...

The young noblemen would take boats out at night and paddle up the river to come serenade the Knox sisters at the Legation.

What a lovely sight it must have been, the small, light golden craft decorated with lanterns, the young men in their bright silk coats and jungraben, the flowers Fanny and her sister threw down from the Legation balconies followed by laughter when Consul Knox, their father, bustled out in his nightshirt to chastise the noisy singers, discovered His Majesty was among them and had to sink down into his best court bow.

'Really? The King went out to enjoy himself at night with his friends? Was that before he married?'

I was amazed, I just could not imagine this grave and serious man behaving as light-hearted boys do all over the world.

Hardly, she replied with a grin. He was married at a very young age, probably before he reached manhood.

But it was certainly before Queen Sunandha and their one year-old daughter drowned.

He never seemed the same after that.

The young Queen and the child were in a boat that capsized at Bang Pa In, and nobody dared save them because it was forbidden on pain of death to touch Royalty.

I blanched somewhat, recalling the many times I had touched members of the royal family, including shaking hands with His Majesty.

But Fanny told me that precisely because of their useless, tragic death the heartbroken King repealed that ancient law.

Nonetheless, I vowed to be more careful in the future when I caress the cheek of one of my little students, or playfully tug them by the hand to make them dance.

Fie was getting nervous, and wanted to return home, she heard from a water-carrier that gangs were looting the shops on New Road.

Of course, we saw nothing, and I am truly tired of all this."

Fie was not the only person who was nervous, Julie realized with a grimace, when she saw Michael, pale with worry and rage, waiting on her verandah, and heard him shouting at her before she could even remove her hat.

"Where have you been? Fanny's house? Are you quite out of your mind?"

It was perfectly safe, she replied frostily, as she pushed past him to enter the house. Had *he* seen anybody in the *soi*? Because she hadn't.

He grabbed her arm.

"You are an impossible, impossible, impossible woman, do you know that?

"Have you no sense at all? If you cannot think of yourself, then what about your son?"

She stared at him until he released her and sank down on the rattan sofa.

"I'm sorry," he muttered. "But I was so frightened when I heard you had gone out on foot, with only Fie as an escort."

She sat next to him and took his hand with a smile.

"Michael dear, I do think you're exaggerating the perils. Pavie doesn't like me, it's true, but even he would not send a gunboat to be rid of me."

He shook his head, looking grim. She could jest all she liked, but everyone at the Legation was under strict orders not go about without an escort, or at least a firearm about their person.

"Look." He pulled a pistol out of his pocket, and held it up rather clumsily for her to see.

"Of course," he admitted ruefully, as she recoiled with a frightened gasp, "I'm not entirely sure what to do with it. I was rather counting on it producing the same reaction that you have just had, and hoping any assailant would run for his life."

Pocketing it again with distaste, he looked about.

"It is rather quiet, isn't it?

I suppose the rumours finally got to all of us. Although, I hear there is a danger of Chinese looters coming downriver from Yaowarat, but I wonder if that's not a rumour as well."

"Fanny heard the French have attacked the Palace." Julie recounted, but Michael just snorted.

"Do you know," he asked, "how many men those gunboats carry? Barely enough to take and hold the bar at the Oriental, so I think the Palace is safe."

Before leaving me and extracting the promise that I will have the gate barred and both the watchman and the gardener patrol around the house tonight, Michael told me that Pavie has repeated French demands to allow the gunboat Inconstant *to steam upriver, and that the Siamese have repeated their refusal. If the French attempt to force their way through, the cannon will fire at them.*

After the tension of the previous two days, the mood at the Legation was almost jubilant: Jones had called in his staff at noon to read a message scribbled in haste by Rolin-Jaequemyns.

"Paris — well, actually, Foreign Minister Develle — has telegraphed Admiral Humann, Governor General de Lanessan *and* Pavie to formally countermand any order to send French ships upriver. He informed Lord Rosebery of the same, and I have just received confirmation from London."

He stretched his arms out, and sighed in relief.

"So it would seem the crisis has passed.

"Sometime today, Pavie is to take a steam launch provided by the Siamese to give a copy of the orders to the captain of the *Inconstant*. Admiral Humann, and the other French ships are to arrive on the fifteenth, and anchor well below the bar. Develle has stated that whatever needs be negotiated will be without threatening Siamese independence.

"Tomorrow the French will be busy celebrating their National Day and that should keep them out of trouble.

"So... and although it is only noon, I think we all deserve a drink."

After pouring the soda water into his whisky, the Minister asked Michael to step out onto the terrace with him.

They both gazed at the sepia-coloured water under the heavy sky.

The usual small canoe traffic of fruit vendors bobbing between the floating houses seemed to have resumed, although none of the huge barges ferrying rice downstream towards the mills could be seen.

"You must have been right, you know, my boy," Jones confided.

"From what I gather, Rosebery protested to Develle about not keeping his promise, and Develle took action to rein in Pavie."

Michael pursed his lips.

"That's almost bad news, Sir."

Jones raised his eyebrows. "How so?"

Michael turned back to look at the river, and spoke very low.

"It means that Pavie is far more reckless than I thought – do you know the French expression *'fuite en avant'*? It means a headlong rush forwards, disregarding the risks.

"I may be wrong, but I think the crisis is *not* over."

"BANGKOK, JULY 13ᵀᴴ 1893

Something is happening.

We heard cannon and gunfire. I want to rush out to find out more, but dare not leave Louis.

At first, I thought it might be fireworks, but of course, I told myself it could not be. Why on earth should anybody have fireworks on this day of all days? The French cannot be celebrating our national holiday yet, and anyway, the noise is coming from downriver.

I cannot bear waiting here and not knowing.

Surely going to the Oriental Hotel is safe."

Michael was about to walk home in the gathering dusk and already planning his evening, a long cool drink, a massage, a bath, and then... He imagined the look of delight on Somboon's face at seeing him arrive earlier than usual and his charming prattle of the small events of the household, the latest rumour by Granny Khop, or memories of his boyhood in his impoverished Isaan village while he smoothed his master's — his lover's — knotted muscles with fragrant oil.

Well, of course, he should stop by Julie's house at some point, but after his bath, certainly. He could not bear his sweaty, rumpled shirt or his creased duck suit any longer.

He had barely started to pick his way through the piles of stinking rubbish on the sidewalks of New Road, hoping the street sweepers would come back soon, when he heard shouts, then, distinctly, what sounded like gunfire, and suddenly, as if from nowhere, crowds appeared running away from the river, yelling, waving their arms, rushing as if to safety.

The sky was orange with the setting sun, but, looking up, he could make out grey-black smears above the gilded rooftop of the small Chinese temple down the *soi* and flights of black crows streaking through upriver, their shrill cawing competing with the cries of the people.

"What? What is it?" he tried to ask a cobbler who was frozen against a wall, his tools gathered against his chest and his eyes wide with crazed fear, but the man just looked at him, as if he could not understand.

He found himself buffeted by a group of shrieking women carrying baskets, obviously fleeing the riverside market in Bangrak. He almost lost his balance and righted himself against the shop front of a silversmith. The merchant glared at him, shouting "You! *Farang*! Go! Go!", and seized a broomstick to chase him from his doorstep, before slamming the iron gate in front of his door with a clang.

He fought his way through the throng and managed to get a few steps down the street, sheltering in a doorway and mopping his face. His hair was drenched with sweat, and he could almost smell his own fear, and his shame at his fear.

"Think, think." The closest haven was the Oriental, two *soi* away.

Head down, pushing people aside, wrenching his jacket away from a nail on a pushcart, he finally reached the double avenue of palm trees leading to the hotel and paused with a shuddering sob of relief once the entrance gate closed behind him.

The usual uniformed doorman had been replaced by guards massed to defend the entrance, looking, he thought, now that he was safe and could take the time to be amused, more terrified than terrifying.

He sat down on one of the garden benches under a tall palm, catching his breath, and fanned himself with his straw hat. How astonishing I didn't lose it, he thought in bemusement, trying to concentrate on his next move.

He needed to recover his calm — or at least, the appearance of calm. It would not do to be seen by all the men no doubt propping up the bar — planters, virile, bullish types — with his face running with sweat, his breath coming in jagged bursts and — he examined his jacket —, a long rip at the pocket, and two buttons missing, no doubt torn away while he was fighting his way against the milling, threatening mob.

"Miserable, cowardly faggot," he repeated. "That's what they will see and that's what I am."

He closed his eyes again, taking deep breaths. He would stop at the gentlemen's lavatory to try pull himself together.

"Have you heard what's happening? I can't get anyone to tell me."

He jumped up.

Julie was in front of him, hatless, hands thrust deep into the pockets of her practical khaki skirt and her sweaty white shirt sticking to her shoulders. He felt so angry he could barely speak.

"What are you doing out?" he hissed. "Have you gone quite mad?", and, so incensed was he by her recklessness that only deepened his own humiliation at his fear, he felt he needed to wound her in some way; he glared at her appearance and spat "Going out hatless! You look like a missionary's wife."

She gaped at him, shaking her head at his irrelevance, then shrugged — "Really Michael, who could possibly care whether I'm wearing a hat or not?" — and took his arm to pull him towards the bar.

"I was inside but I could not stand being stared at by all those men who looked as if they had not seen a woman before, and a French one at that. But now that you're here, it's all right."

He stopped in his tracks, shaking with rage.

No, it was not all right, he said, each word dripping with his barely concealed panic and fury.

For his money, the Chinese were looting the godowns upriver. "Do you know what a mob can do to a woman?

"Do you ever stop to think before you do the first thing that comes to your mind?"

They could not tell what danger they were in, and she should be home with her son.

"Well, I can't be now," she pointed out reasonably. "I tried but couldn't get back through any more. I think I arrived about ten minutes before the worst of the stampede, judging from what I heard from those who came in just after I did. It appears everybody at the Bangrak market fled *en masse*, including the chickens.

"People just let me pass to get here, an old Indian lady even told her son to escort me. He was stopped by the guards at the hotel gate, and I thought that was quite rude. It was obvious he was not trying to force his way in."

It was true she looked remarkably composed, her chignon had hardly slipped loose save a few stray locks stuck to her flushed and damp cheeks. She smiled up at him as they entered the cool foyer.

"Don't be angry, please. I just could not stand waiting and not knowing. Anyway, it can't be the Chinese rioting in Sampheng, I heard the cannon from downriver."

He shook his head. Was she sure? He had only heard gunshots.

They both looked around at the deserted space, usually so busy; there was not a single planter with a wide-brimmed hat loafing in the big bamboo armchairs reading the papers or a grizzled sea-captain guzzling beer and scanning the room for an acquaintance to spend time and money with, nor even a waiter padding silently in bare feet bringing frosted bottles to a table of rowdy English businessmen.

"Where is everybody?" she whispered, when he spotted a bellboy running from the kitchens towards the terrace overlooking the river, where, through the curtain of banana trees and frangipani they could see a crowd of *farangs* and Siamese milling around, pointing at the water.

"Come!" He grabbed her hand and they both ran over the slippery paving stones, just in time to hear the cannon, and someone say, knowingly.

"It's much closer this time. That must have come from the West Point Fort."

They pushed their way to the balustrade, just in time to spot a low white ship steaming up the dark roiling water, thick and powerful from the daily rains. Its rigging was torn and hanging in tatters, while one of its three masts had been shattered. Sailors, so close one could have almost stretched out a hand to touch them, were aiming guns towards the crowds gathered on both banks.

The last ray of the setting sun glinted on the cannon turned menacingly upriver, towards the Palace.

"The flag... look at its flag," Julie murmured, as a low, angry voice exclaimed: "Well, they've gone and done it. The bloody French have attacked."

Behind, a second gunboat followed, with a man lying on deck, his uniform covered in blood, and another seated by him, holding his bloodied head in his hands, his blue beret with its red pompom at his feet.

The sight of the jaunty French sailor's cap, which Julie had always thought so happy and cheerful seemed unbearably poignant, and she suddenly truly realized that it was indeed France, her country, whose ships were threatening Bangkok.

Then it was dark, and in the twilight, Michael kept muttering. "Impossible, it's impossible. Pavie had orders, he *had* orders...

"So I *was* right, and I didn't even believe it myself...".

Monsignor Vey, standing next to him, crossed himself and muttered prayers, his face a mask of misery in the flickering gas lanterns that had just been lit.

From the bar, they heard the first words of a ragged Marseillaise sung by a couple of Frenchmen who staggered onto the terrace, clutching bottles, and toasting the group of onlookers with broad, drunken grins.

Michael turned away in contempt. One of them was the generally disliked Lucien Fournereau who had badgered him and every other diplomat in Bangkok to admit that Siam would profit greatly from France's civilizing embrace. In tow was George Dupont, a hulking, shy, and generally harmless lumber merchant who had obviously imbibed far too many drinks.

Fournereau had lost his foppish demeanour, his usually slicked hair was tousled and his spotted silk cravat was hanging loose. Seeming unaware of the harsh stares that greeted them, he linked his arm with Dupont's, and warbled into the rousing, blood-thirsty chorus: "*Aux armes, citoyens…*"

James Smythe, a burly Scottish railroad engineer, marched up to them, and swatted away Dupont's bottle that shattered on the flagstones.

"I'll thank you to shut up or I'll push that song down your throats," he growled, as the man raised his fists, swayed then lost his balance and fell heavily on his backside.

Fournereau spat out a few inaudible words as he attempted to help the huge man to his feet while Smythe kicked him down again.

The bishop stepped in, and spread out his arms to stop the scuffle.

"No, no, please, my children. Let us not make this bad situation worse."

He was about to be shoved aside when Michael grabbed his cousin, who was standing there, so pale he could see every freckle on her cheeks, her eyes wide and staring and her lips white with shock. He had suddenly become aware that she was the only woman in sight.

"Listen," he whispered urgently pulling her away from the terrace.

"I must get to the Legation. Do not — do you hear me? — do *not* leave the hotel until I come back to get you. Promise me." Stunned, Julie just nodded.

She sat down heavily in an armchair, but Monsieur Malherbe, Léonie's husband, appeared next to her and grabbed Michael's arm.

"Do not worry. I will take her back to her house as soon as the streets are safe."

He shook his head, with a mournful, apologetic look on his ruddy flushed face.

"It's a bad business, and we French who live and work in Siam shall pay for this. Now leave Madame Gallet with me, and go."

With a grateful smile, Michael kissed Julie's forehead, put on his hat, and raced out the door.

The Legation was in an uproar, clerks rushing about to send telegrams and notes amidst a flurry of conflicting reports. Captain Jones turned away from a message he had just received and welcomed him with a quizzical look.

"You know," he said drily, "you are fortunate they don't burn sorcerers and witches at the stake any more. How on earth did you guess that Pavie would ignore his instructions?"

Michael wiped his forehead with his sleeve, he had run all the way from the Oriental, pushing and shoving just like the rest of the milling terrified throng.

He shrugged and gasped for breath.

It was only logic, really. Pavie was too vain to let his erstwhile protector Le Myre do all the negotiating and collect whatever glory was to be collected.

"He still believes he can impose a protectorate, but to do so, he needed to manufacture an incident. He couldn't stand what he saw as the ultimate prize slip out of his grasp.

"What do we know happened?"

Not much as yet, Jones informed him. Except a French pilot boat was sunk, and some French sailors have been killed. No figures for Siamese casualties. "I've just received a note from RJ, who's at the Palace, His Majesty fears for the independence of Siam, and also his life. So, tell me now, Oh, Wise One, what happens next?"

Michael sighed.

He really had no idea.

"BANGKOK, JULY 14ᵀᴴ 1893

Today is the French national day, and I am deeply ashamed of what my country has done.

No, no, it is not my country, I cannot believe it of France, the nation of the rights of man. It is the work of a handful of ambitious, unscrupulous, misguided men more concerned with their own glory than with that of their country.

I would never have told Michael, of course, but I was really rather frightened when I found myself on New Road with those crowds in a panic, cut off from my way back home by a group of youths who looked sullen and hostile, and masses of people pushing me forwards. So I just smiled, and apologized, and said a few words in Siamese to the ones I jostled, and a nice old lady in a saree ordered her rather reluctant son to escort me the few remaining steps to the Oriental.

I could feel the resentful looks from all the men gathered at the bar, for them, I was no longer that unfortunate, rather unconventional widow some of them had actually danced with at the New Year ball. I was a French woman, and, as such, to be despised.

"What are you doing here, and why are you not at home like a proper lady?" I could feel them all asking silently, and indeed, there were no other women to be seen, not even a missionary wife or one of the

simpering, giggling misses who, in any case, would not have welcomed me at their table.

When Monsieur Malherbe finally escorted me home, Fie grabbed me with tears streaming down her face, she had been so worried, poor Somboon had come looking for Michael and they imagined us both lying dead in some dark and deserted alley.

I sent the gardener to reassure Michael's household, he told me he would cut through back gardens so as not to pass in the soi, *and would not believe me when I told him the streets were quiet now, everyone was huddled in their houses, trying to keep safe.*

It was very late, past midnight when Michael finally came by.

I had made sure all the lamps were lit and all the servants were still awake, ready to defend the house had any one decided that they would strike a blow against France by attacking me.

What little news he has is very bad. A French pilot ship has been sunk, at least four French sailors killed. The warships we saw arrive are moored before the Consulate.

Today the streets teem with soldiers, and the city is in a panic. There is no meat or fruit and vegetables to be had as the markets are closed.

If this goes on much longer, we will have to kill one of the hens, but for now, we have eggs.

For men, war is blood and glory, and for women, it's ensuring the family has enough to eat. We are so much more sensible …

Speaking of blood and glory, I have no news of Victor, the post-office is closed, and in any case, would he bother to let me know he is unscathed?

Of course not, it would not even cross his mind.

How I wish I could embroider or paint and had something to do rather than pace from the door to the gate and back. "

Monsieur Rolin-Jaequemyns coughed and finally rapped on the table to ask for silence. The conference room at the Foreign Ministry was buzzing with low, excited voices, barely hushed arguments, and unanswered questions.

Waiting for the muted hubbub to die down, he looked beyond the baize-covered table with its arrangement of flowers at the uniformed Palace servants passing trays of tea and sweetmeats and sighed in exasperation at the clatter of china. "Nothing here happens without food," Prince Devawongse whispered with a bleak smile.

The Foreign Minister had dark circles under his eyes but his smooth face betrayed nothing of the harrowing hours he had just spent by the King's side. To his left, Admiral de Richelieu stared despondently down at a paper on which he had sketched a map of the river mouth and the positions of the various ships.

Seated in the front row, Auguste Pavie was stroking his beard spread out over his waistcoat, and nodding pleasantly at his colleagues.

He had the smug yet greedy look of a cat that not only had eaten a canary, but also felt entitled to gobble another, Captain Jones thought.

"Somehow," he murmured very low to Michael who had accompanied him as note-taker, "if British sailors had just been killed, I don't think I would seem so sanguine."

The French staff surrounded their Consul-General, but all the other Europeans present had chosen seats as far away from them as possible. As if to underscore their mourning at the loss of their sailors, they were all wearing black, a jarring, somber note in the assembly of white suited diplomats.

"Gentlemen, please" the Belgian Special Advisor to His Majesty finally said.

"I have asked you to come so as to inform you of the latest news, some of which you have heard of course, but some aspects of which remain unknown to you.

Yesterday evening," he continued, "against all Treaty agreements, the French warships *Inconstant* and *Comète* had forced their way through the entrance of the river, despite blank warning shots being fired from the forts at Paknam, leaving Royal Navy vessels no choice but to attempt to stop them by force. The French gunships returned the fire, disabling several of our ships, and killing 31 sailors."

Pavie could keep still no longer. Bouncing up, he strode up to the table, chin and beard jutting forward, his whole body quivering in indignation.

"You make very light, Monsieur, of the four French sailors who were killed as well, and did not mention the French pilot ship that was sent to founder on the sand banks so as not to sink at the bottom of the river."

Rolin-Jaequemyns closed his eyes briefly and sighed deeply.

"I had thought it better to let you do so yourself, Monsieur le Consul-General, once I had given you the floor. But you decided to speak before I had done so.

"So, yes.

"We deplore the loss of lives on both sides, as well as the unfortunate fate of the French pilot-ship, the *Jean-Baptiste Say*. But I must point out that none of this would have occurred if the captain of the *Inconstant* — Captain Borey, I believe? — yes, if Captain Borey had abided by his orders, which, I am given to understand, were to *not*, I repeat, *not* force his way upriver."

He paused and stared at Pavie, who shrugged negligently.

"The telegram had not reached us at that point, and *we* had been given to understand that the Siamese naval forces would attack on the fifteenth. So you see, it was just, shall we say, a pre-emptive precaution.

"Furthermore, may I point out that pursuant to article 15 of the Treaty, we were allowed to anchor at Paknam?"

"You did not anchor!" Richelieu roared suddenly. "You went upriver when we had repeatedly, yes, repeatedly denied you permission to do so!" He dropped his voice and repeated, growling, his guttural accent becoming ever thicker with his anger.

"You did *not* anchor at Paknam! No, Monsieur, you went all the way upriver and your guns are now trained on the Palace!

"Which article in the Treaty allows you *that*?"

Pavie rolled his eyes and looked around, as if asking for support in dealing with such an unreasonable attitude. "How could Captain Borey anchor at Paknam when he was fired at? In flagrant contravention to article 15, I repeat."

Rolin-Jaequemyns put his hand on the Danish admiral's arm to stop him from erupting again.

"In reply to your assertion, there was no earthly reason to believe the Siamese fleet was to attack the French ships, either on the fifteenth of July or at any other time.

"You mentioned the Treaty; French and Siamese interpretations of article 15 obviously differ, but given the many repeated threats, it appears to me, as a lawyer, that the Siamese view may well be seen as legitimate, the Treaty pertaining mainly to trade and not to naval disputes between our States.

"However.

"Such was not the purpose of this meeting, convened so as to inform all foreign diplomats of the situation, and, I take it, of France's regrets for this confrontation due to a surprisingly late reception of orders."

He paused, then added in a flat voice, his eyes narrowed at Pavie, "All the more surprising, I may add, given that we ourselves had received them well before this extremely unfortunate event took place.

"So, Monsieur le Consul-General, if you have nothing to add, may I wish everybody a good day and return to my duties?"

Pavie rose again, belligerence written in every line of his face.

"Regrets? You expect regrets? We believe that it would be more fitting for the Siamese government to express them.

"There will no doubt be reparations demanded by France, and, of course, the ultimatum I notified you of last month shall certainly be modified accordingly.

"I am now awaiting my instructions from Paris. You shall be notified in due course"

Prince Devawongse leaned forward, seeming about to make a heated rejoinder but sitting back, he signalled that the Belgian advisor should reply.

"Very well, Monsieur. We shall wait. Is there anything else?"

Pavie shook his head, at a loss for any more protests, got up from his chair, and, still surrounded by his staff, left the room without a backward glance and without the pleasantries he had bandied about on his arrival.

"Captain Jones, if you will?" Rolin-Jaequemyns crooked his finger at the British Minister who, followed by Michael, joined him by the window.

"I am very worried," he whispered. "His Majesty..."

He shook his head, glumly. "His Majesty is most dejected, and veers between all out desperate resistance and complete surrender.

"He envisions massacres, bombing of the city, threats to his very life.

"Richelieu, you may have noticed, believes the same, and wants us to attack the French and put an end to the whole affair, once and for all.

"Neither believes me when I say France will not dare go any further now, at least in military terms.

"Not so if we were to put ourselves in the wrong and sink the three ships — Siam would be far too easy to overrun and subdue from Saigon." He rubbed his drawn, lined face. "Forgive me, I have not slept much, if at all, in these last hours."

Jones put a sympathetic hand on his shoulder. "It's

hard, I know. We shall do all we can to help." His eyes went very hard. "Do you believe what that mountebank Pavie said, about receiving the telegram late? How is that possible?"

The Belgian sighed. It was not totally impossible, albeit unlikely. What one should consider, of course, was an intentional delay in sending this telegram from Paris.

"In any case, what we believe is immaterial, as we cannot call Pavie a liar to his face.

"He has requested an audience en 'tête-à-tête' this evening to discuss the sinking of the pilot-ship with His Highness Prince Devawongse and obviously does not want me to attend. Nonetheless, His Highness has asked me to participate, so I shall. I cannot let him run roughshod all over us.

"Meanwhile, I count on you, my good friend, to faithfully report our situation to London."

Jones nodded. "I shall, of course, as well as to Paris. Lord Dufferin will be quite intrigued to hear that the order not to attack conveniently reached everybody except the very ones it was meant for."

Rolin-Jaequemyns closed his eyes again, briefly, and managed a smile.

"In times such as this, it is good to know we can rely on Britain.

"I shall tell His Majesty so. Good-bye, my friend."

"It was quite moving, really," Michael recounted to Julie over a hurried lunch.

"But at the same time, I could not help but feel that RJ was perhaps expecting more support from Britain than we are prepared to provide."

He helped himself to more rice and chicken and asked where she had managed to get the food.

Julie had a mirthless laugh. Cook had killed one of

the hens, because there were not enough eggs to feed her household of seven adults and two children. And one hen for nine...

"I hope farmers will return to the markets soon. We have plenty of rice, but not much else.

"Mangoes and papayas from the trees, of course, but even that will not go very far."

She looked pale and drawn. She too had spent a sleepless night in an armchair, fearing an attack on her house.

"Get some sleep," he advised her. "There truly is no danger."

If RJ was right, and the French refrained from further attacks — and he, Michael, thought he was — then things would soon return to normal.

He kissed her on the forehead and rushed back to the Legation.

"BANGKOK, JULY 15TH 1893

It is very strange.

Despite what I told Michael so as to sound like a sensible woman for once, I am not afraid at all.

If anything, I feel this mad, slightly hysterical elation, as if I were truly alive at last. Perhaps Mama is right, and living in this climate has addled my brain, but at no time did I believe we might be in danger.

It all seems so unreal to me, although it must be painfully real to the Siamese.

Nonetheless, I do what I feel is necessary or rather what is expected of me, hence the — probably irrational — precaution of barricading the house, to the extent that this wooden building with its jutting verandahs and balconies can be barricaded, and tried — in vain — to keep the servants awake by walking around and clapping very loud when I found one asleep by the barred doors. Fie needed no such recommendations. She slept, as she always does, on the floor next to Louis' cot, but when I went in to kiss him,

I saw that she had a kitchen cleaver by her side. I almost laughed but I was very moved by this rather absurd proof of her courage and devotion.

My only worry is the food supply, and even so — I can order meals from the Oriental, they must not be running short, all the more so as I expect they have lost many customers. I wonder how the ordinary Siamese people manage, they who, heaven knows, do not have that option.

I went walking around the garden in the dark, just to enjoy the coolness of the night, and listen to the bullfrogs sing.

Meou, the one-eyed cat, followed me as it always does and was doing its best to catch one of the bats swooping around when I heard some unmistakable sounds coming from the servants' quarters. As only Mali, Nhu Dam and cook were inside, the other servants being made to stand guard — such as it was — I can only assume that Nhu Dam may soon be joined by another little Nhu. I wonder if Fie knows, and if so, how she puts up with it, she being the self-appointed mistress of this household.

I, however, do not mind anyone snatching whatever happiness they can. Mama would have had the offending maid out on her ear."

"BANGKOK, JULY 16ᵀᴴ 1893

Life is returning to normal, at least on the street. Markets have vegetables and meat again, but there is a subdued, ominous feel to the people, whether Siamese or farang, as if they are containing anger that might erupt at any moment. Still many soldiers patrolling New Road.

I went to the Oriental for tea, and also to try and get news, but all I heard were rumours, the chief ones being that the French are going to blockade the coast and impose a protectorate. No surprise there.

Michael, however, says that Pavie has not yet conveyed France's demands, and that the Palace fears the worst.

That French gunboat, the Inconstant, is still moored before the French Consulate, next to the Lutin, and from the hotel terrace, one could see the sailors always at battle stations and the guns trained upriver, towards the Palace.

I received two telegrams, one from Victor who appears to be in Saigon, urging me to join him there, the other from Mama and Papa, frantic about our safety, and insisting that I return to Paris.

Have answered both saying I am perfectly safe here, and shall not budge for the time being.

My mind is always on what might be happening at the Inner Court, and if my little students think me a traitor to our friendship. How I wish I had news from Keow..."

"BANGKOK, JULY 17ᵀᴴ 1893

Still awaiting official French reaction. However, Pavie is now in a snit about the fact that the Siamese fleet was commanded by Danish officers at the moment of the confrontation and demands that those 'mercenaries' be punished by the Siamese government presumably for obeying orders given by the Siamese government.

He also challenged RJ's right to attend and speak other than as interpreter during the audience he was granted by the Prince — the impudence of the man defies belief — and he trembled with rage when RJ reminded him that he was Special Advisor to His Majesty with rank of Plenipotentiary Minister and thus outranks him.

How could Louis have admired him so, I do not understand. But then, when I think of it, I hardly knew Louis at all..."

"BANGKOK, JULY 18ᵀᴴ 1893

Another British gunship, the Linnet, *has arrived to join the* Swift *and the* Pallas, *but anchoring well below Paknam. Some members of the Legation have taken this to mean that Britain will support Siam in case of a blockade. Michael, who I find is getting more cynical and grumpy by the day, says it means absolutely nothing.*

More petty incidents between the French, the Siamese and the Danish sailors, this time involving a flag that should or should not have been flying on the beached pilot ship. There was a scuffle and

Pavie and one of the gunboat captains have protested at what they call barbarous behaviour.

Do they not see how ridiculous they make themselves?

There is to be a funeral service at Assumption Cathedral for the French sailors who were killed, and I shall attend, out of respect for those poor young men who died in a land they didn't know, for a dispute they didn't understand. And also, because they all had mothers."

"BANGKOK JULY 21ST 1893

I had barely seen Michael these past few days, but he was able to come to lunch, and fell on the food with such appetite I gather he had barely taken time to eat. I was not expecting him, so it was a rather austere meal but he didn't seem to mind.

He looked quite haggard, and told me he had spent the night assisting Captain Jones in composing a report on the finally received French ultimatum. They were called to the Foreign Ministry around midnight to be briefed after Pavie presented his demands to Prince Devawongse."

According to Rolin-Jaequemyns, the interview was very distressing, Michael recounted between bites of the spicy salad and omelette that was all Julie was able to serve him.

He paused to swallow, and shook his head in dismay.

"It really does not bode well, if Pavie believes he can treat Siam this way."

He said the Belgian advisor still looked quite upset when he read them the paper that Pavie had produced from his pocket and practically flung at the Foreign Minister, demanding an immediate reply in writing.

His Highness, who was already exhausted by the events of the previous days could barely contain himself, protesting that he needed to inform His Majesty of the demands and receive his orders, that it was most irregular, indeed intolerable that France expected an immediate reply, it was against all rules of international law not to mention the rules of courtesy.

Pavie just sneered and replied that if within 48 hours France had not received satisfaction to her demands, a blockade of the coast would be ordered, and he himself would leave the country on the *Inconstant*.

"He shan't be missed," Julie remarked bitingly. "So, what is in the ultimatum?"

Michael hesitated.

He had been told to keep the content of the briefing confidential, but, on the other hand, Carlos Xavier, the chief translator of the Foreign Ministry often passed news to the various journalists, and it would most probably be in tomorrow's papers. And Julie was more discreet than most of his own colleagues who were probably discussing the matter over tiffin at the Club.

The usual claims to the left bank of the Mekong including Luang Prabang and the river islands, full control of the river itself, he sighed, along with recognition of Tonkin and Annam's rights — in other words, everything that could not be proved from scouring the Imperial Archives, quite simply because there were no such rights, at least in the case of Annam.

There were also other lesser conditions pertaining the various border incidents, he added, Grosgurin's death and Thoreau's capture.

"Apparently the international court Siam has promised does not satisfy, they consider that the Siamese are guilty, and want compensation even before a verdict is handed down."

But the worse was an absolutely extortionate demand for immediate payment of two million francs in reparations for damages and deaths, plus an additional three million to be deposited in piasters to guarantee the financial indemnities.

"I don't even know if Siam has that amount in her coffers."

Julie absently began peeling a mangosteen, her face grim.

"In other words," she remarked, "they are trying to humiliate the country and bankrupt it at the same time, so the King will have no choice but to surrender Siam to the French."

He nodded.

Yes, that just about summed it up.

What was Siam going to do?

Well, RJ was trying to get London to negotiate the demands down.

That was what he had been doing all night, drafting a request for Lord Rosebery and Dufferin to intercede with Develle.

"Prince Devawongse, however, is so despondent he just wants to give in, as does the King, to avoid the bloodshed they imagine the French will unleash if their conditions are not met immediately."

He rose and crumpled his napkin, leaned over and kissed her.

"Thank you my dear, I needed some food and sane conversation.

"Which reminds me, you had better stock up on butter and the other imports from Singapore you may need. And by the way, write whatever letters you need to write by this afternoon, that will be the last chance to get them out if the blockade does indeed take place — as it must, because I cannot imagine Siam able to ever satisfy the French.

"From tomorrow onwards, we shall be able to communicate with the outside world only by telegram."

"BANGKOK, JULY 23RD 1893

The blockade starts at midday. Yesterday, I rushed to write a long, reassuring letter to Paris, making little of the events and reminding Papa that he always said one should not trust what one reads in the newspaper.

I also gave them my opinion of Pavie and of the shabby, duplicitous way he has been treating Siam.

I decided to go myself to Fusco's general store instead of sending Lek with a list — I am not proud of it, but I knew that a farang *would not need to queue, and that I would therefore be able to buy what was needed, before others who sent a servant bought the shelves bare.*

And also, as I told myself, beyond butter, jam, tea, coffee and biscuits, I could think of nothing, so if I saw the goods on display, I would better know what might be needed.

I love talking to Signor Fusco, who, besides having such a lovely choice of food in his shop, is also Master of the Royal Navy band and is always gallant and entertaining, fussing over his lady customers.

He was there, and indeed, drew up a chair so I could order in comfort, and reminded me that sugar and flour might also be in short supply, so I took a large sack of each, along with his excellent tinned tomatoes, olive oil, macaroni and other delicacies he imports from Italy, and I ended up buying far more than I usually do, and things that I never buy.

It will delight cook, who loves to try new recipes, and who, as I recently found out, used to work in the kitchens of the Bangkok Hotel under Italian management. A little voice was whispering in my head that times such as these were not for buying dried mushrooms and jars of preserved truffles, but I silenced it quickly. What worldly difference will it make what I eat?

I have now become quite used to the oily yellow butter in tins I found so distasteful when I arrived, and there were only three tins of it left, so I bought them all, feeling guilty and selfish, all the more so as Louis will not eat bread and butter, much preferring rice. But Signor Fusco whispered that most of the European households already started stockpiling last week and that Reverend McIlvarny actually took six tins. How very unchristian.

From there, I went to the British Dispensary, and stocked up on various creams, soap, rouge and tooth powder and felt very virtuous and housewifely.

For all the talk of doom I heard in the various shops, I cannot but help being more excited than frightened.

What is wrong with me?

The thing is, I have no idea what a blockade will do to our daily life."

"Trade!" Captain Jones told Michael to stress the point in his coded telegram for Whitehall.

"Britain must be made to understand the value of the trade lost by the French blockade. Remind me of the figures, my boy."

Four and a half million pounds was the total amount of Siam's outgoing trade, Michael replied wearily. Ninety-three per cent of which is in British hands.

"Well, that should light a fire under their Lordships' arses." Jones growled.

"Meanwhile, I have just received several dispatches, one of which is reassuring: Develle assured our Embassy in Paris that Siam's territorial integrity would be respected. Although... how do they square this with the demand for Luang Prabang, eh? He also made a speech at the Chamber of Deputies, repeating the same, not basing himself so much on international law as stating the difficulties and expense of a direct attack on Bangkok."

The other dispatches were worrying, in that French public opinion was on the warpath, not so much about Siam, but about Britain itself. An article in *La Cocarde* — "Never heard of the rag, have you?" — should certainly lead to British official protest, he continued in a belligerent tone.

Etienne, the leader of the Colonial Party, was proposing the immediate seizure of Siem Reap and Battambang, to threaten Bangkok overland, and — "listen to this, I quote:

'so not to always give way to the leopard' — that's Britain, I assume. *'Siam will inevitably be taken over by them or by us, better that it be us.'* The gall of it!"

French, the Consul pursed his mouth.
There was such a thing as freedom of the press, he remonstrated.

Jones eyes flashed in exasperation.

"That's as may be, but accusing a friendly nation — and I suppose we must still be called that, we are not at war, as far I know — of designs on an independent kingdom, is tantamount to libel in my book. All the more so if it is knowingly used as an excuse to take over said independent kingdom.

"Crawfurd, remind me to see Thompson, that *Times* newspaperman. He's a sound chap, he's on our side and will explain the ins and outs of the situation to the British public. If the frogs can use the press as a weapon, no reason why we shouldn't.

"Anyway, I have advised Devawongse and RJ to reject the ultimatum and await Britain's reaction to the blockade."

"Was that wise, Sir?" French asked in the drawling, supercilious tone he had recently began to employ when speaking to his minister.

"Wise?" Jones erupted, "Wise? I'll give you wise.

"Wise is not to go behind your minister's back to our erstwhile Under-Secretary of State for India, the exalted Mr Curzon, in the hope he will communicate your 'wisdom' to Lord Rosebery. Ha! Bet you think I wouldn't find out."

An ugly dark blush stained the consul's cheeks. It seemed to him, sir, he stammered, that Britain was being far too committed into this dispute that did not really involve her and that Lord Rosebery's instructions were being disregarded.

Captain Jones was about to sputter a rejoinder, but cut it off, giving the Consul a malevolent look. "All right. You can go, all of you."

In the hall, with the door firmly closed behind them, French shook his head.

"The old man is getting more unbearable by the day."

Michael cocked his head. "You really shouldn't have gone behind his back, you know."

The consul shrugged.

"What was I to do? Whitehall's instructions were clear.

"I was not about to be blamed for not carrying them out. I have a career to think of."

He looked down at Michael, and dropped in a patronizing voice: "And so have you."

The following day was tense at the Palace.

Prince Devawongse and the King were frightened, and the Foreign Minister drafted an unconditional acceptance of all French demands.

He presented it to Rolin-Jaequemyns, assuring him that His Majesty approved.

"Better to give in, than to risk the destruction of Bangkok," he said. "As there has been no response to our request for advice from Britain, it seems we are on our own."

The Belgian advisor protested that he, too, had been preparing a letter to Pavie, and that total submission to France was premature. What he proposed was to cede the left bank up to the 18th parallel.

Going to the table, he unrolled the map he had brought with him, and beckoned the Prince to his side to show him that his proposal would preserve Siamese control over most of Northern Laos.

"Let Lord Rosebery apply to Paris for better conditions,

Your Highness," he urged, "Such things cannot be done in a day."

The Prince shook his head. He had already sent a copy of his draft to Captain Jones, to be communicated to London. And he had heard that Consul French was advocating immediate compliance, against his Minister's wishes.

Perhaps the younger man was right, and understood Britain's position better.

But if Monsieur Rolin-Jaequemyns thought it useful, he might try to improve the wording of the text.

All this Jones told Michael next morning, after escorting Rolin-Jaequemyns to the door and seeing him into his carriage.

"That letter of Devawongse is impossible," he raged. "RJ is at least trying to save Luang Prabang province, and stresses the duress of each demand. I don't see how the King could hesitate between the two. That's the one I shall send to London."

"Edward French fears, and I think he is right, that the refusal to cede most of Laos will play into French hands," Michael confided to Julie over lunch. "It will just excite the Parti Colonial to push for further, and harsher demands."

She stirred her coffee thoughtfully. "But wouldn't giving in right away without protest just do the same or worse?"

"Probably," he sighed. "From my experience of boarding school, surrendering to bullies never works. But when you are faced with such overwhelming force... And Whitehall has still not replied. Meanwhile, the blockade has been postponed until tomorrow, as Pavie could not sail before."

"BANGKOK, JULY 26ᵀᴴ 1893

The blockade started yesterday evening, not that it seems to make any difference in our everyday lives yet.

But I suppose I should be more sparing in my use of coffee, tea, etc.

Pavie has left Bangkok, good riddance!

I, and it seemed most of Bangkok, watched him leave on the Inconstant, *standing at the poop, dressed all in black. It was all I could do not to cheer.*

Afterwards, had tea at the Oriental, and was snubbed by the Misses Cole and Shakespeare, my fellow teachers at the Palace who also have classes at the Sunandalaya College for Girls.

Miss Cole sneered that I must be pleased that Siam has accepted France's (actually, she said 'your') ultimatum. Of course, I could not set her right, as it would mean betraying something that Michael told me in confidence, so I replied mildly that I knew nothing, and that the ultimatum was certainly not mine any more than it was hers.

The reason for their anger, it appeared, is that I attended the memorial service for the French sailors. I said I would have attended any service for the Siamese sailors as well, had I known where to go.

Both withdrew in a huff, muttering something about 'brazen French widows'.

It seems that the rumour of an unconditional Siamese surrender is going all around town, as I also heard this from Mrs McFarland, who came to sit with me, apologizing for the rudeness of as she put it 'those two desiccated spinsters.'

Still no news from Keow."

Captain Jones was livid.

After an agonizing several days wait for instructions from London, he had just received a telegram from Lord Rosebery which he read out to Rolin-Jaequemyns, his voice quaking and his hands shaking with indignation as he held the flimsy paper: "*I have constantly and consistently advised to make terms with the French quickly. The result of my inquiries in Paris shows me that, if Siamese resistance is continued, the French demands will increase rapidly. I do not see therefore what Siam can gain by further refusal and their best course is to accept the French terms immediately and unconditionally."*

The Belgian paled. "So they abandon us."
Edward French, standing in a corner of the office, smirked watching Jones' face twist with anguish as he replied. "So it would seem. I am very, truly sorry, my friend. I did my best."

Rolin-Jaequemyns sighed as he rose heavily from his chair, and collected his hat and umbrella. "Thank you. There appears to be no other choice but to surrender our pride, then. I must now go inform His Highness Prince Devawongse. I dare not think what His Majesty will say."

Meanwhile, the news from Paris the same day was worrying.

Lord Dufferin communicated mounting rage expressed by the Colonial Party after the reception of the first reaction of Bangkok to the ultimatum and the refusal to cede Luang Prabang.

The Under-Secretary for the Colonies was in open conflict with the Foreign Minister, and demanding the imposition of a protectorate over Siam along with the annexation of Battambang and Siem Reap in the Khmer provinces. The British ambassador to France quoted an article in *Le Figaro* newspaper stating that what was needed was no less than to put all of Siam's foreign relations under French control.

The Foreign Minister had offered his resignation, reminding his colleague Delcassé, in charge of the Colonies, and the whole of the Cabinet that he had promised Britain to guarantee the independence of Siam, and stating forcefully "he had thus given the word of France.

Was France to be known, henceforth, as a nation that went back on her word?"

Delcassé had then folded, according to Lord Dufferin, but insisted on France taking control of what he tremulously called the "lost Khmer provinces."

"One could almost think he was talking about Alsace and Lorraine, so pathetically was he describing the loss," Michael told Julie, "as if Battambang and Siem Reap had long been part of France…"

Julie shook her head in bemused despair.

"I no longer recognize my country. It's as if all of them had taken leave of their senses. To think that practically no one had ever heard of Siam five years ago, and now, nobody talks of anything else.

"At least, one good thing about the blockade is that I shan't receive any letters from home demanding that I fall in line with their thinking.

"So what is going to happen, do you think?"

Michael shrugged. "Well, once the formal acceptance of the ultimatum is received, Paris has to declare itself satisfied. Or so I hope.

"Lord Dufferin concluded his telegram by saying that thankfully, Parliament was breaking up for elections, and that the zealots of the Parti Colonial were all back in their constituencies, which made it easier for Foreign Minister Develle to make good on his promises.

By the way, Captain Jones is having a big dinner party tomorrow, and asked me to give you this invitation. Yes, I know, his timing is unfortunate, to say the least, but he sees it as his way of proving the blockade does not affect us. Do come, please."

"BANGKOK, JULY 30ᵀᴴ 1893

The social merry-go-round continues.
I duly attended Captain Jones' party and a stranger event I have yet to see.

All that Bangkok counts as non-French luminaries were there, the American chargé, Herr Kempermann the German Minister, the Chevalier de Keun, who is the Dutch Minister, and who whispered importantly to me that he was in charge of the welfare of French nationals in the absence of Monsieur Pavie, and therefore of my own welfare — and he actually pinched my waist in saying so. I rapped his hand with my fan, smiling graciously all the while.

There were also the captains of the English, German and Dutch ships, and I suppose that I and the other unattached ladies had been asked to make up the numbers.

Despite their antagonism, Captain Jones had to invite Edward French along with his wife, whom I had rarely met before, because, as she told me with a simper, 'Edward does not approve of leaving the children with the native nurse.'

She is the ideal two-penny romance beauty, pursed rosebud mouth, yellow curls, and huge blue eyes, and talks of nothing but her children, her wonderful husband and of how much she misses the Brighton of her childhood. A stupefyingly boring young woman, and that, I think, is why her husband does not take her out more often into the world.

Mrs Jones was very warm to me, as were the Misses Cole and Shakespeare, who are hardly ever seen without each other and behaved as if our encounter of last week at the Oriental had never occurred. I suppose they feel that if I am good enough for the Minister of Britain, I am good enough for them.

Captain Jones, who is really most amazingly indiscreet and was steadily and methodically getting drunk, revealed at the table that Prince Devawongse had the idea of asking the Emperor of Russia to intervene on Siam's behalf.

RJ, from whom he obviously had this bit of information, glared at him from over his glass, but said nothing.

A newspaperman, a Mr Thompson, noted that down when he thought no one was watching. His eyes scanned all of us, lingering, I couldn't help noticing, on the pretty face of Mrs French.

He also stared at me with what I hope was admiration, but he could just as well have been comparing me unfavourably with her.

The general atmosphere was tense, people were dull, no one laughed, and everybody drank and ate too much of the usual terrible food to make up for the absence of conversation.

After dinner, to make things even more bizarre, there was music, and Monsieur RJ had to play for hours. As if the poor man had not enough on his plate...

At one point, as I stood near the piano to help him find the sheet of music he wanted, he whispered to me, his eyes twinkling: 'Do you not think our good Chevalier de Keun the most perfect ass?' I wholeheartedly concurred.

Captain Kirby, of the Swift, sang Scottish ballads very well.

I, as usual, begged off from performing at all.

The acknowledgement by Paris of Siam's unconditional acceptance of the ultimatum arrived on the last day of July, and was anxiously received in Bangkok.

"In truth, it is both almost good and very bad at once," Rolin-Jaequemyns told the whole of the British Legation diplomats gathered to hear him, "and as to the conditions, given the intentions of Delcassé to impose a protectorate, I expected much worse. I was imagining Pavie as my master here and having to literally kowtow before him.

"Siam has lost the entire left bank of the Mekong. It is a fact, and they shall have to learn to live with it, as," he added with a touch of malice, "France has had to learn to live without Alsace and Lorraine, which is a comparison I intend to make when I have the opportunity.

"Withdrawal of Siamese troops from Battambang and Siem Reap provinces, as well as from all areas 25 kilometres from the Mekong on the right bank starting at the

Cambodian border, but local police forces shall remain to ensure order in those regions.

"No Siamese armed boats or launches on the Great Lake in Cambodia or on the Mekong.

"And finally, the establishment of French consulates in Korat and Muong Nan.

"Well, that is not a problem, unless, of course, they decide to turn it into one by claiming French protection and jurisdiction for any number of Khmer and Indochinese to enable them to escape Siamese justice and taxes.

"No, the real hardship is an additional guarantee they demand, besides the financial one: until the entire left bank is surrendered to them and all border posts, garrisons, etc., are dismantled, they want to occupy all of Chantaboon province."

Michael who was furiously scribbling notes raised his head in disbelief, Jones whistled very low, and even Edward French looked stunned.

Chantaboon was a province on the Gulf of Siam, close to Cambodia, and also directly opposite the strategic islands that gave control over all shipping bound to and from Bangkok. And, besides its famous orchards and gardens that made it one of the main supplies of fresh food for the capital, it was rich with ruby, sapphire and topaz mines — exploited by British companies — a major source of revenue both for Britain and the Crown of Siam.

"*Oui mes amis*," Rolin-Jaequemyns continued, lapsing into French in his dismay, "it is excessive, is it not? And quite unjustified, coming as an additional demand after the others were accepted. But I believe — no, I hope, rather — it is imposed only symbolically by Develle to satisfy the Parti Colonial, rather than actually to be carried out.

"In any case, what choice does His Majesty have?" Public opinion in Bangkok, whether Siamese or amongst the foreign community was aghast and scandalized at hearing that the French flag was flying on the royal island retreat of Koh Si Chang, chosen as command base for the blockading fleet.

This was not just a military action; it was a deliberate humiliation.

His Majesty, by all accounts was demoralized and fearful that the conditions imposed by Paris were but a pretext to create incidents with Siam and that the occupation of Chantaboon would continue indefinitely.

Meanwhile, all the silver reserves of the kingdom were loaded on the *Lutin*, and, as Rolin-Jaequemyns recounted to the German and British ministers, the Crown was as good as bankrupt.

"Members of the Royal family have also contributed from their own fortune, as has His Majesty. It is said — but I doubt I shall ever know — that secret reserves of silver coins amassed by previous kings were used.

"Whatever the source of the monies, it is one condition met, and beyond met, might I say. The sum was supposed to be deposited as a guarantee, not an outright payment! Shall Siam ever see it again, I truly wonder...

"Accordingly, I received a telegram from the Foreign Ministry in Paris saying the blockade was to be lifted yesterday, August 2nd."

"I received one as well from Lord Dufferin," Jones chimed in. "He was told by Develle."

The Belgian sighed. "However, nothing has happened, French ships still patrol the gulf and Pavie, Admiral Humann and the French Navy do only as they please. This might explain somewhat the attack on the 13th of July and the delay in passing on orders not to force a passage upriver.

"Did I tell you a reply was received from the Emperor of Russia? He expresses his most sincere wishes for the re-establishment of peace and the removal of difficulties with France. In other words, I am sorry for your troubles but I shan't lift a finger and good luck.

"The king and Prince Devawongse, however, were very heartened, I do not understand why...

"Ah, believe me, had I known what was going to be expected of me when I was offered this position, I would have thought twice before accepting it."

"BANGKOK, AUGUST 5ᵀᴴ 1893

For the first time in ages, Michael managed a leisurely lunch here.
Cook had somehow found quite delicious beef, which he stewed with dried Chinese mushrooms and served 'en croûte'. It was as good as anything served at the Boisenfray's table, and Michael arrived with a bottle of Burgundy and the news that the blockade is lifted. So we needn't worry about our wine supply!

We played in the garden with Louis, who now speaks a few words, but only in Siamese. Michael tried to teach him 'Baa baa black sheep', but Nhu Dam was much quicker in repeating the words, being several months older. He is a most endearing child as well, with an open, smiling disposition. He has bright intelligent eyes and big ears that stick out, all the more so as Mali, his mother, shaves his poor little head.

It is quite delightful to watch the two boys, the blond with his ringlets and the shaven-headed, dark-skinned one, occupied together at a game I do not understand, but which keeps them pouring buckets of water in the dirt and floating twigs. Whenever there is an argument between them, Mali and Fie force Nhu Dam to give in, so Louis is becoming quite imperious.

It is useless to try to have them treated equally, because, as Fie explained, 'Nhu Dam must not expect to be equal to his master.' I was rather appalled by this, but Michael pointed out there is wisdom in what she says. That's as may be, but I do not believe that Louis should be taught that everyone is to do his bidding. Michael says that boarding school will cure him of that, but boarding school is something I refuse to even think about at present.

He brought them a ball, but neither was interested.

What I most enjoyed about today, I think, is that for once, we did not discuss Pavie, France, or — outside of boarding school — anything unpleasant.

"BANGKOK, AUGUST 7ᵀᴴ 1893

Received a letter from Victor, as nonchalant and uninformative as ever. He is in Saigon, and enjoying life, women and wine.

I understand he is not to mention anything confidential, but surely, he might acknowledge what has happened here?

Nonetheless, he did write that Monsieur Le Myre de Vilers is due to arrive in Bangkok next week and that I must make sure to be introduced, as he is an acquaintance of Papa's and should be cultivated.

The blockade is indeed lifted, and stores full of goods. I indulge myself at Signor Fusco's once more, then actually bump into Monsieur RJ at Falck's where he was buying Rhine wine and I had come to order a delivery of aerated water. He tells me with his usual twinkly eye that Pavie is stalling on returning to Bangkok, because of some nonsense about insisting upon a twenty-one-gun salute from a Siamese ship in front of the French Consulate. But the Prince is holding firm on his refusal, quoting diplomatic customs, tradition, etc. Nobody can out-protocol the Siamese, as he said.

We both laughed.

Pavie's return, which he had planned to be sensational and thunderous to the sound of a twenty-one-gun salute, was actually discreet and almost unnoticed, to his great disappointment.

Not so the arrival of Monsieur Le Myre de Vilers, he of whom Michael said that his nomination as plenipotentiary was certainly not good news.

The French envoy was coming to hammer out the Franco-Siamese Treaty that should put an end to the dispute in a spirit of renewed friendship.

All of Bangkok was braced and tense, following his progression from Saigon and his prolonged stay in Chantaboon, ostensibly to inspect this new French outpost, but above all to ensure that he would be received with due honours.

"They say that Develle regretted appointing him before his signature was dry on the nomination decree," Edward French reported from the dispatches received overnight. "What this says is that Le Myre wants to add to the ultimatum several points of detail that would lead to a real protectorate, and that Develle is trying to rein him in."

"He should have known better than to entrust this negotiation to a candidate from the Parti Colonial, and he has only himself to blame," Michael replied grumpily, decoding another telegram from Whitehall's Asian desk. He paused, then held up his hand and read it out.

"Listen to this, Sir:

"Secret. The French still seem to intend to take the provinces of Battambang and Siem Reap, which would be very grave. It is very important that the Siamese strictly execute the conditions agreed and avoid giving any pretext for complaint. Can you ascertain if the Siamese Government has reason to believe the rumour is founded?"

Captain Jones exploded. "For god's sake, what do they expect the Siamese to say? They have every reason to disbelieve the French.

"If the Foreign Legion troops had arrived from Algeria, believe me, it would be done already!"

He leafed through a sheaf of papers, and paled, pulling out a cable marked Reuters. "Now you both must hear this: *'The French will occupy the port and river of Chantaboon until the left bank of the Mekong has been evacuated. The cession to France includes that portion of Luang Prabang lying on the left bank.'*"

Edward French shrugged and rolled his eyes towards the others. "Well, sir, no news there, we already knew."

Jones stared him down over his spectacles and snapped. "Do you think I had forgotten? But then Reuters adds '*M. Develle and Lord Dufferin have signed a protocol creating a neutral zone between the new French territory, Burmah and China. Parleying is proceeding between France and England regarding the limits of this zone.*'"

"Well," the Consul ventured patiently in his patronizing way, "that seems a rather good idea, Sir."

Jones closed his eyes, and made an obvious effort to restrain his anger.

"I'm not saying it's not. But why the hell aren't we, and I suppose, more importantly, the Siamese, informed of it?

"Why is Whitehall going behind our backs?

"RJ was already disappointed in us, wait till he hears of this!"

The portly Belgian just nodded with a dejected look.

He too thought it might be good to create a buffer zone between the two great colonial powers. But of course, it would be scandalous it Siam were thus cut off from China.

He picked up a pen from his desk and played with it, speaking without raising his eyes. "In truth, my dear friend, I am discouraged. Not only at this cable you have just brought me, although it does confirm that Britain has completely lost interest in our claim to Luang Prabang.

"But it would seem that the negotiations with Le Myre de Vilers shall go on without me."

Jones stared. How was that possible?

His Majesty and Prince Devawongse had surely not lost faith in their adviser? He could not be blamed for anything that had happened since his arrival in Siam.

No, no, he was reassured. It was nothing like that.

But when Le Myre de Vilers, the French plenipotentiary,

had arrived in Chantaboon, he had made it known that he wanted an audience with His Majesty.

"Nothing more normal, naturally. But as you know, the King is unwell again, and has retired for several weeks to Bang Pa In — although the French flag no longer flies over Koh Si Chang, he did not want to even be near the fleet, which is still in the gulf — and Prince Devawongse replied to Monsieur Le Myre that he would be received by himself, and not His Majesty.

"The reply was a curt summons to His Highness to wait on M. Le Myre in Chantaboon. That was not acceptable, as you may well imagine.

"So I wrote that I would be the one to welcome him to Siam. No reply for a week, then finally, this..."

He shuffled the papers on his desk, and produced a sheet with a République Française letterhead and read out: " *The instructions of my government prescribe me to categorically refuse to enter into relations with other persons than His Majesty the King or his ministers and to spurn the intervention of foreign advisers.*' It was not even sent to me, but to His Highness — I, apparently, am not even worthy of the courtesy of an answer.

"And His Highness has accepted this shameful condition. It is of course because they expect to take advantage of Siam and do not want me to prevent them from doing so, and in their own language."

He gave the Englishman a pained smile and patted his damp cheeks and forehead with a huge square of checked linen. "So you see, I wonder what use I am here... I shall not lie, I often think of packing up and returning to Egypt, or any place sunny. But the Prince says he wants my advice behind the scenes, as it were, and I would feel guilty leaving him alone to deal with the likes of those two jackals — nay, three — ! I think Hardouin just as bad as Pavie and Le Myre."

He sighed deeply once more. "I am so tired, I want only one thing, for Emilie to be back and to spend a quiet evening with her."

He made an effort to brighten up.

"Have I told you the latest idea? His Majesty wishes to travel to Europe.

I think it would be a capital plan."

Jones made a face. "Would it be wise, though, to leave his country precisely now with the French on the brink of taking it over, to go and spend months a pleasure jaunt?"

Rolin-Jaequemyns shrugged and carefully folded his handkerchief. It would not be before next year, at best.

Such things took time to organize.

"And in any case, the talks with the French should be over by then, and either Siam remains independent, or, by hook or by crook the French will have achieved everything they set out to achieve.

"His Majesty's presence or absence will then make no difference."

Chapter XI

Such a surprise!

A reception was organized at the consulate for the French community to meet Monsieur Le Myre de Vilers, and, to my astonishment, I received an invitation.

To say I had no wish to attend is an understatement, but Léonie and her husband were most insistent, claiming my absence would be seen as an insult, and even Michael advised me to go, saying I could not afford to be on the wrong side of the French authorities here, and I suppose he was right.

Whatever I think and feel, I am after all a French citizen, with a French passport, and depend upon the protection of French diplomats.

I wore one of my plainest gowns — let them not think I primped specially for the occasion — and a simple hat with a veil along with my most frozen expression.

The receiving line was long and slow, and unfortunately, I was waiting behind Monsieur Fournereau, who was smirking and fluffing his moustache for all he was worth, congratulating himself on what was going to be at last proper standing and recognition of France in this benighted land.

Thankfully, I had Léonie to chat with so we could both ignore the odious man, freezing him out with our shoulders each time he attempted to draw us in conversation.

Suddenly, I was seized from behind, kissed in the neck, and 'Guess who?' was whispered into my ear, as everyone around looked quite scandalized.

Victor!

I spluttered an introduction to those around who had not met him on his previous stays, and he dragged me out of the line and onto the verandah.

'No point in waiting with the crowd,' he laughed, 'I shall introduce you myself later.' He was part of Le Myre's military escort, and had not written of his arrival, he wanted to surprise me, and Heaven knows he did.

He looked marvellous, very dashing in his uniform with his sunburnt face. I, however, did not pass muster in his eyes and he looked me up and down critically.

'Didn't make much of an effort, did you?' he asked with a smile. 'How very like you! Let's see if we can fix you up somewhat.' He took my shawl away, gave it to a bearer, lifted the veil from my hat, and rearranged my hair.

I was getting quite annoyed, happy as I was to see him.

He then took me by the hand to meet the great man, and I was irresistibly reminded of Louis introducing me to Pavie, who was standing there next to Le Myre, of course, and looking at me with ill-concealed dislike.

'Ah, of course, Madame Gallet, the most unconventional French lady in Siam,' he murmured, as Le Myre nodded at Victor's gushing words of introduction.

'You are unconventional, Madame? How so?' he asked, although he seemed to care not a whit. He does not have a pleasant face, and looks haughty and contemptuous of our ragtag group of provincial, old-fashioned Bangkok denizens.

I explained that I did not see myself that way at all, but some might think it because I opted to remain in Siam after the death of my husband.

A death in the service of the Pavie Mission, I added pointedly.

'To pass the time, Madame teaches French to the ladies at the Palace,' Pavie murmured with a sneer. Le Myre was looking me up and down.

'So you are Captain Lucas-Sauvain's sister? I know your father somewhat,' he finally said. 'A very worthy man, with great common sense. I wonder he let you come all the way here, and once here, that he let you stay.'

'Had he been able to, he would have stopped me,' I replied with as gracious a face as I could muster. He grimaced a sour smile in return — he obviously does not like unconventional women — and turned to the next person, but not before saying with a swagger, 'We shall make this a more worthwhile country for you to live in, then.'

I was then introduced to a young, rather handsome lieutenant, with a curly moustache and brazen undressing eyes who kisses my hand politely.

'*My friend Jean Le Myre de Vilers.*'

Well, he certainly seems pleasanter than his father, but even I with my limited experience can tell he is quite the roué.

Victor cannot stay with me, he has been given a room at the consulate as he may be called at all hours.

He thinks I was not very pleasant to our exalted plenipotentiary, and takes me to task as if I were a child.

'*Did you want me to curtsy?*' I asked in anger. '*I am past the age when someone can tell me what my father should or should not have done about my choices. Really!*'

'*It's because you look so young,*' he replied with mock gallantry, before telling me with great pleasure that he expects to be sent to Chantaboon to command the garrison there. '*So we shall be able to see more of each other.*'

I cannot say I welcome the prospect, much as I love him.

If I am ever asked back to the Palace, how can I tell them that it is my very own brother who is occupying their land?"

"*BANGKOK, AUGUST 25ᵀᴴ 1893*

Victor escaped the Consulate and joined Michael and myself for lunch here. I had suggested the Oriental, but my dear brother does not want to be seen in Michael's company in public.

I was incensed, but Michael advised me to drop the matter. '*Truth be told, I'd rather not be seen with him either.*'

Victor is full of glee, because Le Myre and Pavie were able to force Prince Devawongse to begin meetings at seven in the morning.

'*Pavie knows the Siamese council of ministers begins after midnight and can last until dawn, particularly these days when there is so much for them to discuss. So our good prince is exhausted even before it starts!*' he crows munching happily on cold chicken. '*'t will make it so much easier for things to go our way.*'

Michael said very little over the meal, as did I, blessing Louis' presence and antics to conceal the distaste we feel.

However irritated I am at his enthusiasm for the French side, I cannot blame him, and neither does Michael.

He is a French officer, acting and doing as he was trained to; anything else would be treachery on his part, as Michael stressed, and we cannot expect him to be otherwise.

Nonetheless, I wish he had stayed in France.

Prince Devawongse was pale, disheartened, and sickening from fatigue.

After briefing Rolin-Jaequemyns in secret, raging the while at being forced to hide so as to seek the views of His Majesty's Special Adviser, he then had to go to the Royal Council and spend the night listening to his fellow ministers' views.

"He is holding firm in resisting those bullies for the time being, but he shall not be able to go on much longer," Jones told Michael.

"RJ has repeatedly told him to try and curtail those council meetings to get some sleep, but he says it is just not possible. Meanwhile, Pavie, Le Myre and Hardouin threaten, cajole, and push, push, push.

"Now, they want Siam to remove its custom posts in the entire demilitarized area on the right bank. That was most emphatically *not* in the ultimatum!

"Can you imagine the losses in customs duties, while all the goods will flow to Saigon, and the Indochina government will just sit there gleefully counting its piasters!

"There has also been talk of piercing a canal through the isthmus of Kra, to enable ships to reach Saigon without passing the Malacca Straits, and Le Myre is dangling that in front of Devawongse as a carrot, saying it will develop shipping traffic in Bangkok. My aunt Fanny, it will!

"Well, that would be the end of Singapore as an international shipping port, which is of course what they want.

"Furthermore, what the hell gives the French the right to even consider such a project so close to Malaya?

"I tell you, those goddam frogs are going to beggar us all, and I will bloody well write to London and tell them to start doing something about it!"

London replied expressing concern, and appending a long message from Lord Dufferin, to whom Develle had confided his frustration and anger at Le Myre de Vilers' and Pavie's actions.

"Pavie, who is an agent of the Foreign Ministry can be brought in line — he was instructed most strictly not to aggravate the conditions imposed upon the Siamese by making them lose face — but Develle finds it impossible to control Le Myre." the British ambassador to France wrote.

"The plenipotentiary now refuses to accept amendments Paris has made to the draft treaty and ignores any instructions given to him. He has put back in entire paragraphs he wrote and which the Foreign Ministry deleted, and announces further, harsher measures.

"This treaty, which was supposed to put an end once and for all to this dispute, is now worsening it. All that Develle can do is threaten not to ratify it.

"He also tells me that there is a general folly amongst the zealots of the Colonial Party, who almost seem to be pushing for a war with England."

Jones dropped the letter and looked around at the Legation staff who had listened with increasingly dismayed faces.

He had also received a private letter from a friend in Whitehall who was told by Lord Rosebery that never had France and England been so close to war since Waterloo.

"Can you imagine, gentlemen? Going to war with France over Siam?

"Well, to quote our good RJ, had I known what was going to happen, I never would have accepted to be posted here. I am much too old and tired to play these games, and with such people." He ran his hands through his hair and shook his head in disgust. "Prince Devawongse is tired too.

"Pleading illness, he has interrupted the meetings, and gone to join His Majesty in Bang Pa In." He stopped, struck suddenly. "You do realize, don't you, that Koh Si Chang is in Chantaboon province?

"Which means that the Royal retreat there will be occupied by the French? Well, you can just imagine Monsieur Pavie spending his leisure in that lovely teak palace..." he snorted. "French sailors sunning themselves on that beach and bringing their mademoiselles to be wooed in the moonlight. All I can say is I'm truly appalled at what is happening in this world."

"BANGKOK, AUGUST 28TH 1893

As the negotiations are interrupted, Victor is quite free when he is not escorting Monsieur Le Myre de Vilers around to visit Bangkok.

Naturally, he also spends a great deal of time with his fellow officers — including, of course, the dashing young Lieutenant Le Myre — enjoying the amenities of the various hotels and pleasure establishments, whatever these pleasures are, but I ask no questions. He has brought several of his colleagues to my house after sending me a chit to make sure that Michael won't be there.

I do my best to entertain them, but I am no better at it in Bangkok than I was in Paris, which is very strange, as I have no problems receiving my own friends here. I find myself becoming once more the Julie Victor knew ten years ago, and cannot seem to shed that diffident and abrasive role.

My brother is quite incensed at not being welcome to play tennis at the British United Club — he was courteously but firmly shown the door, whereas he played there at New Year — and speaks darkly about this being remedied 'next year, at the latest...'

Meanwhile, he comes to lunch or dinner, and talks perhaps overmuch when the wine has been flowing. Needless to say, and I am somewhat ashamed of this, I keep pouring.

Yesterday, he told us that although he enjoys not being constantly on call, he is rather annoyed that his stay in Bangkok might be extended for who knows how long because he is in a hurry to start installing his garrison in Chantaboon, and does not believe in Prince Devawongse's illness.

'It's obviously a ploy,' he sneers, 'so as to scurry to the summer palace and have that Belgian go with him there! The dishonesty of the man!'

Michael choked on his food at hearing this, but said nothing, so as not to start an argument. I ask Victor quite mildly if the King and his foreign minister have also been prohibited from meeting Monsieur Rolin-Jaequemyns, as was, from what I understood, Monsieur Le Myre.

No, he splutters, not for want of doing it, but because it was just not possible. But pretty soon, that so-called international lawyer would be sent packing.

Anyway, the pause in the meetings was probably a good thing, and enabled the Siamese to, as he put it, 'stew in their fear.'

'It will make it all the easier to force their hand,' he said. 'As Monsieur Le Myre de Vilers always says, European diplomatic customs do not apply in Siam. With Asians, you impose your will when you are the stronger, or you stand back when you are weaker. And as far as possible, you don't waste your time in negotiations.

'From what I have seen in Indochina, it's a very wise policy.'

When he left, Michael just grinned at me and said that Victor is no doubt a very good officer, but would have made a terrible diplomat.

He talks too much.

My little acts of rebellion to enable Michael to gather information for England by making my brother speak out of turn may not amount to much. But somehow, I have the impression that I am striking a blow for Siam...

"*Bangkok September 4*TH *1893*

I know I wrote I did not blame Victor for so whole-heartedly adopting the French point of view, but I realize it is not true, and although I do try, I cannot help blaming him.

But, I ask myself, what would I be feeling, or thinking if I were still in Paris? And, what troubles me, what would Louis be thinking?

I spend so much time alone these days that I find myself examining the past, and desperately trying to preserve my memories of my husband, so as not to have them vanish in a misty haze and to be able to tell Louis about his father.

And I always come back to the stark fact that I hardly knew him at all.

Would we have lived happily ever after, as in a fairy tale, or would we have tired of each other, as some married couples seem to after a few years?

I hear Léonie, who, while undeniably devoted to Monsieur Malherbe, speaks of him with the exasperated indulgence often reserved for unruly children. Or Amélie, who, just a few months after her wedding, seemed to fear Jean-Baptiste's judgement in all things, be it her choice of hat or the quality of a roast lamb, and appeared to have abdicated her own preferences so as not to incur his annoyance.

Louis and I did not have time enough together for me to ascertain what his favourite food was, if he enjoyed reading poetry or if he preferred me wearing blue or red.

What I do know is that he is all the easier to love now that he is dead.

How sad…

I received a big packet of French newspapers from Saigon, and spend a pleasurable morning getting angry reading them.

They have no words harsh enough to describe Monsieur Rolin-Jaequemyns who is accused of being a fraud in English pay, a dishonoured lawyer, a bankrupt traitor to Belgium, etc.

It must be extremely difficult for him to read such things.

Michael to whom I was saying this, tells me that the Paris press is just as bad, and that Emilie and her children who are vacationing in the south of France only use the name Rolin so as not to be shunned even by hoteliers and restaurants.

Prince Devawongse has returned from Bang Pa In and the negotiations have resumed, therefore keeping Victor busy and away from my table.

When he is not so ridiculously nationalistic — and there I certainly see the influence of his friend Jean Le Myre — he is very good company though, and I miss him, as do little Louis and Nhu Dam, for he seems to have the ability to play with them and enjoy it as if he were their age.

Also, received an infuriating letter from Mama who by now seems to treat me as if I were simple-minded and in need of a firm hand to guide me out of the darkness I wallow in, according to her.

Thank heavens my money is my own, and that she can in no way cut it off, otherwise, I am convinced she would 'for my own good, of course.'

"Listen to this," Julie said, waving her mother's letter at Michael and at Victor who had just come in for a quick drink before joining friends at the Trocadero Hotel.

"*My dearest daughter, I sometimes feel that I have not done my duty by you, and have let your Papa encourage you in an unbecoming and dangerous independence.*

Of course, you are of age and, as you have been at pains to repeatedly make clear, your own mistress, but have not as yet given me any evidence that your sense of responsibility to your son and yourself are equal to this claim.

When I meet with friends and family, I am at a loss to explain your continued absence after these three years and your preference of Siam over France, as a home, is not a valid reason, particularly these days.

I take no stand on the political matter, as it seems to involve both my country of birth and my adopted homeland, but the more I read about it in the press, the less I understand you, particularly as as you have mentioned in your letters being friendly with some of the people described in the papers here as veritable and ruthless ruffians.

I almost hoped that an 'affair of the heart' was what detained you, but all the information we have received says not, and that you lead a blameless life.

Will you not come home, and seek a husband to guide you and your son through life?

It is probably in vain, but I beseech you to reflect on this and see the light.

Your loving mother."

Victor burst out laughing. "Well, how do you like that? Our respectable Mama, hoping that you were having a passionate affair with a teak wallah!"

Julie did not smile.

What information had her parents received? Who from?

"Me, who else?" her brother laughed. "Mama just asked in a letter if anybody seemed particularly attentive, or if you had expressed any preference for any gentleman. So I said no. I didn't think you wanted me to mention that little schoolmaster from the Palace, whatever his name is."

"Joseph. Joseph Caulfield James." she snapped. "He is younger than I, and he is not particularly attentive, or at least, has ceased to be.

"What business is it of yours what I do?

"How would you like it if I were to write about your Chinese landlady's nieces, or any other *mousmé* you might keep in Saigon."

Victor shook his head in amusement.

"Do! Please! She — and Papa as well — will be delighted at learning their son is sowing his wild oats in the Colonies, because, after all, isn't that one of the advantages of being young, wealthy, and a conquering master?

"The world is unfair, kitten, the sooner you finally accept this, whether about your own life or Siam, the happier you will be.

"And now... I must go, or I shall be late." he drained his glass, blew her a careless kiss and slapped Michael on the shoulder in passing.

They heard him still chuckling on his way out of the door.

"He's right, you know." Michael said, his head cocked, then he slapped his forehead in exasperation. "Just listen to me! I am so, so tired of spending my life saying 'He's right, you know' to absolutely everyone.

I say it to French about Jones, and to Jones about French, to Jones about RJ, to RJ about Devawongse, to you about Victor, to.... When will I stop being the universal mediator?"

Julie came over to sit on the arm of his chair, and kissed his balding head.

"And who, besides me, says, 'he's right, you know,' about you?"

Michael laughed shortly. "Just about everybody.

"For my sins, I seem to have been right about most things in the crisis, and Jones even joked I should be burned at the stake."

He hesitated, after taking another gulp of whisky for courage, gripped her hand then finally blurted, "Dear girl, do you remember when you suggested we got married? Just before the Foreign Affairs ball?"

She nodded with a smile. "Had it been after, you probably would have accused me of drinking too much."

"Well... I was thinking... and in view of your Mama's letter, perhaps we should. You said we would be happy as tinkers, and we probably would."

She got up, feeling the blood withdraw from her face and her whole body become cold suddenly and turned to face him.

"I often think of it," she said slowly, "and I would be lying if I said I was not serious that night. But I have come to realize it would be unfair to us both.

"We accept each other as we are, because we are friends,

and I am closer to you than to, heaven knows, my own brother.

"Would we still be quite so understanding as man and wife?"

"In fact, my darling, except in name, we would not be man and wife..." he replied gently.

And what if she were to meet someone, to "guide her in life" as her Mama said?

"You could divorce me of course.

"I would never stand in the way of your happiness. All I ask is that you do not humiliate me publicly. And, of course, neither shall I humiliate you, but that goes without saying."

She sat down, stunned. "I don't know. I shall think about it."

He rose, and in his turn, gave her a kiss.

"I must get back home. Please don't lose sleep over it. But you will see, once you have given the matter due thought, you'll say: 'he's right, you know.' "

"*Bangkok September 5*TH *1893*

I did not sleep a wink, despite Michael's advice. But when I got up, I had made up my mind. He's right, of course."

"Are you sure?" he asked.

She nodded. "The question is, are you?"

He took a deep breath. Yes, he was.

He sat down, and took her hand. "Now, for the practicalities."

She would not find him very romantic, but it was important that they decide.

She would of course keep full possession of her money — he stopped her embarrassed protest that there was no need to discuss that. There was every need, he declared firmly, and with the Married Women Property Act, her fortune remained hers and Louis'.

About Louis. He was willing to adopt him, if she wished. She shook her head.

Louis was to remain his father's son and keep his father's name. He agreed.

"Another advantage I see," he added, "is that you will acquire a British passport. That should save you the harassment of Pavie and Hardouin."

Wordlessly, she nodded again.

He suggested that he move into her house.

It was more comfortable, larger and better staffed. As she knew, he had no furniture worth mentioning, so he wouldn't clutter it up. All he asked was to bring his books, his ceramics and his two bronze statues.

Besides Somboon, of course, and if she didn't mind, he would like to add Pon to the household, he could not bear dismissing him, and they would need the coachman. He would keep the horse and buggy at nearby livery stables.

She would be delighted to have Pon back, she said. She missed his antic way of serving dinner.

"When shall we do it?" she asked at last, feeling strangely dizzy and wondering why. After all, she had happily shared a house with Michael for two years.

"I thought just before this French mission is over, so Victor can be your witness, and lend an air of propriety to the whole affair?

"But if you agree, I suggest we inform our respective families once it is done, so as not to have to deal with the inevitable questions about the advisability of cousins marrying each other."

She grimaced. "Actually, I was wondering about that. Is it legal?"

"My dear, royal families do it all the time."

"Yes, but look at the result for their offspring."

He looked at her strangely.

"You do realize, don't you, that we shan't have children?"

"Bangkok, September 7ᵀᴴ 1893

Somehow, I had not realized until then. Not that it will induce me to change my mind.

We have decided to keep the news to ourselves for the time being, so as to keep the inevitable gossip to a minimum, and to have a civil ceremony at the Legation. Michael says that Captain Jones will accept to shorten the banns to a day.

Bangkok society, however, would love to have something other to talk about than the piecemeal disintegration of Siamese territory at the hands of the French, and will fall on this piece of news with glee.

"Can't do it my boy. Nothing less than a week, otherwise your marriage wouldn't be valid and anyway why the secrecy?

"I won't say I'm not surprised — you could have knocked me over with a feather just now — but it seems highly suitable for the two of you. And no one can say you don't know what you are getting into."

The British Minister leaned back in his chair, with a huge smile on his face.

"You are a dark horse, aren't you?"

Michael returned his smile with some embarrassment.

"It must seem fairly ridiculous to you, Sir. After those years of being cousins, and also best friends, and my seeing her through those awful times… well…"

"Nothing ridiculous about love, boy.

"You say she wants her brother there to give her away, as it were. Most proper. Although, I must say that what I know of your fair Julie, nobody gives her away but her own good self.

"From what I hear, that rat Le Myre wants to leave by October 1st, so shall we say September 25th?

"I'll publish the banns on the 18th, just before going to Bang Pa In to celebrate His Majesty's birthday.

"Now, if that is agreeable to you, would you mind getting back to work?"

As Michael took his leave with a nod of gratitude, he heard Jones chuckle in his back "Don't know when I've been so tickled in my life."

Two hours later, he called his staff together.

"It's a day for good news," he crowed, "listen to this telegram I have just received and decoded — Good Lord, His Lordship must have got up at dawn, it's barely eight in the morning back home — Lord Rosebery strenuously advises Siam to accept nothing beyond the terms of the ultimatum without consulting England.

"At last, Whitehall is getting off its collective backside!

"That will stiffen the backbone of Prince Devawongse in his fight against France. Ha!"

He got up and practically danced out of his office, shouting to a little Siamese clerk who waited by the door. "Tell the boatman to be ready. I'm off to tell RJ."

French stared as Jones rushed down the steps. "What other good news has he received, do you know?"

Michael shook his head. "Possibly something personal."

The Belgian adviser sighed with relief.

It was very good news indeed, because the additional demands were mounting every day. "Each time, he brings something new to the table. Last week, it was the customs posts. Yesterday it was the trial of Phra Yoth, who has to be declared guilty, or else!

"Now it is the Danish officers. He wants them expelled from the country.

"His Highness is quite overwhelmed with this onslaught of conditions, and always the threat over our heads: do it, or we shall remain in Chantaboon indefinitely; which is of course what they want to achieve, by forcing down our throats exigencies that are impossible to satisfy.

"I do my best to bolster him, have all the demands put in writing, and go over them at night so as to enable him to present a response the next day, but his nerves are exhausted.

"This will prove a veritable balm to him."

But despite the support, albeit belated, of England, the Prince's resistance was no match for the ruthless determination of the French plenipotentiary.

"Of course, he is not only negotiating for France," Victor exulted over a Sunday lunch en tête-à-tête with Julie, "but ensuring his election to the Chamber as Deputy for Indochina.

"Because of that lily-livered Develle, Battambang and Siem Reap were not returned to us, so the least he needs to achieve is the commercial control of the entire Mekong basin. And once there are no Siamese customs there any longer, well, imagine the trade advantages flowing to Saigon instead of Bangkok. All thanks to Monsieur Le Myre."

Julie gazed at him with distaste over the rim of her glass.

"*Returned to us*?" she repeated in chilly tones. "When were they ever ours?

"We are not talking of Alsace and Lorraine, to my knowledge."

She shook her head in dismay. "What I do not understand," she continued, "is why this matters so much to you."

Victor stared at her in surprise.

"It should matter as much to you.

"We are French, our Papa stands to gain greatly by being awarded contracts in Indochina, and our Empire, thus our prestige and position in the world, shall be immeasurably enhanced.

"Unfortunately, our aim of making Siam a French protectorate appears to have failed, at least for the time being. But did you not want to see the Bangkok you love so much become a modern city, with an opera, theatres, good schools for the natives, a proper social life, and the amenities of civilization?"

Julie grimaced slightly.

Not really. She quite liked Bangkok as it was.

"You only speak thus to be contrary," Victor snapped, "and have no idea of what is at stake. I begin to believe Mama is right, and that it is time for you to return to Paris."

Perhaps, she agreed. So he should tell her more. Did he want some cognac with his coffee?

"I am despicable," she told Michael the same evening. "I refused to spy on you for France, but I actually get my brother drunk to make him talk.

"And he did not tell me anything I didn't already know, whether from you or the Saigon papers."

He probably did not know that much, Michael replied.

In any case, nothing new was happening, still the same round of demands, which Siam rejects, and Le Myre presents once more under a different form, making increasingly dire threats.

At last, Prince Devawongse was able to achieve a small, but heartening, breakthrough. The Danish naval officers, contemptuously referred to as "mercenaries" by the French, were not to be expelled, merely chastised.

"It took an intervention of the King of Denmark going through the Emperor of Russia to achieve this. Can you imagine?" said Rolin-Jaequemyns.

Jones laughed. "It might take an intervention of the King of Belgium for you not to be hanged publicly in Saigon."

The Special Adviser gave him a wintry smile. What defied imagination was the level of pettiness that permeated the demands.

Besides the unfortunate Danes, what excited Le Myre-- and Pavie above all — these days, were claims by the missionaries. "The good fathers, they mean well, but they accept anyone who claims to convert, whoever he may be, even common criminals. And once they have converted, well, the priests fight tooth and nail for them.

"There were several cases on the right bank in the neutral area where mission churches and schools were established, and where it is impossible to bring wrong-doers before Siamese justice if they wear a cross or know the words to 'Our father.' And even in Bangkok... a matter of a house sold to a Catholic Chinese who refuses to pay... but it is all too ridiculous to describe."

Lord Dufferin wrote again on his meetings with Develle, who was increasingly incapable of controlling Le Myre de Vilers.

"*He is violent, brutal, and outrageous in his demands,*" the ambassador quoted the French Minister as saying in despair. "*I tell Monsieur Le Myre de Vilers that he is jeopardizing the Treaty as a whole, and that as concerns the French Government the affair with Siam is settled.*

"*He instructions are to allow the Siamese to challenge any clause beyond the original ones included in the ultimatum, otherwise the Treaty would be no more than an ultimatum in itself, but he has refused and is now preparing a completely unauthorized version of the Convention of enforcement to be appended to the Treaty — he gleefully describes it as containing the truly harsh clauses.*

"I have warned him that this may lead to a complete breakdown in the negotiations, and what would happen then?

"But he cannot be recalled without creating an uproar from the Colonial Party and endangering the stability of the Government.

"Perhaps," Lord Dufferin continued in his dispatch, *"it might be wise to warn our friends in Bangkok of the existence of said harsh clauses in the convention, and to be prepared to challenge them."*

"I know already," Rolin-Jaequemyns cried in despair.

"It is an insult to international law just to present this so-called convention, and you cannot imagine the tone of the letter to the Prince that accompanied this... this... the words truly fail me. I do not know what this document is except perhaps the basest of provocations. And they expect Siam to sign? As to that letter, you should have seen it: contemptuous, mocking, and without even the pretence of courtesy.

"I swear the Prince had tears in his eyes when I translated it for him. 'Has France fallen so low?' he asks."

"What are these objectionable clauses?" asked Jones who was getting somewhat uncomfortable with such a Gallic display of emotion.

Rolin-Jaequemyns took his heavily annotated and underlined copy from his desk and read out in a quivering voice that all, yes *mon ami,* all Siamese border posts in the neutral 25 kilometre zone are to be evacuated, pending the conclusion within the next six months of a commercial Treaty — "and mark my words, there never shall be such a Treaty"— the remaining military garrisons on the left bank are to be evacuated within a month—"one month! How is that possible?"— and all fortifications razed to the ground —"you do understand, do you not, that I am only giving you the more unexpected and hurtful elements?

"Finally the Phra Yoth trial — remember, the man accused of murdering Inspector Grosgurin in his bed?

"*Eh bien*, if the verdict does not satisfy French authorities — in other words, if he is not declared guilty — he will be re-tried by a tribunal whose composition is to be decided by France.

"I see you shrug, my friend, and you are right in part. The fate of Phra Yoth is of little importance, and he may well turn out to be guilty.

"But the insult implied in having France decide to retry him, and how, and by whom... That is unforgiveable.

"Now, for the venom in the tail: Chantaboon will continue to be occupied until all clauses of the Treaty, and therefore of the Convention which is part of it, are executed. No provisional date of when it is to end: it is indefinite, at the pleasure of La République.

"And in his letter, Monsieur le Plénipotentiaire implied that had it been up to him, Siam would actually pay the expenses of the Chantaboon occupation."

"The gall of the man," Jones interjected with feeling. "I knew from the moment I laid eyes on him he was a wicked rat. It's in the jaw, you see. He has a most inferior and obstinate jaw.

"But I cannot be as pessimistic as you as to the duration of the occupation. Surely, once Siam has executed her obligations, the French will have no earthly reason to stay."

The Belgian shook his head slowly, and raised his finger, speaking like the Professor of Law he once was.

"You are a soldier, my good friend, and I a jurist. I know how jurists think.

"There are too many ambiguities in this treaty not to create disputes that will then be exploited by French lawyers and create reasons to prolong the occupation.

"Take for instance the clause on the neutral area, that is, the twenty-five-kilometre zone along the Mekong plus Battambang and Siem Reap provinces. It is said *'that police activities will be carried out by the local authorities'*. How do you understand this?"

The British minister raised his eyebrows. The Siamese authorities, of course. It was still Siamese territory.

"Yes, it is obvious to you. But I maintain that that the French will claim that the local authorities must be Khmer or Lao, because these are Khmer or Lao provinces under Siamese rule. Everything will hinge on the word 'local'.

"Siam shall never accept this, *et voilà!* Here you have a case of non-execution of the Treaty."

The Englishman looked out of the window. A downpour had started, and he was loath to face the weather in his boat, but it could not be helped.

"Don't be discouraged, I shall forward all you've said to London.

"And tell His Highness to stand firm. After all, if both Develle and the Prince refuse to sign, what can Le Myre do?"

What he had threatened to do, was the terse reply. If the Treaty were not accepted by the 1st of October, the blockade would resume.

So British support had best be made known very soon.

"BANGKOK, SEPTEMBER 13TH 1893

The telegraph line is down, and we are cut off from the world. How nice.

It certainly releases me from having to send the telegram I shall need to write very soon to Mama and Papa, and I feel rather guilty about not letting them know beforehand.

Michael and I were discussing the upcoming ceremony and the reception we will have afterwards. The Oriental is the only possible place, as I cannot entertain fifty-odd people here.

He would have liked Captain Jones as his witness, but as he will be marrying us, that is not possible.

He says there is no one at the Legation whom he might want to ask, and has no other friend, which I think is unbearably sad. So I suggested that Victor stand by him, and I ask both Fanny and Léonie to be my witnesses.

We shall need to start telling people soon, starting with Victor.

Afterwards, I asked Michael why he is marrying me.

He gave me his lovely crooked smile. 'Because when the time comes, you will make a rather satisfactory Ambassador's wife.

More seriously, you know that I do love you dearly, and I could not be more fond of Louis if he were my own son.'

He paused and looked at me very seriously and said he had no words to express how grateful he is to me for making this sacrifice of my youth and beauty that will quiet any questions about his life anybody might start asking.

Youth and beauty, ha! I wish Mama could have heard.

Then he asked why I am marrying him, and I found I could not really answer. I stammered that there was no one I love or trust more, or whose company gives me greater pleasure, and that when I am with him, I feel a better person. All this is true.

But it certainly isn't for romance and I suppose I must give up that side of my life. After all, I had romance with Louis, and can live on those memories.

Victor stared open-mouthed at his sister, and dropped in the nearest armchair.

"You? You are going to marry Michael? It's impossible!

"When was this plan hatched?"

Very recently, two weeks ago. The real question was why it had not occurred before she replied airily.

But they were cousins.

Yes, they were. But royal families intermarried all the time.

Victor finally managed a reluctant smile. "Well, *that* should go a long way in convincing Mama of the merits of the match." He leaned forwards, and grasped Julie's hands. "Are you sure?

"Truly sure? It's not just that idiotic letter Mama wrote that has pushed you into this?"

She smiled and shook her head. "I actually proposed to Michael last spring.

"It has taken him this long to accept that I was serious about it, and that I could be happy with a man other than Louis."

Victor was still not convinced. "I like Michael, of course. He is no beauty but he has a certain distinction, and good manners and education.

"There can of course be nothing against him, or his family, but... I don't know. He doesn't seem like the marrying kind. I suppose I shall need to get used to the idea."

Well, did he think he could get used to it by dinner time?

Michael was coming so as to celebrate together and she did not want him offended by any reluctance on Victor's part.

"I shall need to have a talk with him, in loco parentis," he warned her.

"Oh, don't be so ridiculous," she laughed, "We are of age, we are certainly used to each other's ways, and you cannot seriously intend to question him about his career prospects or his fortune."

No, but he could threaten to beat him to jelly if he did the slightest thing to cause his sister pain.

Very well, he agreed when she asked, he would be Michael's witness, if there was no one else, although he found it surprising that a man should have no close friends.

But a civil ceremony... he kept shaking his head, and at the British Legation... why not at the Cathedral, and do things properly?

Because Michael was not Catholic, she answered patiently. The Bishop would refuse to marry them, and – her voice took a warning tone – Victor was not even for a moment to suggest Pavie marry them at the French Legation.

She loathed the man.

"Yes," he drawled, "he is rather... how shall I say... well, I think 'uncouth' is the best way for me to describe him. You should hear how Monsieur Le Myre de Vilers and his son make fun of him behind his back, calling him the little telegraph man, and suggesting he get to work to repair the lines. They are still down, have you heard? What an impossible country!

"So... tonight is your engagement party, I suppose?"

She laughed again.

An engagement party? At their ages?

No, tonight was just a dinner for Victor to wish them well.

When Lek opened the door to Michael, she realized how tense he was, and gave him a quick reassuring smile, and Victor got up and slapped him heartily on the back.

"I can't say I'm not surprised, old man. But I give you my blessing."

"That's one down," Michael sighed once Victor had left. "Everyone else to go." He fumbled in his pocket, and held out a dark red leather case.

"I wanted to be alone with you to give you this."

It was a large sapphire set in diamonds, glinting brightly on the white velvet.

She slipped it on her finger "Michael, it's beautiful. And it fits perfectly."

Fie had helped, he smiled, entrusting him with one of the rings Julie rarely wore for the jeweller.

"Probably one of the last sapphires from Pailin before the French get their hands on the mines." he remarked drily as she moved her hand in the candlelight to catch the stunning azure heart of the stone.

She looked up. "Are things bad?"

They were not good.

The unending theatre of proposals, counter-proposals, coding them, sending them to London, getting London's view, communicating them to RJ... It was exhausting because it seemed to go round in ever worsening circles.

"I've had an idea," he said.

When all this was over — and it should be over soon, one way or another — why shouldn't they go on a honeymoon to Paris and London for two or three months?

He was overdue for home leave, she had never brought her child to his grandparents, and they would certainly be forgiven for their hasty marriage if they were to go in person to ask for their parents' best wishes.

He warmed to the project, as she cried out in delighted acceptance.

They would take both Fie as both nurse and lady's maid and — he stammered as he said it — Somboon as his valet, spend a few days in Singapore, Marseille perhaps, with a stop in Nice, then Paris, then London.

"What do you say, Mrs Crawfurd? "

"Yes!" she kissed him, feeling that it was becoming more natural.

"I say yes!"

"BANGKOK, SEPTEMBER 15TH 1893

Mrs Crawfurd. I am to become Mrs Crawfurd.

Well, why am I surprised?

But it is one of the things I had just not thought of. I suppose that is the difference between a first and a second marriage — there is far less to get excited about. I don't even care that much about what I shall wear.

Fanny swore by a cloth merchant in Pahurat, the Indian bazaar of the old city. "I know it's not where you elegant ladies are used to shop, but trust me," she said when Léonie raised her eyebrows in disbelief."

He has far more choice than anyone else."

Picking her way over the broken sidewalk, Julie hitched her skirts to sidestep the dirty and malodorous puddles and ducked under the tattered tarpaulin awning dripping rain in the lane leading to the merchant's doorway.

The barouche had dropped them at the entrance of a warren of spice-wallahs, incense merchants, tea-shops, and ironmongers crammed alongside small dark temples and vegetable stalls.

She looked around in amazement, her senses assaulted by the smells of cinnamon, cumin, incense and frying fat, the raucous cries of food sellers and the yapping dogs. They were shoved aside to make way for a naked man with long, matted hair, his entire body smeared with ash, and found themselves hovering in a dark doorway that offered a glimpse of a many-armed bronze statue draped with garlands of marigolds, dancing in the light of tiny candles.

"I've never been here before," she murmured to Léonie, who sniffed and made a face as she snapped her umbrella shut, looking down at the filthy pavement. She hadn't either.

Surely, this cloth-wallah might have brought some bolts of silk to their homes.

"Ah yes," Fanny agreed, "and charged far more. Anyway, you would not have seen all of his stock."

"Yes, yes, madam," Patel, the merchant agreed, bowing them in, his white turban askew in delight. "You must see my stock, the very extraordinary best in Bangkok, madam, Chantilly lace from France, yes, brocade and chiffon from Italy and crepe de Chine.

"For a wedding, is it? I have white lace, madam, just look. And illusion tulle for a veil.

"Devi, bring tea for the Maems. No veil, madam? Oh, no white?"

His face fell, but he quickly grasped another bolt from the shelf and flung a misty mauve cloud of silk before them. "Then embroidered gauze, perhaps?"

The words rolled out of his mouth as quickly as he deftly unrolled lengths of taffetas and satin, transforming his dark shop into a rainbow of silk glimmering under the oil lamp.

"No, absolutely not", Léonie said firmly as she saw Julie fingering a sensuous oyster grey satin crepe.

She sat down on the chair a small child with enormous dark eyes had brought, took the tea a servant in a saree had offered her and considered it carefully before wiping the edge of the cup with her handkerchief.

"You cannot marry in white, of course, but I shall not let you marry in grey, chérie. It is a day for happy colours."

"We spent hours deciding on our gowns — mine is to be a pearly pale blue, to match my sapphire — and, with great embarrassment, I suggested to Fanny that the one she chose be my gift. What is so wonderful about her is that she has no false graces or pride. She accepted without even trying to hide her pleasure and selected a lovely soft changing silk of pink with a mauve and gold shimmer, whereas Léonie will wear a very dark heliotrope.

Léonie had also determined what styles we shall have — she brought several books of the latest Parisian dress patterns.

Signor Locatelli, the Italian couturier, seems rather worried about the intricate designs and having a client as demanding as Léonie can be, but he assures us all will be ready in time, he will employ all of his seamstresses for the task.

'I should very much hope so,' Léonie declared shortly, 'after all, there is no embroidery work to be done, so I fail to see how our dresses might not be ready.'

Fanny burst out laughing at that, Léonie glared at her and Signor Locatelli seemed relieved at showing us out.

The manager of the Oriental Hotel received me in person and expressed his best wishes when I went with Fanny and Léonie there to organize the little afternoon reception for our wedding.

My two friends did not disappoint: they neither expressed any surprise or misgivings, claimed to be honoured and delighted to be my witnesses and seemed to enjoy choosing the menu and the floral decorations even more than I did, because for me the Oriental will always be the place where I saw the gunboat come upriver with its cannons still smoking to threaten Bangkok.

How different from the organization of my first wedding, when I was giddy with nerves and happiness and Mama was sniffing in her handkerchief all the while.

I wish there were a way to send word to Keow."

"So, Crawfurd? How is the bridegroom to be?"

Such were the words that greeted Michael on the morning the banns were posted at the Legation and the invitation cards had been sent.

He replied with a tight smile that he was very well, thank you, deliriously happy, and attempted to push past his colleagues who had gathered in the stairwell to rib him on his arrival. But Charles Stringer was not satisfied and followed him into his office, standing there and watching him as he went through his mail while the others clustered in the doorway. "Quite the dark horse you," he commented.

The very words used by the Minister, Michael replied evenly, and slit an envelope.

"So you managed to pluck up your nerve and ask her? I thought you never would, although everyone could tell you were aching to get hold of her before anyone else did."

So. His secret life was still secret, apparently. He smiled coldly.

Indeed? Did everyone?

How gratifying to know they were interested.

"I hear she is quite the heiress, as well."

He raised his eyes. "As well as what?"

Stringer was taken aback at the icy tone.

As well as being rather attractive in her quiet, Frenchy way.

And everybody knew about French women, he added with a leer while the others sniggered. But what about the brat?

Michael got up, took Stringer' arm, and guided him firmly to the door. He had brought up the brat, to use Charles' charming word, since he was born. And it was really none of his business.

Edward French who had just arrived on the scene looked at Stringer and the others in disgust.

"You men are beyond crass. Leave him alone. You all would be fortunate to marry such a charming woman."

Michael had returned to his chair. "Thanks, Edward." he said simply. "I felt like punching him, but he is twice my size."

Not at all, the Consul shrugged. He found all those lurid steamy comments about French women unbearable. "Probably because of my name. You can imagine what boarding school was like for me. Anyway, the old man wants you."

Jones was about to leave for Bang Pa In for the anniversary celebration, and was busy assigning tasks for his expected three-day absence.

"Can't say I'm looking forward to this celebration, I have the feeling it's going to be more like a wake.

"In fact, it's not to be a reception, did you know that?

"It's a non-reception, whatever that is.

"Hope they'll nonetheless see fit to give us some food, or maybe it will be non-food, you know, like those paper feasts the Chinese burn for the hungry ghosts.

"RJ says that the King is so depressed that he cannot bear facing his subjects, that he feels he has failed them, especially his poor Lao.

"Not sure the Lao feel the same, although being under French rule won't be any better. And the devil you know...

"Anyway, I don't need to tell you to keep on the alert for anything from Whitehall.

"Also, you are to expect a Mr Scott, who is due to arrive sometime in the next days, with his wife. He is commissioner for the Shan States and has been sent here to advise me on the borders between Burmah, China, Siam and now France, for what purpose I have not really been told.

"What does this mean to you, Crawfurd?"

It meant a buffer zone, sir, and French nodded.

The minister agreed with a frown. That was what he thought, and it disturbed him that the Siamese had not been informed.

"Don't know how I'll tell RJ, though.

"In any case, I won't need to right away, he won't be at the event in Bang Pa In, has to stay in Bangkok with the Prince to continue monitoring the negotiations, poor man, and make sure that Devawongse doesn't get hounded into accepting something he shouldn't."

He stretched his arms out.

"If it doesn't pour with rain, I will really enjoy that day sailing up the river. The quiet, just gazing at the landscape and not having to deal with anything." His eyes misted surprisingly. "I really love this country, and it will be a heartbreak to leave."

French raised his eyebrows. "Are you being posted elsewhere, sir?"

Possibly. Probably. "And all thanks to you and Mr Curzon. Never mind, as they say here. My time has come. No, let's not talk about it.

"And the day after I return, Crawfurd, is your big day."

Michael smiled.

"Well, I'm certainly going to enjoy getting you hitched, and you know what I'll enjoy even more? It will be removing that delightful girl from the ambit of that dog Pavie's authority and putting her here where she belongs."

"Bangkok September 19th 1893

Victor is shocked that I did not send a card to Monsieur Le Myre or Pavie.

I am shocked that he is shocked, and we had words.

I pointed out that as RJ is to attend — he sent a delightful note of acceptance with a lovely gift of silver coffee spoons — it would be most awkward for everyone.

Still, my brother insisted it is the correct thing to do, and Le Myre would certainly find an excuse and send his regrets.

Michael agrees that it must be done — we cannot appear to take sides, he says — and that there is no risk of having them come to the reception, so wary are they to have to be forced to greet RJ for politeness sake.

He told me an amusing anecdote of RJ and the French negotiating party crossing in the Outer Court of the Palace two days ago, as RJ was leaving and the others just arriving. Pavie ignored RJ with his nose up in the air, Father Schmidt, the missionary who is serving as interpreter, dared not acknowledge him and kept his eyes on the ground, and Le Myre was trying to twist his head away so much he missed the carriage step and almost fell flat on his face.

So I sent the cards, reluctantly.

"*BANGKOK SEPTEMBER 20*TH *1893*

Indeed, as expected, Le Myre expressed his regrets along with a bouquet of flowers and Pavie did not even deign to acknowledge the invitation.

Perfect! So the sin of discourtesy is on his head and not mine.

Prince Devawongse has also promised to be there if he possibly can 'if his diplomatic health permits' as he wrote in his charming English, and implied in his letter that I shall soon be able to receive in person the 'wishes for great felicitations from many grateful students at the Palace.'

I am very excited at the prospect of travelling back to France now that I know I shall not be cajoled or harassed into staying and have begun preparing Louis for the voyage, telling him about Paris, Notre-Dame and that Eiffel Tower I still had not become used to seeing in our landscape by the time I left France.

I have had the house and garden decorated with lanterns, candles and pennants to honour the anniversary of His Majesty's birth. The years before, I just let the servants put up a flag, but this year I am resolutely, defiantly Siamese.

Victor and some of his officer friends came to dinner and Michael's presence is now accepted, as he is Victor's brother-in-law to be, indeed, anything else would be most strange.

They were asking about the reason for the extravagant display of lights and lanterns that would make the garden quite an enchanting place for dinner al fresco if it were not for the mosquitoes. When I told them it was to honour the King, young Le Myre de Vilers gave me a pitying smile. He obviously thinks me a simpleton, which I do not really mind as I find him a vain and ill-bred snake with far too much influence on my brother.

It was however a very merry evening. I overheard some officers saying the negotiations were certainly going according to plan and that Victor would soon be in Chantaboon. There was much teasing about how Saigon would be a duller place without him and what would he do to entertain himself in that malodorous swamp, besides attending mass at the Cathedral some Catholic Annamese refugees built in the town.

I, for one, shall never visit him there."

"BANGKOK SEPTEMBER 26ᵗʰ 1893

The sky was clear on my wedding day.

Léonie and Fanny came early to lunch and to help me dress, Fanny wove jasmine into my chignon and loaned me a pendant of diamonds and rubies that was far too grand for my gown.

'One of the last of my mother's jewels,' she said.

What will she do when she has sold them all? She has hope that her husband's estates will be returned to her and her son — and if not... she laughs, she will manage.

I was far more nervous than I had expected to be, and heard my voice quiver in making my vows, but far less than Michael who was quite pale and stammered somewhat.

Captain Jones made a little speech that purported to be witty and failed, and afterwards, at the reception, Victor gave a rather moving toast.

Prince Devawongse came in briefly looking harassed and spent most of his time talking in a corner with RJ who told me Emilie sent her best wishes.

The champagne flowed, the Legation men drank too much and kept aiming dirty looks at my brother.

Louis, after eating too many tartlets and cakes was sick over his white sailor suit, and had to be taken away by Fie who was proudly wearing a new silk phasin and beamed as if she were the mother of the bride, which I think she somehow believes she is.

I was very surprised and touched to find two packages from the Palace when we arrived home — an English-style silver salver from His Majesty engraved with the royal emblem and a tea set of the precious Bencharong porcelain from Keow. I had tears in my eyes when I unwrapped it.

It was a relief to have a quiet dinner, after having sent the telegrams to our families. To soften the blow, we announced our arrival for later this year.

They must have received them by now, and I am trying to imagine what is being said on Boulevard Malesherbes. I do not see how they can be anything but happy.

Michael says his family as well will be delighted. I wonder.

After dinner, we each went to our rooms after a chaste kiss, a sad pair of newly-weds. I feel that Michael regrets as much as I that we can never be more to each other and I lay awake for a long time remembering my first wedding night, the passion and the happiness.

Well, I am not unhappy — but it seems I shall no longer know passion."

"Is married life treating you well, boy?

You look quite in the pink."

Very well, sir, Michael answered patiently. It was the third time he had been asked that morning.

He had been given a day's leave after the wedding, which he devoted to unpacking his books and ceramics and awaiting in vain his family's reaction to his nuptials. In the evening, Julie had received a reply from her mother that managed to be both ecstatic and reproachful.

He knew his own mother would support his decision, despite her private misgivings about what she must have guessed about his life, but his father... well, his father, might find the Lucas-Sauvains a bit too brashly wealthy and French.

He blew the dust off a perfect Sawankhalok dish engraved with fish and wondered where best to place it away from Louis' grasping fingers.

Curiously, after the many, many times he had come to this house and treated it as his own, he now felt uneasy about putting his things on shelves, where he should leave his straw hat or should he give an order to Lek.

"Goodness, Michael," Julie finally told him in amused exasperation after he had asked her where she might prefer to see the bronze Vishnu or if she did not mind his leaving his shoes in the hall, "you always leave your shoes there, and have never hesitated to ask Lek for anything.

"Just accept that this is *your* home now, please. That's what you told me when I arrived in Bangkok, and I certainly did."

"Women are so much more practical and less romantic than we are, sir," he finally blurted.

Jones looked at him over the newspaper he was perusing.

"Don't I know it," he replied with a short laugh. "My lady wife hasn't a romantic bone in her body. Now, see here.

"I've left a note from RJ on your desk to be coded for London and Paris.

"It says that it would be expedient for Siam to sign the Treaty with some modifications and to refuse to sign the Convention.

"Get on to it now, please, it might be good for Lord Dufferin to give Develle some warning, see if he can't muzzle that attack dog Le Myre so as to avoid a last minute incident and threat of renewing the blockade.

"Meanwhile, I am going to brief that nice Thompson chappie from *The Times*. We want to start giving the world a true idea of what France is up to here."

He returned home in a violent storm with gusts of wind that rattled the buggy's canopy and sent people to huddle under the few metal awnings of New Road, thinking of Captain Jones' likely departure and wondering about his replacement.

He knew he himself would not be transferred for another two years at least.

Given the crisis and its inevitable aftermath of quarrelling diplomats, particularly with the prospect of the future buffer zone if it ever happened, someone who spoke fair Siamese and fluent French could not easily be replaced.

But then?

"I am too young for an embassy, naturally, but perhaps Minister-Counsellor somewhere like Rome, or Madrid?" he told Julie the night before. What did she think?

It would be nice, she agreed, but was in no hurry to leave Siam.

Somboon was waiting crouched on the verandah, being buffeted by the gale, and rushed up to help Michael out of the buggy and to ease off his drenched canvas shoes in the hall.

"Why don't you wait inside? Are the other servants unpleasant?"

Somboon beamed. No, Lek was a good-mannered person and made all the others good mannered. He just wanted to be first to see Khun Mykin.

Something wistful in his tone made Michael's heart stop.

"You know, don't you, that the marriage with Maem changes nothing for me and you? Look at me. I swear."

Somboon fumbled with the wet laces and nodded. If Khun Mykin said so, he believed.

"Darling boy, father and I send best wishes for happiness to both. Am writing Daphne to rejoice with her. Your loving mother."

"Well, that's a relief," he muttered after reading the telegram Julie handed him when he entered the drawing room.

What else did he expect? she inquired. There was, after all, no other possible reaction.

"Listen," she told him after he had changed to dry clothes and was sitting with a whisky and soda at his elbow, "I know your family may think we are not quite up to yours socially.

"Just as I know mine must certainly wish yours were wealthier. And I also realize that if anybody, anybody at all, had an inkling of what our life together is to be they would recoil in horror.

"But it is completely unimportant to me, as, I hope, it is to you."

He toasted her with an ironic smile.

For once, Pavie was right, he declared. She was a most unconventional woman.

By the way, and before he forgot, she should not expect him to dinner the following day. Captain Jones and he were expected at Rolin-Jaequemyns.

Thompson, *The Times* correspondent was also to be there.

"His Highness is in perfect agreement with me.

"The treaty may be signed if the little modifications I wrote down for him are included, and are no more than a promise to loyally execute the articles of the ultimatum, all the ultimatum and nothing but the ultimatum.

"If, however, Le Myre de Vilers repeats his threat to leave by tomorrow at lunchtime without discussing the convention, then the convention will not be signed.

And good riddance to him. But I do not believe it will come to that."

The Belgian helped himself to lamb cutlets and sighed in satisfaction, looking at the table set with old-fashioned Belgian crystal and heavy silver epergnes.

"I believe I have made the best of a very bad business."

He certainly had, Jones concurred with feeling, taking a chicken breast from the tray offered by an uniformed servant.

What he knew from Lord Dufferin is that under no circumstances would France authorize another blockade. So Le Myre could bluster all he liked, nothing would come of it.

Rolin-Jaequemyns grimaced as he tried to cut the tough, dry meat.

"This lamb is overcooked, forgive me. The cook is just

useless when Emilie is not here." He smiled at Michael.
"That is a problem you do not have with a new charming
French wife," and turned back to the British minister.

"Yes, and I am grateful for all your support, for which,
as I well know, you needed to force the hand of your
Foreign Secretary at times.

Your articles in *The Times*, Mr Thompson, have also
helped a great deal."

The young journalist raised his hands in polite self-
disparagement, and brushed his long hair from his eyes.

He had only reported the truth — it was his good
fortune that in this case, the truth made for better copy,
his readers enjoyed hearing about French treachery — as
their host continued in his sonorous voice: "All's well that
ends — not quite well ... but certainly better than what I
had feared at times."

Now that this unfortunate and time-consuming affair
seemed to be drawing to an end, he had set his mind on
several courses of action.

First, he would sue the despicable Mr Lillie of the *Siam
Free Press* for libel. The latest articles were intolerable and
insulting, based solely on easily verifiable lies.

"Hear, hear" Captain Jones muttered.

Then, he would set the King on a series of reforms.

France thought she could behave thus because she
considered Siam a backward, feudal country.

Not so, he posited gravely, raising a finger, when
dealing with a modern state.

And that, my friends, is what he intended to encourage
the King to bring about. "Think of it. A reform of the
judiciary must come first, putting an end to corruption,
for, although I am told there is none, I am not blind, no,
and I see what I see.

"In parallel, regulating mining concessions, logging

concessions, so that the money goes to the kingdom, and not into the pockets of the local lords.

"Developing the telegraph, and, eventually, the telephone to reach all villages.

"The administration, the ministries, above all, accountability, accountability, accountability!

"Therefore, the French could not claim to bring to Siam the benefits of governance she already had.

"What do you think?"

"Well, Gustave," Ed Thompson drawled, "I think you have your work cut out for you."

The Special Adviser took a sip of Mosel wine and smiled with some embarrassment.

He knew he was over-idealistic at times, and let himself carried away by his enthusiasm, Emilie often said so. But would it not be a beautiful thing if he were able to achieve just a fraction of it?

"What a dreamer," Thompson laughed with a hiccup in the boat bringing them from the Sapathum area, where the Belgian had elected to reside, back to the New Road landing.

"Still, just being *seen* to be reforming would be very beneficial to Siam's standing in the world," Michael said musingly, slurring his words. At least, that was what he wanted to say, he was finding it difficult to gather his ideas. Of course none of this could be done in months or even years... but it was worth the effort.

"Be quiet, both of you" said Jones whom they had both thought asleep in the stern of the boat and had in fact been heard snoring off the cognac that ended the evening.

"I know you think me an old soldier who does not know the ways of the world, and you are probably right. But I don't want to see Siam change at all, and am thankful I shall have left before it happens."

"Ah," Michael said as he gave the older man his hand to help him off the boat, "if RJ is a dreamer, sir, *you* are a real romantic. What does Mrs Jones make of it?"

His wife would not know a romantic from a pincushion, the Minister snorted, and weaved his way unsteadily up the Legation path.

"You certainly look the worse for wear," Julie dropped critically, seeing Michael's pale face at breakfast the next day.

He groaned. It was the cognac on top of the port on top of the burgundy on top of the mosel on top of the champagne. "Good Lord, those men can drink. I don't think I can face anything."

But Somboon appeared with a bowl redolent of coriander and ginger, which he placed firmly in front of his master.

"*Jok*" he beamed. "Rice porridge with fish sauce, ginger and chilli. Very good when too much wine. With ginger no vomit."

Julie exclaimed. She loved *jok*, Fie used to give it to her when she was expecting Louis. "If you don't have it, I shall."

No, no, he pushed her offer away with a raised hand and dipped the china spoon in the steaming gruel. He didn't want to offend Somboon, and he needed his wits about him.

Today was the day when everything might come to a head.

"Have you heard anything?" he asked French as he crossed him in the stairs.

The Consul shook his head. Was it a good sign?

Who could tell? Michael replied, dropping his hat off in his office, and then rapping on the Minister's door.

No news, he was told tersely. But there would be nothing before eleven when Le Myre was supposed to carry out his threat and leave. Unless, of course, he left before that in a huff and attempted to bluff his way to a takeover of the country.

Jones paced, called for coffee, and told Michael he looked as if he needed it. He himself was chipper and clear-eyed.

"You need to learn how to drink if you want to be ambassador someday, y'know."

Pushing his hair back from his throbbing forehead, Michael considered the statement. "Actually, sir, I'm not sure that's quite true."

Steps came thundering up the wooden steps and Thompson pushed in, looking, Michael was pleased to note, as queasy as himself.

Anything yet?

"Have some coffee, Jones replied pushing a cup towards him. You're as pale as a nun's wimple. These youngsters..."

An hour went by, then two.

"Shall we go to lunch?" Jones suggested.

Thompson shook his head. If he could borrow the legation boat, sir, he would go to see RJ and hear from him directly. He needed to telegraph *The Times* very soon in case of success.

"And all the more so if it's a dismal failure and Le Myre threatens fire and brimstone. And though I would personally regret it, it would make for better news."

The sun was almost setting when the little steamer flying the Union Jack came gliding downriver on the strong current.

"I think RJ's on board, sir," Michael said, making out

the familiar heavy silhouette in a white suit against the darkening sky.

Thompson helped him onto the deck, and held his arm to steady him up the slippery flagstones.

"*Mes amis, mes amis,*" the Belgian cried out in a mournful voice, raising his arms in despair. "Despite all our agreements, and the notes that I gave him, despite it all, His Highness has signed everything he was given to sign, the Treaty and the Convention.

Everything is lost."

Chapter XII

"I do not blame him," the Belgian stammered when they had finally sat him down in Jones' office with a large brandy in his hand, his moustache drooping woefully, his face ashen and dejected. " I do not blame him.

But those jackals... "he repeated almost in a sob," Those jackals! "

"Now, now, Monsieur," Jones said firmly. "Pull yourself together and drink. You will feel better."

He looked around at Michael and French who were hovering helplessly, while Thompson had pulled out his notebook and started scribbling notes. "Thompson," the Minister said "Not sure you should be here, be a good chap and go outside, and I'll brief you later."

"*Non, non,*" Rolin-Jaequemyns had straightened up and his cheeks recovered colour. "The world must know what has happened. The world must be told how weakness was taken advantage of.

"Oh, France, where are your ideals?" he moaned "Oh, *France, mère des arts, des armes et des lois...* what has become of you?"

Michael, seeing his superior's puzzled face whispered quickly. "France, mother of laws. Du Bellay, sir. Renaissance poet."

Renaissance? Oh, right, Jones answered with a worried nod, as the Special Adviser continued.

"Listen. His Highness was given yet another draft treaty and convention, and told they incorporated the changes I had suggested, and they seemed to, only seemed to.

"Ah, they are clever with words, those French... Xavier, the Ministry interpreter, is a willing man, but perhaps not of the calibre to deal with such matters.

"On the other hand, Father Schmidt, who was interpreting for the French — well, I prefer to believe the good father was gullible; it would grieve me to think a missionary could lend a helping hand to this.

"When His Highness attempted to stall to seek my counsel, they forced his hand, they threatened violence in the streets, and, finally, Le Myre proposed that His Highness make a list of objections, that he himself would write the answers to, and that this 'proces-verbal' be appended to the convention. I need not tell you that the so-called answers were nothing but diktats sweeping the objections away.

"Evidently, when His Highness attempted to call their bluff about a renewed blockade, Pavie implied Lanessan and Humann have far greater latitude than is the case. And then..." He raised his arms to the sky, "Then, *mes amis*, the apocalypse. No trade, no rice, prices of food reaching sky-high levels, riots, famine... Was that what His Highness wanted for Siam? Le Myre asked.

"No? So sign here, here and here."

So all of England's efforts had been in vain, Jones snapped, pale with anger.

Such as they were, Rolin-Jaequemyns dropped sourly. He could not help feel that...

A bit embarrassed, Jones cut him off. What was past was past. It remained to be seen what Whitehall might decide to do next.

Lord Rosebery wouldn't be best pleased, he could tell them that without needing to await instructions.

"I need to see the Prince. No, it can't wait, I really don't

give a tinker's cuss if he's too depressed to receive me,"
he countered, waving away Rolin-Jaequemyn's objection.
"Now, Crawfurd, you come with us to take notes.

"Thompson, our friend is right, you need to get this
out as soon as possible. Just wait until I've telegraphed
London before sending send your story.

Right, let's get cracking."

"BANGKOK, OCTOBER 2ND 1893

*Michael sent a terse chit to warn me he would be back late if at all that
night, so I had no trouble in imagining what had happened. My fears were
confirmed when Victor arrived unannounced at the door in a jubilant mood
and gave me an inkling of the events of the day. My brother appears to have
no idea of what my feelings are in this matter and behaves in a completely
insensitive manner.*

*When Michael finally arrived past midnight, he was exhausted and
resigned.*

*Far more resigned, he says, than Captain Jones who almost forgot
himself in the very harsh tone he used to His Highness.*

*The prince was dejected and defiant both, Michael said, and asserts that
he acted in the best interests of Siam.*

*So defiant was he, in fact, that Captain Jones suspects him of a secret
agreement with the French about opening a canal in the Isthmus of Kra, the
Siamese part of the Malayan peninsula.*

*Nothing would be easier for the French who have indeed proved
their engineering ability, Kra would be a far simpler project than Suez,
and, as did Suez, it would completely change the shipping routes to and
from Asia.*

*That would be most serious indeed for Britain, and would in no way
serve Siam.*

*Day after tomorrow, to rub salt in the wound as it were, there is to
be a big dinner in His Majesty's presence at Bang Pa In celebrating —
celebrating!!!— the signing of the Treaty.*

Victor is to attend, of course, and very excited because Le Myre has demanded and obtained that the French delegation be conveyed in the Royal yacht Gladys.

I was delighted to inform him I had already sailed on that ship, and that she was the second best, generally used to convey the ladies. His face fell somewhat. Hah!

He leaves on the 5th for Chantaboon, where he shall remain.

His friend young Le Myre is too important to be posted in such a backwater, and I am delighted that Victor will be cut off from what is a very harmful influence."

"You know what the worst of it is, my lads?" Jones asked in disgust.

"Develle is astonished that Siam folded because he himself had guaranteed Lord Dufferin that in no case would the ultimatum be exceeded.

"So Devawongse gave away everything for nothing — unless, of course, Develle is lying and that blasted canal happens. Which may well be the case.

"But that is something London can prevent — we've still got muscles we can flex, after all, particularly in negotiating the buffer zone.

"So, any idea what Scott is up to?"

"For the time being, nothing much really," Consul French reported.

Touring the canals with his lady, enjoying the food at the Oriental. Bangkok is so much more cosmopolitan and amusing than Mandalay, Scott says, and he only gets to Mandalay twice a year.

So this advisory role for the buffer zone — although he was very close-mouthed about it — came as a holiday for him. Also, he spent much time at the dental clinic of the British dispensary, having his dentures adjusted.

Well, yes, Jones, commented with a snort, the dentists in the Shan States probably didn't amount to much.

But he was hanged if he knew where the buffer zone might start and end, and when and to whom they would start talking about it. Scott was probably waiting for instructions, same as he was, pending discussions between Paris and London.

"And there you have it, gentlemen.

"The fate of Siam is being decided outside of Siam, which is no more than the board on which our masters play chess.

"Crawfurd? You wanted to say something?"

The French-language press from Saigon had wind of a secret agreement passed in July between Develle and Lord Rosebery to create the buffer zone.

"That cable from Reuters, that we never heard about again, Sir, yes.

"It's pretty hazy about the demarcation of the zone — probably intentionally so — but implies that it will involve, I quote here *'mutual territorial sacrifices and concessions.'*

"Saigon is up in arms, not surprisingly, I suppose, as they got less territory out of the Treaty than they expected, given their failure to annex Battambang and Siem Reap."

So his beloved Le Myre didn't deliver all Lanessan wanted, Jones grunted.

Good.

Yes, Michael replied, it was not a bad thing to see that bully returned somewhat tarnished to his constituents.

"However, we can expect strong protests from the Parti Colonial very soon.

"London probably realizes it, but still... It might be well to remind them somewhat forcefully."

"BANGKOK, OCTOBER 5TH 1893

I have started to prepare for our trip to Europe, and Michael is inquiring about obtaining the necessary documents, visas, etc. for Somboon and Fie.

Somboon is delighted and excited at the prospect, Fie is terrified, but, as I point out to her, would be even more worried if she were not in charge of Louis for several months, at which she stares as if the idea were inconceivable, and she swamps me with questions as to what she must pack.

Rice? No. Bananas? No. Dried squid? No. Shrimp paste? Absolutely not, though I then relent, as I doubt she will like French food and may occasionally need to have something that tastes familiar.

We leave in eight weeks and have decided to stay in hotels in both in London and Paris, so as to avoid the awkwardness of bedrooms, etc. and the probable hostility of our respective families' servants. I wonder what Constance, my mother's maid, for instance, will make of Fie's black teeth and cropped hair.

We shall need to purchase warm clothes for all in Singapore, and I hope there will be snow so as to show Louis what it is.

I show him a picture book about the life of a rabbit in winter, but he just laughs "Naam, naam" apparently thinking all the white is water and that the forest is flooded.

Mama is going to be quite shocked to find her grandson speaks no French; I must do my best to remedy this during the voyage."

"BANGKOK OCTOBER 10TH 1893

Yesterday, we held a dinner party for a couple newly arrived from the Shan States, Mr and Mrs Scott, and that amusing and cheeky journalist, Mr Thompson. Captain Jones and his wife were there of course, along with Mr RJ who was greatly gratified to see I used his gift of coffee spoons.

Mrs Scott is an unfashionable woman with intelligent eyes — she was wearing a very plain cotton gown more suitable for market going than for a rather formal dinner — and had bedecked herself in native silver jewellery that tended to clang and rattle with every move.

I found her a bit of a prig but I rather liked her husband, who has grey hair and a very strong and painful handshake, although he constantly belittles what he has seen of the Siamese and finds them less moral and hard working than the Shan.

He seems to have problems with his teeth, so Michael had warned me to plan for something soft.

Cook made a delicious mousse of fish followed by little flaky pastry cases filled with prawns, quenelles of chicken with mushrooms then soufflés for pudding. It was just like a dinner for children, only tastier.

I very much enjoyed seeing Edward Thompson again, he is the very embodiment of the cosmopolitan journalist, slightly dishevelled, well informed, opinionated, adventurous and witty. He is not really handsome, but when he smiles, one forgets it, so engaging is he.

He has arrived from Japan, recently covered Spain and Morocco, and before that was in Chili. Mr Scott himself used to be a journalist, so the conversation was lively with anecdotes.

RJ looked tired and sad, his many chins drooping, but claims that it is from missing Emilie who shall return only in November.

A disturbing moment occurred, when Thompson asked him outright if it were true that the evening before Prince Devawongse signed the Treaty and convention, therefore, when they were having dinner at his home, Edward French had gone to the Foreign Ministry in a closed carriage to advise His Highness to give in to Le Myre.

RJ looked as if he had been slapped in the face, and replied slowly that he had invited Consul French to that same dinner, but that French had begged off, pleading an indisposition.

It was rather a relief, he admitted, because he had extended the invitation only out of courtesy and with reluctance.

"We shall never know," he finally said, "and whoever spread that malicious rumour may just be intending to harm him, as, from what I gather, he has not only friends here."

He asked Thompson not to publish this, as he is sure that Prince Devawongse shall never mention it — if indeed it did happen — and warned him he will be liable to be sued for libel if he does.

"'Don't I know it!' Thompson said, but I am not sure he will heed the warning, he appears to be someone who enjoys taking risks.

Captain Jones said he couldn't abide Edward French, never could, Mrs Jones kept her opinion to herself and the Scotts proclaimed to be shocked.

True or not, it revealed an underhandedness in Bangkok's foreign community that is very unhealthy and repulsive, Mrs Scott stated very firmly. One would never see such doings amongst the Shan.

I can well believe it."

"BANGKOK OCTOBER 20TH 1893

Captain Jones is recalled to London, ostensibly on leave for his health after the travails of the crisis, but we all know that he is being made the scapegoat for the British failure in stemming French greed and will not return.

It appears Edward French will take his place as chargé d'affaires, and he shouts it from the rooftops.

I am livid, thinking that Michael would be much better suited but he says not, that he is still too young and would find it difficult to be seen with sufficient authority by the various ministers.

Anyway, I wouldn't want to leave this house to move into the Legation that is vast, gloomy, damp and poorly furnished and staffed.

"BANGKOK OCTOBER 23RD 1893

At last!

Michael received a message asking me to resume my classes today at the Palace if he had no objections. I suppose that now I am married to an Englishman, there is no point in snubbing me any longer.

So I went forthwith and was welcomed with great delight by all of my butterfly ladies.

I found Keow aged since I had last seen her, the tension of the past five months has added grey hairs to her head and lines to her face. But her *waistline is as ample as ever and she showed it off ruefully, all the while munching crisp fried banana slivers. 'When King worry, Queens worry. Queens worry, I worry. I worry, I eat.*

'Also, I gamble much and lose much money, never mind.' "

She told me that Captain Jones is to be received at Bang Pa In next week to make his farewell to His Majesty and that Michael is invited — which I already knew — but that she has asked that I too be included in the party.

When we are there she will take me to pick lotus stems, she promised and show me how to cook them although I am not sure I really care to know.

I cannot travel upriver with the Palace ladies, she said regretfully, as I am now married I must go with the farangs.

Never mind, as Keow would say, I am nonetheless very excited.

I had to inform my friends that I shall be away several months but when their faces fell — 'Teacher Chouli,' Chuttarat cried out, 'we are just knowing you again!' — I promised to bring them all presents from Paris."

"This is heaven," Julie sighed, resting her arms on the railing of the royal yacht steaming steadily though tangles of water hyacinth up the churning reddish waters of the great river. She waved at naked children who were casting nets on the edge and turned to Michael. "Why haven't we done this before?"

He leaned next to her and smiled. "I suppose it's because we don't have our own steamer," then added more seriously that venturing outside of Bangkok could be dangerous. There were groups of dacoits roaming the countryside robbing travellers and worse.

"Which RJ is trying to remedy, by attempting the reforms he will submit to His Majesty. Better central administration means better law enforcement."

She shook her head and gazed at the landscape of flooding rice fields, dotted with the occasional golden spire of a temple. Who could think of violence in such quiet beauty?

"Men are violent animals, my beautiful, or didn't you know that yet?" drawled Edward Thompson who had come to stand on her other side.

"A woman sees a flower, plucks it and thinks, how lovely, a man sees it, plucks it, and crushes it with his boot."

"Or sells it," Michael remarked pleasantly but with a frown at hearing the forward way the journalist was addressing his wife.

"Yes, Crawfurd, you're right. If it's an Englishman, he sells it at an inflated price to the natives."

Michael made a face. "Edward, you're drunk."

Not really, the journalist declaimed, just tipsy although he'd rather have liked to get drunk as a lord on the wine they had been given at lunch. It wasn't so often he could get drunk on such good stuff; he certainly couldn't afford to do it out of his own pocket.

"I suppose that's why you came to dinner at our home," Julie said drily. "Michael is known for his cellar."

Thompson straightened up, pulled off his hat and gave her a mock bow.

No my lady, the wine wasn't why he came, it was the sight of her face in the candlelight, and he turned on his heel to go ask for another drink from the servants in white uniforms who were dispensing tea and stronger refreshments on the deck.

She shouldn't mind Edward, Michael said, watching her follow him with her eyes. He meant nothing.

She didn't mind, she replied thoughtfully, and as to meaning nothing, she wasn't so sure.

On arrival at the country residence of Bang Pa In, they were all assigned ships to sleep on, as the rainy season flooding had made it difficult to access some residences, and Julie, to her great joy and relief — the idea of sharing a bedroom with Michael was awkward and embarrassing — was told that as a special favour to Princess Keow, she was to join the Palace ladies in their sleeping quarters on an old fashioned teak houseboat, "if Khun Mykin allowed…"

"I thought you happier with us. Easier." the Princess said matter-of-factly, as they were paddled in a small boat past a red and gold Chinese-style palace and an ornate triple-roofed pavilion shaped like the abodes of the gods in the Emerald Buddha Temple frescoes.

"Easier?" Julie asked in surprise, and understood suddenly what was meant.

Keow nodded gravely. Servants talk. Teacher Chouli's servants knew servants from Palace. Easier, never mind.

"Easier, easier, easier," Julie repeated in peals of hysterical laughter. "Oh Your Highness, so much easier! If you only knew…"

She knew, was the answer. She understood. "You do right for your son. Son need man."

Julie sighed and wiped away a tear of laughter or sorrow, she couldn't tell which. Yes, she did right for her son, and wrong for her. And did she not need a man?

"Men!" the older woman snorted. "Men come and men go. If come, good, if go, never mind."

Sons were what mattered.

Julie shook her head stubbornly. Her Highness was a traditional Siamese lady, she was a modern European woman, and thought differently.

"We make you think like Siamese lady then, never mind." the Princess said firmly. "Now we go pick lotus stems from boat."

"Think like a Siamese lady, Keow told me.

I don't know if I ever can.

Talking about it with Keow has finally enabled me to admit my own misery to myself and yet, I do not understand why I am so unhappy.

Our life is no different from what it was when we shared Michael's funny unkempt house, so why should anything have changed?

I love him as I always have, I prefer his company to anyone else's; he is as perfectly understanding and affectionate as he always was, but I resent his happiness, and indeed, why should he not be happy?

He has all that he had before plus a wife who offers a perfect cover for any suspicions that might be raised against him.

Now, when he kisses me on the forehead before retiring for bed, I could scream with frustration although the idea of sharing a bed with him is as foreign as it always has been.

I suppose it's that somehow, I thought that my life as a woman was not over, and now it is.

And yet, I do not regret marrying him, it was the right decision — the only possible decision.

I may not yet be thinking like a Siamese, but I am trying.

The reception at one of the Palaces in Bang Pa In (the one called 'Shining and Heavenly Abode') was very moving as it was to be Captain Jones' last meeting with the King.

I was very struck by His Majesty's dignity in what must be a very trying time for him being forced to cede a large piece of his kingdom but he let none of his private anguish transpire and said many affectionate words to Captain Jones who had tears in his eyes.

To me, he was as usual very kind, congratulated Michael on our marriage and gave me his best wishes for happiness.

RJ told Michael in confidence that during that humiliating reception in Bang Pa In to 'celebrate' the signing of the Treaty, Le Myre strongly advised the King 'to write to the President of the French Republic and consult him whenever there is a problem' — which would be tantamount to giving France an unofficial protectorate over Siam.

Did he really think he would be heard, after those weeks of insults and double-dealing?

Of course, His Majesty declined politely.

At the dinner, I was seated next to Prince Damrong, who is as witty and urbane as ever, and frightfully elegant in beautifully tailored tails; we had a long chat about Siamese art — actually, he chatted, I listened, as I know very little about it. He promised to show me some remarkable pieces of statuary when we return from Europe.

He also discussed his plans for improving education, assuming I am knowledgeable — I dared not tell him that playing shop and singing songs at the Palace were the extent of my expertise — and I stressed the need to educate girls as well as boys.

Thompson was sober, thankfully, because he was granted a Royal Audience and came out of it quite dazzled.

The Scotts were invited as well, she wearing a better gown but still bedecked in her sonorous silver necklaces, he upright and busy, commenting on everything and taking copious notes with sketches of the various palaces.

There has been a great controversy in the newspapers these days, the Siam Free Press having attributed to His Majesty a completely spurious speech to a Captain Gerard, who, apparently, is one of Victor's fellow officers, dispelling any rumours of mistreatment of the Siamese in Chantaboon, and actually thanking the French for 'prudent management'!

Well, as it was the Siam Free Press, nobody here paid much attention knowing it was French-paid propaganda, but The Straits Times of Singapore picked it up and printed it.

Thompson fired off a rebuttal.

He himself went to Chantaboon on the "Linnet" a week or so before our Bang Pa In excursion, but had to admit that besides confiscating the weapons of the local Siamese garrison, he hadn't really noticed any particularly hostile measures on the part of the French troops.

However, he claims that he was not allowed to see much — 'If they had been raping and pillaging, do you think they would have asked me along to watch?' — and said darkly that that any such piece of shameless propaganda means that the local population has been mistreated.

Could that be true? And could my own brother be responsible for such despicable acts?

We leave on December 3rd, on the same ship, as it happens, as Captain Jones, we shall miss Christmas but, if we are lucky with the weather, shall be in Paris for the New Year."

"Bangkok, October 28th 1893

There is a party almost every night, to either bid farewell to Captain Jones or to celebrate the interim appointment of James Scott as his replacement, because French has been passed over to the great and vocal delight of Captain Jones.

Poor Edward French takes it very badly.

There had been too many complaints against him, including from RJ, who had received a cable from Whitehall asking his opinion of the man.

Finally, Thompson took it upon himself to send a 'vitriolic', as he put it, telegram to Lord Rosebery informing him of his own views, stating, inter alia, that when he confronted Her Majesty's Consul in Bangkok with that rumour about urging Prince Devawongse to sign the Treaty, the man did not deny it.

'He did not confirm it either, did he?' Michael asked him over a drink, as now, ever since the dinner party for the Scotts, Thompson stops by our house every evening for whisky soda and gossip. 'He may have thought the rumour not worthy of a reply.'

Thompson ('call me Ed' — he has frequented American journalists) just shrugged off the objection.

Of course, he now takes credit for Scott's appointment.

He really is most exasperatingly vain, but Michael finds him useful and I find him amusing to chat to. Of course, I realize I am flirting with him, which is quite a novel experience for me — I don't think I have ever flirted before, and finally understand the pleasure it gives. Michael does not seem to mind."

"It would seem our friend Ed has quite a pash for you", Michael remarked quietly once the journalist had taken his leave.

"A *pash*?" Julie repeated, with laughter in her voice. "What's a '*pash*'?"

Michael was surprised to hear she did not know. Well, of course, she had been completely spared the English school experience.

A pash, short for 'passion', he explained, was when a young girl — or boy, he added with diffident smile — in boarding school falls in love with an older, usually glamorous student.

"All very harmless, and part of the boarding school experience... Did I ever have a pash?

"Well, of course. But not for one of the virile brutes on the rugby team.

I've always fallen for the bookish, sensitive types."

"BANGKOK, NOVEMBER 1ˢᵀ 1893

I was getting ready for a ball the Scotts were giving at the Oriental yesterday and seated at my dressing table when Michael entered my room and sat down on the bed to watch me. This is unusual in itself, and I was expecting him to make some distressing announcement, that our departure was to be delayed or that he had received bad news from Paris.

Then he said, very gently. 'My dear, I've been thinking. Why don't you have an affair with Thompson?"

I was so startled and shocked that I smeared the lip salve over my cheek and wiped it off with what sounded like a very hollow laugh, pretending it was all in jest, but my hands were shaking. 'No,' he said, 'hear me out.

'I know that this... partnership... we have entered is unfair to you and that I cannot make you as fully happy as you deserve to be, as a woman.

'You will grow to hate me, and that I could not bear. Thompson wants you; it's clear to me and must be to you.'

'And, of course, what I want counts for nothing?' I asked in a cold voice, to mask my distress and shame at having so poorly concealed my feelings.

'You want him too, as you would know,' he replied a bit sadly, 'if you allowed yourself to admit it. Of course, he is not worthy of you, but I cannot think of anyone who would be so suitable.

'There would be no danger to your reputation. He is so boastful that nobody believes a quarter of what he claims, so if he were to be indiscreet, it would not be taken seriously — and for that matter, I have never heard him

brag about any of his conquests, so I do think he has some sense of honour where women are concerned.

'Just think about it. Please.'

He smiled and added. 'I am right, you know.'

I was trembling so that I could not fasten the clasp of my necklace so he got up and did it for me, then kissed my shoulder.

'I want you to be happy,' he repeated before leaving my room.

I just sat for a moment trying to imagine it and it is of course impossible.

Yes, he is right, Thompson wants me, I am not such a ninny that I cannot interpret him pressing my waist too tight when we dance, the lingering way his hand holds mine, the smouldering looks he gives when he thinks I do not notice.

But he is brash, and boastful and uncouth — and were he a very Prince Charming from a fairy tale, it would be just as unthinkable.

Although I was not married in church, I did take a vow to be faithful.

The ball was a rather grand affair and all the silks and jewels were on display. Mrs Scott was in bright and unbecoming green, with a huge bustle that must have been the height of fashion when she last left England some fifteen years ago.

I asked her if Fanny had arrived yet, but she said she had preferred not to invite her. 'Some people might be uncomfortable, you know. She's a nice enough woman, and yes, I have of course heard her father was consul here, but… a bit of the tar brush?' She lowered her voice. 'One can barely see it, but did you know her mother was a native?'

Actually, I do not like Mrs Scott at all.

It was all I could do to remain civil, and probably would not have if my mind were not so very much occupied and upset by Michael's … what can I call it? Suggestion? Advice? Permission?

I was determined to avoid Thompson at the ball, I did not want to dance with him, feel his eyes on my bare shoulders, the heat of his breath when he spoke, but that was impossible without seeming rude, and he claimed me as a partner within minutes of our arrival.

When the waltz was over and he brought me back to my seat, I was

intensely aware of him wherever he was in the room, hating Miss Mitchell
for being in his arms and cursing Michael — had he said nothing, I would
have been perfectly comfortable — well, less confused and upset, certainly.

I went out on the terrace for air, and he followed and just stood next
to me looking at the lights on the water. He asked finally why I married
Michael —

'You seem a very unlikely couple,' he said, 'but I suppose it was a
marriage of convenience, arranged by your families?'

I said no, that our families had actually been surprised and probably
a bit reluctant when we informed them. He raised his eyebrows looking —
cynical, perhaps, or amused.

'Seems to me you are rather wasted on him... I never took Crawfurd for
the marrying kind,' he drawled.

So he has guessed....

I told him that my husband is dearer to me and loves me better than
anyone, more, I said very forcefully, than any man could, and was about to
leave the terrace rather abruptly, when he caught me by the arm."

Julie put down her pen and stared at her hands clasped
before her, feeling herself flush at the memory of
Thompson's dark eyes gazing intently at her. He then
released her and leaned on the railing, looking down at
the river, and spoke quietly.

"Have you ever heard Paderewski play Chopin?" he
asked. "I did, once, in Vienna... the 'Revolutionary'
étude. It was quite an experience. I was merely listening at
first, feeling, yes, yes, I have heard all this before, I know
where this is going — then suddenly, something surprising
happened, was it a change in rhythm, a different intensity,
a new meaning to the notes?

"I don't know, but it was as if I heard Chopin for the
first time and he had composed for me alone."

He turned back to look at her, and she felt, to her
surprise, that she was disappointed, she didn't want him
to talk about music, she wanted — what did she want?

He was staring, and she felt she needed to say something, but the words coming to her mind were too dangerous, so she nodded with a non-committal "Well?"

"Well," he continued in a hoarse, rasping voice, "that is what I feel when I see you, hear you, dance with you, as if I had never seen or heard or danced with a woman before. And I wonder how it would feel to have you in my arms."

I managed to laugh as if it were a joke, yet another meaningless flirtatious exchange, and said I had rarely heard such drivel, and to keep it for Miss Mitchell. Furthermore, as to holding me in his arms, had we not just danced together?

'You're not a fool, nor an innocent so don't pretend to be. I mean naked in my arms, and you know it,' he snapped.

I was speechless with shock, and thankfully, a couple joined us on the terrace so he had to stop, and I avoided him for the rest of the evening.

I came home still all hot and bothered and resolved to put any thought of Thompson out of my mind.

Michael said nothing on the way back."

"BANGKOK, NOVEMBER 4ᵀᴴ

I cannot believe that his ridiculous words about Paderewski and Chopin actually moved me, they sounded so… pat, so rehearsed — There was something so insulting and mediocre, as well, in having him assume I would be won over by being compared to music….

I am sure he has used them countless times, his great seduction piece…

How many women, I wonder, have been taken in by such nonsense?

I am almost tempted to confide in Michael, and say, well, this is the man you want me to have an affair with.

But I cannot get him out of my head.

This evening, there is a reception at the German legation.

I am tempted to plead indisposition, but I know I cannot resist seeing him.

I am playing with fire.

Later.

*Fie has just brought me a chit from Edward, asking me to his rooms ...
'for luncheon'.*

    Of course, I shall decline — or better still, ignore it."

Folding up Edward's note, she rested her head in her
hands; she could hear Louis' laughter warbling up from
the garden, and Fie's low voice chatting with Mali. She rose
to pace her room, stopped at the looking-glass to stare at
her flushed reflection then walked out to her terrace to
watch the scene below her, her son using a coconut shell
to scoop up water from one of the huge earthenware jars
for collecting rain water, the cat scurrying to safety, the
gardener cutting back the blue blossoming vines. She did
not want anything to disturb this happiness, or at least this
peace she had carved for herself.

    No, she decided, with sudden resolve.

    Ignoring him or just writing a curt note to decline was
cowardly, and, whatever else she was, she was not a coward.

    She had to have it out with him, once and for all, and
not let this troubling situation fester. It would be kinder
for him, and kinder for her, and leaning over the railing,
she called Fie to help her dress.

"NOVEMBER 5TH 1893

What have I done?
I am appalled and elated and feel I have lost my mind."

Was it only yesterday that she had decided to put an end to
all this, "once and for all"?

    What was she thinking?

    Although, heaven knows, she was determined to be

firm, but kind, and when she entered the dusty, poorly furnished set of rooms Edward rented over a Chinese tea-merchant's shop in a narrow *soi* off Windmill Road, she immediately started the little speech she had been rehearsing in the buggy.

But Edward rushed up to her, gently lifted the veil off her face, and unpinned her hat from her hair.

"You came!" he whispered, "I hardly dared hope you might."

"He laughed when I said I had only come to ask him to stop pursuing me,

'So why did you not bring your maid?' he asked.

He laughed when I lifted my hand to slap his face after he attempted to kiss me, caught my wrist, and said very low 'So that is the way you want it, then?', forced me against the wall and kissed me again when I tried to resist. He laughed when he began to fumble with the buttons on my dress, and to my immense shame, I struggled at first then laughed as well, and helped him, and I can still hear the whisper of silk as my clothes fell to the ground.

Dear God, we laughed, and afterwards, as I lay sated on his bed, on the rumpled sheets, I laughed again at the thought I would see him later at the German Legation reception and that nobody would suspect how we had spent the afternoon.

We ate nothing at all of the cold 'luncheon' he had ordered from the Oriental, we hadn't the time before I needed to go home to change.

If this is a dream, please let me never wake up and face what I have done.

I haven't so much taken leave of my senses — my senses have taken leave of me. To think I've been married only six weeks.

It was a moment of madness, and cannot and will not happen again."

She shivered as she wrote, reliving every shameful, thrilling moment, hearing her own voice in her head, gasping "You, sir, are a cad" when he released her mouth, and his low growl "Perhaps I am, but you, my lady, are a teasing little hypocrite. You want it as much as I do." And when he kissed her again, she felt first her body yield and then her mind.

Then later, as she was dressing to leave and he was helping lace her stays, he ran his mouth down her naked back and murmured, "Well, well, well. I take it back, in fact, you are not a lady", she replied ruefully that her mother had always said so, and he lifted her and tossed her back on the bed.

"Then let's prove her right again, shall we?"

It must not, would not happen again.

But she found herself planning every detail — couldn't take the buggy, the servants would talk, shouldn't wear a corset, too long to dress and undress, she would tell Fie she was shopping for gifts to take to Paris — no, wait, how could she come back without any purchases? Never mind, she would say she hadn't seen anything she liked —, and counting every minute until she could rush up the dirty dark steps to Edward's rooms and be once again naked in his arms.

"Bangkok November 10TH 1893

I am so ashamed of the woman I have become and cannot stop crying.

But neither can I stop seeing Edward when it is possible and rush to his rooms as soon as I receive a chit saying he is in.

He is not the gentle lover Louis was, however gentleness was not what I needed or wanted.

We are forced to meet in public constantly, whether at parties or for the Loy Krathong ceremonies and do our best to act as naturally as possible and the strain is sometimes such that I could scream.

At times I am fresh from his bed and feel that everybody can tell from my bruised mouth and languorous eyes, clouded with lust.

But everyone is blind and Mrs Scott just chided me for looking, as she put it, 'peaky'. Not enough iron in my diet, she says.

We are sailing soon and I long for that moment to release me from the spell I seem to be under and leave me only the anguish of remembering.

Michael is carefully absent most of the day, and returns very late at night claiming that he has much to do before his long absence.

Some remnant of the convent girl I once was urges me to confession, but it is impossible, so I shall have to bear this guilt alone."

"So, are you truly leaving in three weeks?" Edward asked idly, running his hand over Julie's naked shoulder. She stretched and nodded with a smile, and turned to offer the nape of her neck and her back to his caresses.

"Yes," she finally replied, "I can barely believe it. There's so much to do, and I must find time to go to the bazaars and silk merchants with Fanny and Léonie, otherwise they will start wondering why I haven't seen them — and," she added with a low, sensuous laugh, "I can't very well tell them what I have been doing with my afternoons."

He remained silent a moment, then tangled his fingers in her hair and tugged gently.

"What about your husband? I should imagine he has greater cause to wonder what you do with your afternoons," and when she just shrugged, twisted the tresses tight around his hand to turn her face to him. "And does he not wonder when he comes home and takes you to bed why you are not in the mood for love? Or are you?" he snarled. "Is that it? Can you be with him as you are with me? Are you that two-faced?"

She closed her eyes and sighed. "Stop, Edward, you are hurting me."

He pushed her away, then got up and started to dress, and she barely heard when he groaned that it was the other way around.

She was hurting him.

"Bangkok November 15ᵀᴴ 1893

I refuse to discuss my husband with him, but he presses me to, asking if Michael does this in bed or that, until I feel like screaming and finally say no, otherwise, did he think that I would come to him almost every afternoon, endangering my marriage, my happiness and reputation?

But nothing is enough to reassure him.

I thought at first he had guessed what Michael is, but it seems not, or perhaps he is so eaten away by jealousy that he no longer believes it?

He wants me to postpone our trip and when I refuse and explain it is impossible, and that as it is, we shall barely make it to Paris for the New Year, he sulks.

'And what about me?' he asks.

What about him? I ask in return. Will I miss him? Do I love him?

I say yes, I say of course, I say I shall think of him every day, but the truth is I do not love him — I am sure I do not love him, how could I?— and I hope that in time I shall be able to remember him without despising myself."

"I do not understand you." Edward said with a dangerous look on his dark face as Julie sat on his bed and smoothed a stocking up her bare leg.

"No?" she replied easily, "well, I'm not surprised. Very few people do.

"Except Michael, of course."

He jumped to his feet and stared down at her while she fastened her garter.

Did he understand her correctly? Did her husband know about him?

She winced and bit her lips, already regretting the facile retort she meant as a way of asserting the closeness she shared with her husband.

"I did not say that," she finally answered, keeping her face down, pretending to concentrate on a reluctant shoe button.

"But he would understand, I take it," Edward continued in a heated voice, "if I were to go up to him and told him I love his wife."

Julie rose and straightened her gown, checked her reflection in the looking glass, then began to pin up her hair and mumbled with her mouth full of hairpins that Michael would no doubt find him rather impertinent.

"Although he would be sympathetic, I expect," she added lightly, putting the last pin in place. "After all, he loves me and would think it normal for others to."

Edward snatched the hat she was reaching for away from her, and began to pace the room, raising little puffs of dust from the carpet and floor.

So then, what would happen if he were then to ask her husband to release her?

She closed her eyes wearily. "He would release me, of course he would, if I wanted it."

Did she not see then? They could be happy. They could move to America, or China, or Japan, or Argentina...

In disbelief and consternation, she watched him yield to his excited dream, and snapped angrily. "You fool, did you not hear me say 'If I wanted it?' " Then, turning her back on him so as not to see his stricken face, she stalked out of the room and slammed the door.

"*December 2*ND *1893*

We leave tomorrow.
I have made my farewells to Edward who begs me to give up Michael and my life here and follow him, then accuses me of being nothing but a cold-hearted vixen and a rich unthinking bourgeoise who used him for her own amusement. I suppose that is a fair description.

We parted very badly, and I am relieved, as his angry words are what I shall remember whenever I am tempted to think of him with regret.

Of course, I am convinced that his love for me is no more than wounded pride.

And a dark, rather unpleasant little voice in my mind whispers that my fortune might also have something to do with this passion he professes.

Fanny and Fie held a little ceremony at the spirit house to ensure that our household gods protect us on our journey. We made special offerings and burned incense.

Fanny looks at me queerly, but asks no questions and Fie is much too excited and upset at her first voyage beyond Bangkok to have noticed anything, I think. Louis is impossible, has tantrums, kicks and bites; he senses the upheaval to come in his life, the ships, the hotels, but we cannot really explain it to him.

Michael is particularly loving and kind and has said not a word about Edward.

Victor travelled up from Chantaboon to bid us bon voyage. He claims the local population welcomed the French troops 'with open arms' and that it was hardly surprising as there are practically no Siamese there, only Indochinese and Khmers, who are registering 'en masse' to be French protégés, which will put them under French jurisdiction and exempt them from their royal labour obligations and their taxes.

I ask if that is not the reason, rather than out of love for France, but he just shrugs.

'Who cares? With a couple of thousand more,' he laughed, 'you'll see, the entire province will be French without our having to fire a shot.'

Michael was rather concerned when he heard that, and made a note to Mr Scott to be particularly vigilant.

I feel sad to be leaving, and thankful to get away.

I am not taking my notebooks and shall lock them in a drawer; I do not want them to fall into the hands of someone who could read them. Servants are indiscreet whatever their country, but here there is no danger.

Chapter XIII

"BANGKOK MARCH 14ᵀᴴ 1894

I am so happy to be back.

It was a long and tiring journey until we finally boarded the ship in Liverpool and we both sighed with relief when we finally sat down in our stateroom and shut out the world.

The three weeks from Singapore to Marseille were rather trying, with Louis, Fie and Somboon getting seasick, then colds and coughs.

In the evenings over dinner, poor dear Captain Jones lamented being dragged away from Siam and after a whisky or three berated the treachery of Whitehall in a loud and maudlin voice. It was all Michael could do to quiet him down.

We never saw poor Mrs Jones, as, from what I gathered, she took to her bed and stayed there until the trip was over.

We decided to skip our stay in Nice and took the train to Paris, Louis was entranced by the steam engine and Fie was terrified.

I had forgotten the noise and bustle of Paris and found it quite bewildering when we arrived, but Fie and Somboon were in shock, staring at the trams and hansom cabs, and jumping out of their skins with each whistle of a policeman and shrill hoot of factory sirens. Louis howled with fright, as he did when he met his grandparents, and refused to kiss them.

Fie finally managed to get him to perform a wai, *and Papa asked me if the boy thought he was some sort of God to be prayed to like that?*

At first, I was received by my family like a queen —'to imagine you shall be ambassadress of England, one day,' Mama kept repeating in a trance — and Papa was very affectionate to Michael with whom he had serious talks about his expectations of postings and was reassured when told that under British law, my money and inheritance are my own.'

'So that is what detained you in Siam... ', he tells me with a sly smile. 'I had thought so, but your Mama just laughed it away.'

Finally, it seemed, I have done something that pleases my family.

They regretted we felt it was necessary to lodge at the Grand Hotel, but admitted that with Augusta, her baron, her sons and their nanny, maid and valet staying Boulevard Malesherbes, it would have been a strain.

Augusta has become rather stout and rather provincial, but she is very much 'Madame la Baronne' and won't let you forget it, and professes a stunning lack of curiosity about our life in Bangkok.

Her baron talks of nothing but his cows.

Louis' meeting with his cousins Edmond and André-Charles was not a success. He will not share his toys nor accept any authority, and, as Augusta's Scottish nanny pointed out, 'he don't even speak the King's English. And he don't know his prayers either.'

The encounter between Fie and that po-faced woman is best not described, each of them glaring at the other from opposite corners of the old nursery, and of course, each of them with their own methods of education, Fie's being that Louis can do as he pleases.

Mama was also dismayed and disapproving that her grandson can say practically nothing in either English or French — and perhaps even more so when she heard me speaking Siamese to my child.

So after the initial approval I garnered by virtue of marrying Michael, I quickly once more reverted to being the Julie who is a constant disappointment to her Mother.

My shortcomings in supervising my son's education and manners were brought up daily, and she could not understand that Louis is hardly used to wearing shoes and why he hated the tasteless nursery food he was given.

"What <u>does</u> the child eat?" she demanded to know.

I said he ate rice, chicken and fish but she pinched her mouth when I added squid, and crab and dried pork. When I said he loved fruit and had pineapple daily, her eyes opened wide. Pineapples are such a delicacy in Paris, she could not believe the descriptions of the piles of them sold very cheaply at the market.

She suggested I might want to look for a 'proper' nurse when in London,

'That native you have is no doubt well meaning, but with two children..."

Because, as I discovered some time between Port Said and Marseille my lingering sea-sickness did not come from the swell of the waves but the future swell of my belly and is the result of several afternoons of passionate love-making in shabby little rooms off Windmill Road.

Although three years ago, it took me several weeks to realize I was expecting, this time I could have no doubt.

So there it is.

Michael claims to be delighted; he also claims to have guessed from the first time I rushed away from the ship's dining-room — 'after all, my dear, I am an old hand at this now. I am not angry, why should I be? And I shall love this baby as I love Louis.'—So I am trying to be delighted as well and not to think how this unexpected child came about.

I firmly resisted Mama's repeated and increasingly irate suggestion that I spend the rest of my pregnancy in Paris and give birth there, knowing that I can no longer go back to being a dutiful and obedient daughter and she accused me of having become quite foreign and ungrateful.

Michael finally came to my assistance and assured her that the quality of medical care in Siam was quite excellent, then gently reminded her that a diplomat's wife must be supportive of her husband's career and be by his side.

Mama is so determined to see me as ambassadress that she immediately yielded.

Paris was very gay, very elegant, but I saw a great deal of squalor and poverty behind the beautiful orderly boulevards, a different, less cheerful poverty from that in Bangkok, which seems worse because of the cold. There were beggar children outside every church who cursed you if you gave them nothing and the office workers, huddled shivering under their black umbrellas and waiting for tramways, looked resentful of the high-living Parisians in furs piling out of restaurants or theatres and climbing into their carriages.

One afternoon, I had to discharge a duty I dreaded but could not avoid, and took Louis to meet Monsieur and Madame Gallet, my former parents-in-law. We were all very distressed, as I expected.

They say he is the image of his father at that age, brought out lovingly preserved books and toys of their son's that Louis threw down, and commented on my marriage — which of course I had written to announce — saying sadly that although they understood, they felt they had lost their only grandson forever.

'He will become English, now, and learn to hate the country of his father,' Monsieur Gallet said mournfully, and this child, all they had to remind them of their son, would be a stranger to them.

And there was no hope of ever having another grandchild, his wife sobbed, as Marie, their daughter, has become a nun.

I expressed some surprise, I had not known her as religious, and Madame Gallet, wiping her eyes, said gently that Louis was as well.

'Had he not told you why he became a botanist? It is because in the infinite intelligence and variety of plants, he saw the glory and artistry of God. He was a mystic.'

I broke down in tears, and was reminded once more how little I knew that gifted and unfortunate man, my first love.

I had brought her a dress length of Siamese silk in vibrant blue and green, but she put it aside saying she only wears mourning now — why, why, why had I not thought of that? — I left feeling both insensitive and stupid.

I spent an afternoon with Amélie, who asked me many questions about my life in Bangkok and listened to none of the answers, her eyes darting around to make sure there was nothing in her drawing-room, the cakes served for tea or the deportment of her frighteningly well-mannered daughters that Jean-Baptiste might find fault with.

We parted with promises to write more often.

We were also invited to dinner at the British Embassy, and I discovered that Lord Dufferin, the very same Lord Dufferin I heard about every day at the height of the crisis is 'a friend of the family' and Michael's godfather.

Michael said he had not wanted to tell anyone in Bangkok, he didn't want people being overly careful around him in fear that he might tell tales — still, I feel he might have told me!

They both spent most of the evening talking about Siam and about the latest news, which is the creation of an 'Upper Mekong Border commission' to ensure that French Indochina and British Burmah do not step on each other's toes in Siam.

Lord Dufferin regretfully informed us that Monsieur Develle was no longer Foreign Minister — the man was no doubt weak, he said, but nonetheless honest and did what he could to resist the pressure of the Colonial Party.

Monsieur Casimir-Périer, who is also Prime Minister, replaces him pending the appointment of someone else whom the Colonial zealots will approve of.

Lord Dufferin apologized for boring me, but Michael said I know as much about Siam as any diplomat in Bangkok.

'My wife is a true Siamese pasionaria,' he laughed, 'and the only one these days who can enter the Inner court and converse in Siamese with the princesses.'

I told Lady Dufferin that he exaggerated greatly, but she asked me many questions and told me about her own experiences in India and Canada.

I hope that when Michael becomes ambassador I shall be as remarkable a hostess. They are both charming and entertaining, and at the end of the evening, she kissed me good-bye and said with a smile. 'You'll do.'

'Oh?' Michael said, rising his eyebrows. 'Mother?'

'No, no, Zinnia trusts your judgement.' she laughed in reply, but her eyes were serious.

So it was his father who wanted me examined and vetted. Just as I thought... he fears me too nouveau riche and vulgar for their family.

Then London, and it was very much the same, except this time it was I who was sat down and questioned about my fortune. I believe they were satisfied with my answers.

'A diplomat needs money,' Aunt Zinnia warned me with a smile. She occasionally looked at me quizzically, as if trying to understand, but asked no questions.

I like her very much, far more than I expected, she has Michael's wit, his way of speaking and smiling and flyaway sandy hair. She seems not to take anybody very seriously, especially not her husband who is kind, but rather remote and forbidding.

All are naturally delighted about the expected birth, and Michael behaved as proudly as any ordinary father-to-be.

Dahlia, Michael's sister, asked if I was going to follow the 'idiotic tradition of flower names if it turns out to be a girl,' and I said I would. 'I'll call her Lily.'

'Lily,' Michael repeated with a smile. 'Yes, I like Lily.'

I do so hope it is a girl.

If we are thankful to be back, it is nothing compared to Louis, Fie and Somboon who walk around the house and garden touching everything as if to make sure they aren't dreaming, and laughing for no reason, just the pleasure of being home and away from the general greyness of Europe, be it the skies or the cities.

They sickened constantly, from the food, the cold and the frightening strangeness of it all.

Louis has resumed his undisputed dominion over everyone, and I wonder how he will accept this new brother or sister.

We have received many visits since our return three days ago, Fanny, Léonie and her husband, the Scotts, both Mr and Mrs, and I handed out the gifts of hats and gloves and books for my friends and toys for Nhu Dam.

RJ and Emilie came by for tea and told us Thompson had left 'rather suddenly' for Hong Kong in late December. 'He said there was nothing left for him to report here.'

I expect that's true, Michael commented and drank his tea, carefully avoiding my eye.

I am giddy with relief.

"So you back," Keow said in a gruff voice belied by a huge smile.

"Yes, Your Highness," Julie replied with delight. She was back, and had no wish to leave before a long time.

"Good. Girls need to work."

Instead of wanting to work, the little princesses were picking up Louis with squeals of laughter, exclaiming how much he had grown, and Fie had settled in a shady corner to gossip with friends and regale them with the tales of her travel to mysterious lands beyond the seas.

The Siamese lady leaned back against the cushions on the floor, arranged the pleats of her *phasin* and looked at Julie critically. "You have baby. Who?"

"Who?" she replied, attempting to sound outraged. She was not expecting Keow to notice so soon and even with her all seeing network of informers, she couldn't have known. It was impossible.

Who? Her husband.

Keow shook her head, unconvinced and pursed her lips, but decided not to pursue the matter. "Good, good. You think like Siamese lady. Another son."

Well... she would prefer a daughter.

The Princess considered the reply carefully and nodded. "Daughter good too, never mind. Men need both. Now we eat."

She called a servant and snapped a few words, and when the woman returned with an open coconut, pushed it towards Julie. "Drink. Coconut water. Good for baby. And pumpkin pudding. Eat, eat.

"But no banana blossom. Never banana blossom."

After the class, which was taken up by the distribution of gifts of fans, reticules and feather hair ornaments, and quelling the arguments that inevitably arose, Keow walked her to the Great Gate and nudged her elbow with a grin.

"So, I say to you, man come, man go, if go never mind.

"Man go."

"Your Highness," Julie replied opening her eyes as wide as she could, "I have no idea what you are talking about," and stepped high over the threshold.

As she turned back, she saw the older woman shaking with laughter.

The sun was already high in the white cotton skies and

Michael decided to walk to the Legation, relishing the warm puffs of wind rising up from the river, the cries of the street vendors and the smells of fruit, hot oil, fish sauce and frying pork wafting up in clouds from the food stalls.

It was good to be back.

Somboon, in Europe, had at turns been exhilarated at the novelty but tearful at spending so much time alone, and required careful handling, not understanding the strictures of secrecy his master imposed. "But Maem knows!" he moaned in despair when he was exiled to the garret rooms of the London and Paris hotels and once, when Michael had taken him along for a sightseeing visit to show Louis the Tower of London, had to be told not to grasp his arm in his amazement at the Crown jewels.

"You're worse than a bloody woman, you know that?" Michael had hissed under his voice in his fear of being noticed, and Somboon had snivelled all afternoon. He had also to be restrained from kowtowing to Michael's parents when they arrived from the boat train. "So, this is your man servant?" Mother had asked, gazing at the crimson silk pantaloons and yellow jacket he had insisted on wearing. "How... how colourful."

Here, back in the household where his position was known and accepted, he was once again the quiet, loving companion who eased his mind and quickened his body.

Julie, however...

He did not know. The restless and brittle moods that had so worried him before they left had given place, while they were travelling, to the Julie he knew, quick-witted and amusing, interested and interesting. And when they had returned, for the first weeks, she had seemed happy to be home, commenting on how much she had missed the luxuriant vegetation, the scent of flowers and the heat.

Now, she alternated between a quiet and remote cheerfulness that he could not really believe in and that did not resemble her in the least or raging outbursts when she lashed out and appeared to hate him.

Perhaps it was indeed her pregnancy, as she claimed in the tearful collapses that followed her explosions.

Perhaps she had lost the knack of concealing her feelings.

But she seemed less exhausted than when she was expecting Louis, spent long hours at the Palace or with Fanny, coming home in the evenings telling him of this Princess or that bazaar, and refused to discuss anything to do with themselves.

"But you are pleased about the baby, are you not?" he finally dared ask last night.

"Yes," she replied coolly, "but less than you, it appears. Whenever you want another, just tell me whom I am to sleep with."

"Listen," he snapped. "If you think I engineered that… interlude with Thompson so as to have you get pregnant and better protect myself, I'll thank you to rid that notion from your mind."

He had just wanted…

She knew, she knew, Julie had wept. But why was she punished whenever she stepped out of line?

She married against her parents' wishes, and her husband died, leaving her stranded in Siam with an unborn child.

She then decided to marry him for her son's future and happiness, and she cut off her own. She gave in to Thompson, and here she was…

"He wanted me to leave you and follow him, do you know that?"

He could well believe it. She was a prize above rubies, but why did she not accept?

She snorted as she wiped her eyes. "Actually, it's a 'price' above rubies, and the quote refers to virtuous women, and you know very well why I didn't accept. I can throw myself away for a few days, not for a lifetime. And I never could have done that to you."

She gave a hiccupping sob. "Whatever I do benefits you, and destroys me."

The only thing that might benefit him was to see her happy, he had replied quietly, and gone to his room. This morning, when he left, she had not yet come down.

He settled at his desk, resolving to put her out of his mind, and picked up the papers.

Although the news that Thompson had left for Hong Kong had been a godsend, he had to admit that the press was far less interesting now.

The French were complaining, as usual, seeing the buffer zone as an English ploy somehow intended to rob them of what public opinion, or rather the Parti Colonial, felt was rightfully theirs.

Everything appeared now to hinge on a Lao territory in the Upper Mekong called Mong Sing, over which both France and Britain claimed suzerainty, and possession of this tiny pocket of land was threatening to derail any possible agreement between both Colonial Empires.

Did any of the paper's readers even know where Mong Sing was? he asked himself, but "*Le Courrier de Saigon*" provided the answer, describing it as a province peopled with "peace-loving natives in their colourful garb" who, some twenty years ago, had welcomed a French garrison post that "brought them the joys of civilization".

The unfortunate farmers and fishermen had to be abandoned ten years later when the "iron rule of Siam was once more asserted in this mountainous Eden" which was "indispensable to access the riches of Yunnan". It was on the "French side of the river" and thus, as the Gallic newspaper man wrote, "It is ours, by right."

He shook his head, marvelling at how people could

come to see as indispensable places they had never given a thought to before.

Except Pavie, of course.

That was his old stomping ground.

Well, it would all be decided in London and Paris by that Border Commission his godfather had told him of.

Scott bustled in without knocking, carrying a telegram to be encoded and looked at him brightly. He was still revelling in his status of interim Minister – officially, Captain Jones was on extended sick leave – and hinted at every opportunity that what he really wanted was to be confirmed in this post. Michael briefly wondered if he somehow had found out about the relationship with Lord Dufferin.

"Good day, good, day, weather not too beastly, eh?"

"Here's the latest for Whitehall, you'll see that in just a few months I've really understood this country and I think my views will certainly open some eyes. Oh, yes, say I, that, they will."

He clicked his dentures and rocked on his heels with satisfaction, watching Michael read. "First rate, eh, what do you say?"

Michael was appalled.

Still holding the telegram, he looked up and said, speaking slowly and stressing every word to make sure the man understood how seriously he was alarmed. "You can't send this, sir. It's just not possible."

What, what? How could Crawfurd object? What the hell was wrong with it, eh?

Michael took a deep breath. "What's wrong? I will tell you.

"For starters: '*His Majesty is seriously ill and depressed.*'

"That's probably a fact, although neither you, nor I, nor anybody outside the Palace Inner Court, not even RJ, knows how serious it is, and as to being depressed, well, it's not unexpected, given he had to surrender a large chunk of his Kingdom and have the French occupying the richest province of what he has been allowed to keep.

"But when you continue to say that *'he is thought to be close to suicide...'* Not only have you made that up, you go too far.

"And here: *'The King is as uxorious as King Solomon.'* A bit at odds with being suicidal, isn't it?

"And *'Prince Devawongse is a childish debauchee.'* What on earth allows you to say something so very insulting and untrue about one of our allies?

"And *'The King being incapacitated, the Siamese Crown Council is powerless and considers offering France a protectorate over the Kingdom?'*

"It's absolutely false and you have no right to assert such things."

Scott frowned, very displeased.

He had been asked to analyse the situation at Court, and by George, he had. And Crawfurd was to encode the telegram and send it.

It was an order, he didn't care who his godfather or uncle or whoever was.

Understood?

Michael closed his eyes and clamped his jaw in anger to bite back words he would regret. Understood, he finally managed to utter.

Before leaving the office, the older man gave him a patronizing and contemptuous sneer.

"You look down at the mouth, laddy. Missus troubles?" and without waiting for the answer that Michael, his eyes on his desk, refused to give, continued with a chuckle. "Ah, well, when they're breeding, they're either mad as hornets or over the moon. Don't know which is worse.

"You get cracking on that telegram. Now."

He almost laughed.

The man was a fool but he had, quite unwittingly, made him feel better — about Julie at least. Mad as a hornet... well, yes, she was. It was good to know that she perhaps did not hate him.

He would encode the telegram because he had been instructed to, but he would also write to Lord Dufferin in Paris, who would know how to inform Lord Rosebery. He didn't like going behind his superior's back, and never had for Captain Jones, even when the bluff and outspoken old soldier had gone too far in promising the Siamese British support, but now, with this preposterous buffoon at the helm of the Legation, he had no choice.

He laughed ruefully. Mad as a hornet...

Julie was contrite and tearful at lunch.

"I don't know what possesses me at times. It's as if some demon took over my mind. In fact, Keow says that evil spirits often plague the souls of pregnant women, and it is only by practising meditation that one can be rid of them. But meditation... I don't somehow feel that it is made for European minds."

He laughingly quoted Scott's description of expecting mothers and she brightened. That sounded exactly how she felt.

"So, you think when this child is finally born," she looked down with distaste at her thickening waist, "I shall be myself again?"

Of course she would be. When little Lily or Frederick came — "I think calling him after my godfather would be nice, don't you? And it's pronounceable for his French grandfather."— she would be a perfect mother and he a perfect father, and they would all be as happy as tinkers once more.

He then, to engage her interest in something beyond herself, recounted the interview with Scott and the shockingly inappropriate telegram he had been forced to send.

"How dare he?" she demanded. "I almost think that Edward French would have been a better choice."

Michael shrugged. He didn't think Whitehall would take Scott seriously. The man was just making himself ridiculous.

And as to French, he just went about with a sour look on his face and shirked his duties as best he could, claiming there was no need to serve a government that had treated him so shabbily.

However, did she recall the visit Prince Henri d'Orléans made to Bangkok some three years ago?

She furrowed her brow. Was it not when she was in mourning and accepted no invitations? Yes, yes, it was. She remembered now. What of it?

It appeared that the Prince had written a book about his travels, Bangkok being only the last leg of a journey that took him from Annam and Tonkin to the upper reaches of Laos.

"One must admit the man is intrepid and hardy, such a trip must have been difficult and uncomfortable. Anyway, on the strength of his six-month trip, he is now an expert, as all those travellers are, and his book, besides being a paean to French rule in Indochina is also violently anti-British.

"And there are as well some very nasty descriptions of Siam. Apparently, it's selling very well in the Parti Colonial circles.

"As I've told Scott, that certainly will not help the deliberations of the Border Commission."

The Upper Mekong border Commission was indeed plagued with dissent and mutual suspicion. The flames of discord were stoked by the various articles written by the Prince d'Orléans who was making maximum capital out of the success of his recent opus, and stressed the dangers of the long considered but never implemented British railway project from Burmah to Yunnan.

According to the well-travelled aristocrat, that was the true reason for Lord Rosebery's push to create a buffer zone, so as to withhold the Upper Mekong from French influence – and the French railway line.

Having cowed Develle into submission last December with a article in "*La Politique Coloniale*" describing the project not as a neutral area, but the 'English buffer', Prince Henri now called for a sweeping vote at the next opportunity to "*show that public opinion resolutely rejected the very notion of a buffer state and was determined to maintain all of France's rightful claims to the Upper Mekong.*"

Michael marked the newspaper with a red pencil, and sent it in to Scott's office along with letters to be signed. At the end of the day, before heading home, he put his head in the door and asked, "What did you think, sir?"

"Think of what?" the older man snapped as if he were being disturbed at a very important task, although, from what Michael could see, he was perusing a month-old issue of *Punch*.

The article by Monsieur d'Orléans about the buffer zone, it could complicate things, didn't he think? France might not lend a complaisant ear to the Monarchists, but when they advocated extending the dominion of La République, they were certainly heard.

"Oh, that's what it was about? I don't read French, and anyway, I never thought any opinion of theirs was worth the paper on which it is printed.

"Be a good chap, close the door, will you? Those smells of fish cooking in the street are getting all the way up here."

"So there you have it," he told Julie.

An idiot as head of the British mission, a dishonest

bully at the head of the French one... It almost made him want to get back on the first steamer for London.

"What *is* Pavie up to?" she asked with a laugh.

He would not have sworn to it, but she appeared slightly better and had had no outbursts for ten days, or at least not in his presence.

Pavie was applying his usual ingenuity to exploiting the slightest incident in Battambang or Siem Reap, he replied, and inventing them when there were none. It kept him busy and infuriated RJ. And had she heard from Victor? When was he finally coming to visit?

She shook her head and frowned. Nothing since the hurried note they received at their return. "Why? Are there problems in Chantaboon?"

"No...," he replied slowly. "Not problems — It's just that what was supposed to be a temporary occupation now appears to becoming entrenched."

Camps were built, with moats and fortifications, a depot for more than 500 tons of coal created. He would have liked to hear more from her brother about French intentions.

Of course, there still were reports of mistreatment of the local population, but none had been verified. So she shouldn't worry about that.

In fact, she should worry about nothing.

"BANGKOK, MARCH 27TH 1894

Fie has just brought me my notebook and pencil, so distraught is she at seeing one of my dreadful bouts of anger and melancholia about to seize me, and so, to pacify her, I accept to write a few words.

I feel I cannot go on much longer plunged in such despair, and it is all that I can do to hide it from everyone.

Each morning as I awake I am reminded of the enormity of my sin and each night as I toss under the mosquito net to seek sleep and a few hours' oblivion I relive every minute I spent with Edward.

Shall I be able not to hate this child conceived in sin and guilt? I pray — oh, how fervently I pray — that neither of us survive the birth,

I can barely bring myself to see Fanny or Léonie, they keep on expressing their pleasure at seeing me pregnant, talk about embroidered swaddling clothes and wet nurses and it is all I can do not to blurt out my disgust with myself.

The only place where I find any comfort is the Palace, I am given a room to withdraw to, sob and beat my pillow, and I come out somewhat better.

Keow is quite concerned and considering a ceremony to recall my soul before the evil spirits carry it away forever."

In London, the Prime Minister, Mr Gladstone, offered his resignation to Her Majesty the Queen, who appointed Lord Rosebery as his successor and Lord Kimberley became Foreign Secretary.

"What d'you make of him?" Scott wanted to know.

Michael shook his head. He knew nothing of the man, save the fact that he was Liberal and had been Secretary of State for India.

"Oh? I thought all you toffs knew each other."

The Border Commission talks broke down in total disarray, and accusations of underhandedness and treachery, if not bandied openly at each other by its members, were vicariously exchanged in the press.

"Mong Sing, Mong Sing, Mong Sing" was the general clamour and that small mountainous province where nary a local had ever seen either a Frenchman or an Englishman became the prize in a vicious competition to access the Chinese markets.

It was thus decided than only a local investigation commission might allow a better understanding of the respective claims.

"Do you hear, do you hear?" Scott rushed up to Michael even before he had removed his hat. "I go to Mong Sing."

He paused an instant and cocked his head reflectively.

"Actually, the correct pronunciation is 'Muang Sing', but that matters not."

"Congratulations, Sir," Michael smiled with unfeigned pleasure. The mission should keep the chargé away for a good four or five months.

"So you are returning to your beloved Shan."

"Not at all, not at all, the tribes of Muang Sing are Tai Lue. Although..." he paused and thought. "I suppose you might say that the Tai Lue are a subdivision of the Shan. They're also called the Dai, and wear turbans, like Mussulmans or Hindoos. Strange, that, eh? So remote and yet all sharing characteristics...

"Monsieur Pavie is to be my counterpart on the French side."

"Sir," Michael stated with conviction. "I cannot think of any two better choices."

He walked home, stepping lightly all the way, and changed his mind when he reached the *soi* leading to the Oriental, deciding to stop for a celebratory drink.

At that hour the cool lobby was full of men in white suits talking business and drinking whisky-sodas, while wealthy-looking Sikhs in rainbow turbans whispered the latest price of pepper under the potted palms and a few English women lingered over tea and gossip.

There was no one he felt like talking to and headed for the bar, nearly bumping in to Rolin-Jaequemyns, who, he said, was looking for his wife.

"You've heard?" Michael asked, incapable of keeping his satisfaction to himself any longer.

"About the appointments of the good Mr Scott and

Mr Pavie as Border Commissioners?" the Belgian replied with an ironic smile, and nodded.

Yes indeed. A very sound decision, yes, none better. It would make all their lives easier.

But Mrs Crawfurd, how was she? "A delightful lady, yes, delightful. Lovely, intelligent and unaffected."

He put his hand on Michael's shoulder. Being a father, he said, had brought him the greatest joys of his life. "You shall soon discover all this," he said with moist eyes. "Ah, to do it again... You are a lucky man."

I suppose I am, all things considered, Michael mused as he pushed the gate open. I suppose I am.

Louis was sitting on the verandah steps, looking disconsolate and dragging his bare feet in the gravel, pushing leaves around with a bit of bamboo. Michael's heart went out to him. Poor little chap, his life had been so unsettled lately.

"Mama is not well?" he asked sitting down next to him.

The boy nodded, and answered in Siamese, although he understood everything said in English. "Fie is with her."

She would soon be better, and all would be fine, he attempted to reassure the child and himself both.

All would soon be as before, except there would be a little brother or sister for Louis to play with. The child nodded again, looking unconvinced.

They sat side by side for a moment, then Louis took him by the hand, "Ma du, ma du." — "No, Louis, say: "come see,"to show him a dead bullfrog that he had found in the garden.

Crouching on the ground, he prodded it with his bamboo. "What's inside?"

Michael got down on his haunches. If Louis asked "What's inside?" in English, he would get a knife from cook, and they could find out.

Yes, good boy, very good.

Julie found them dissecting the frog on the verandah floor when she came down looking wan and tired, and they both glanced up guiltily, expecting her to shriek in disgust, but she just squatted uncomfortably next to them.

"What's that? Oh, Louis..." The tears that were never far, overflowed and she clasped him to her. "That's something your Papa must have done when he was a little boy like you. He would be so proud..."

"And that, my darling, is one of the reasons I love you," Michael told her afterwards over dinner, once Fie had dragged the protesting Louis off to take a bath, shaking her head at *farangs'* strange ways.

"Any other woman would have told him to get rid of that horrid frog."

He took her hand and kissed it. " RJ told me I am a lucky man, and he is right. He just doesn't know how lucky."

But she shook her head and looked away.

"BANGKOK APRIL 12ᵀᴴ 1894

Victor has come for the Songkran celebrations. I do my best to be cheerful and he appears to notice nothing of our strange, tense, household.

He is perhaps less ebullient than he was during those dreary negotiations of last year, and the absence of his officer friends, most notably young Le Myre de Vilers, probably explains this. My brother is easily influenced, as I have always known, whether for better or for worse.

His talk of Chantaboon is all about a clinic to be opened for the locals, as well as a school, where only French will be taught.

Why only French? I ask, and he tells me that now they have registered so many natives, whether Lao, Vietnamese, Chinese or Khmer, they must be considered as French, and educated accordingly.

Michael pointed out mildly that, from what he understood, the occupation was due to end soon — practically all of the conditions of the ultimatum have been met, and the last few ones remaining — the judging of Phra Yoth, and also something to do with policing the neutral area — should be met soon, so what was the point of these lengthy and costly projects?

But Victor replies that there never was any intention of surrendering Chantaboon, all the more so, he adds, 'that Battambang and Siem Reap were seized from under our noses. Don't you see that some of the clauses were drafted precisely in such a way that they offer infinite possibilities to challenge their application?

'It was exactly as Monsieur Le Myre de Vilers and Pavie intended.'

And did Victor think that honest dealing? Michael continued in the same quiet and amicable voice.

'I am a soldier,' Victor replied, looking embarrassed at last, 'not a diplomat.

'But you know better than I that nations often resort to double-dealing, take England with India, for instance.'

We left the subject at that.

My brother really does talk too much.

I drag myself to the various ceremonies and politely pour water on Keow's head and hands, and she does the same to me.

'Songkran water wash away misfortunes and sins of past year,' she remarked in passing. If only it were true…

She also tells me she has arranged for a soul-retrieving ritual next week. I dare not tell Michael.

Bangkok April 19ᵗʰ 1894

It seems my soul — my 'khwann' — was difficult to call back, so far away had it gone. The special monk who performed the rites told Keow that he had felt that I did not want the **khwann** *to return to my body, that I was pushing it away.*

I have no memory of the actual ceremony, only of an elaborate tray of flowers and offerings, much chanting, the little princesses looking suitably concerned, that monk who was not wearing the usual saffron-coloured robes and kept his hand on my wrist, and Keow who remained seated at my other side throughout.

But my mind was escaping far away, I could see Louis, with the beard he had when I last saw him and his eyes shining with light, looking down on me with infinite kindness, a strange cawing black bird, not a crow, something less threatening, whose flapping wings made a leathery sound as it rose from me — 'Not crow.' Keow said when she asked me what I remembered of that strange moment. She considered for a moment. 'I think hornbill. Perhaps sad man, perhaps sad you. Perhaps both.'

She presented me with a wide gold bracelet, saying the thread that ties my soul to my body is inside. I am to wear it always.

'Better?' she wanted to know.

I was probing my mind the way you feel for bruises after a tumble, and could not tell. 'Lighter. I feel lighter,' was the way I finally expressed it, and she was pleased. 'Better come later, never mind.'

Meanwhile, in London, Lord Kimberley, becoming acquainted with what Whitehall was referring to as the "Siamese problem", was increasingly exasperated with French claims to Mong Sing.

His terse instructions to the Legation in Bangkok were to verify Pavie's claim that Prince Devawongse had indeed confirmed French title and deed to the province. "Please advise soonest."

As Edward French had decided to wash his hands of the whole matter — "It has only brought me troubles, you can go to inquire from the Belgian mountebank yourself" — Michael took the boat to the Foreign Ministry and asked Rolin-Jaequemyns if he might find out the status of Mong Sing from the Prince.

"How I should know?" cried the Special Advisor whose syntax was unravelling in his pique. "His Highness is annoyed with me, and answers not my questions. He says

I blame him for all the problems with the French refusing to evacuate Chantaboon.

"Well, *mon Prince*, always I reply, is it not the case that we had agreed you would not sign and you signed? And he now sulks.

"Prince Damrong tries to mend fences between us, but even he is not heard. And His Majesty is still not well."

Michael murmured his sympathy.

"So the possession of Mong Sing, I cannot tell you, but if it was Siamese and on the left bank... well, that seems to make it French, does it not?" Rolin-Jaequemyns continued. "But Mong Sing is of no concern to me, it is all I can do to try and start all the reforms I had projected...

"His Highness balks at changing anything in the Kingdom in His Majesty's absence. We were doing very well before the Europeans, he says, the Kingdom had dominion over Cambodia and Laos, and now look at us.

"Why should we do as the Europeans tell us to do?

"What right have they do decide how we should educate our people or judge our criminals? They come from the other side of the world to bring us what they call civilization, but gave us nothing but discord and unhappiness.

And...," the Belgian looked at Michael sadly and opened his hands. "When I hear him speak thus, I find that he is right."

Of course he was right, Julie commented forcefully when Michael recounted his conversation. Who had ever heard of Mong Sing and what right did they have to fight over it like dogs over bones?

And France and England now poised for a conflict, because of that remote place no one could locate on a map?

She had never heard anything more ridiculous.

Michael snorted. He had, just that same afternoon: some French politician called Flourens was accusing the

English in the press of attempting to create a northern Mekong base to invade Indochina from the river.

"And meanwhile we British fear that if the French take possession of Mong Sing, it would allow them to carry out incursions into British Burmah and try to take over the Empire.

I tell you, everyone seems to have lost their minds."

"BANGKOK MAY 17TH 1894

I still manage my classes at the Palace, but I know not for how long...

Although I recently started feeling as if I were walking on air, and my body were weightless, the lurching of the carriage on the uneven paving may be dangerous, according to Doctor Hertz.

I get treated there with tremendous care, massaged — except for my feet, as that could precipitate a premature delivery, according to Keow — oiled, anointed, and fed all the delicacies a royal mother-to-be receives along with superstitions as laughable as those of my mother's maid who always told us you shouldn't look at a chimneysweep if you didn't want to have a black baby.

Here, when I tell Keow that it is perfectly safe for me to use scissors, drink cold water or take cool baths, she just stares me down.

'Khwann you, back, yes? Happy now, yes? No cold, never mind,' and she gives Fie very strict instructions on what I am allowed to do.

Childbearing, it appears, is a 'hot' condition, and as such, is sensitive to chills.

Tempting as it is to remind her that she herself has never herself borne a child, I bite back any disrespect and promise to obey her instructions.

It is indeed true that, as she had promised, 'better came later' and the black moods seem to have flown away a month ago with that bird — or was it the day after, when I first felt the baby quicken?

Is it the child? Is it because my khwann has returned?

I have grown to accept what happened, all that happened, and try not to look back.

Michael does not yet seem to believe it and treats me as carefully as a keg of dynamite. Six weeks ago, it would have enraged me. Now, I feel guilty and sad at how badly I must have bruised him.

He is overworked, the entire weight of the Legation resting on him, with Scott as erratic as ever and French who has not emerged from his sulk.

But as Pavie — who has already left for Mong Sing to whip up a sudden love for France among the natives — cannot manufacture his usual crises, there is one thing less to worry about, all the more so as Phra Yoth, the official accused of murdering the Frenchman, Inspector Grosgurin, was acquitted last month by the special court, only one witness having been produced by the prosecution against seven who were called by the defendant's lawyer.

It would seem Inspector Grosgurin was neither in bed or ill at the time, and that the Tirailleurs Annamites attacked the Siamese column.

That is not going to go down well in Saigon.

Meanwhile, a new Minister of Foreign Affairs has been appointed in Paris, a Monsieur Hanotaux, known for his dislike of anything and anyone English.

The Parti Colonial will love him."

The Government-General of Indochina was indeed incensed at having Phra Yoth acquitted, and although no new elements to prove his guilt were produced, a new trial was demanded, pursuant to the agreement forced upon Siam the year before.

When Michael returned from the Legation, he found Julie in the sitting room, surrounded by French newspapers sent from Saigon.

"Did you see this?" she demanded, waving a recent copy of *Le Matin*, in which Le Myre de Vilers was quoted as saying that he was not in the least surprised at the acquittal — not that he believed Phra Yoth innocent, far from it — but because he was familiar with the Asian mind and the manner in which treaties were interpreted in this region of the world. "Le Myre is in fact accusing the Siamese and the court of being biased and liars," she spat with disgust.

Michael considered her warily.

She had been much better these past weeks, certainly, and had suffered none of the dark spells that left her trembling with rage, and he with fears for her sanity, but he worried anything might set it one off again.

Still, she had not taken any interest in Siamese affairs for so long, he decided to see it as a good sign.

"Yes, I did see it," he replied easily as he sank into an armchair. "Infuriating, isn't it?"

She pushed on the arms of the settee to rise heavily from the cushions, and picked up another paper, which she waved in front of him.

"Here, they imply that Le Myre and Pavie will force another trial. Do you think it likely?"

Most likely, he said, and rang for Pon to bring him a drink.

If fact, he had heard it was to happen in June — "but it's not official yet. Some French officials are in Bangkok to discuss the setting up the joint tribunal that will re-try poor Phra Yoth — and will no doubt this time find him guilty."

That would make for an interesting spectacle, she mused. Well worth seeing, *n'est-ce pas?* Just as he was about to agree, he caught her studiedly careless tone, and peered at her bland face.

"No," he said with finality, "You cannot attend the trial. It's unthinkable."

She shrugged.

What made him imagine for a moment she would want to attend?

He shook his head. "You. I know you. And I know that tone of voice."

She laughed. "I can't deny I would like to see for myself how shameless Le Myre and his clique can be."

Well — it just wasn't possible, he repeated. Did she not realize how much her pregnancy would show by then?

"Not to mention," he added with finality, "that you would not be allowed in."

"I suppose you are right." She dropped the newspaper on the settee, and sighed as she moved towards the door, leaving him a bit surprised at her acquiescence — it was very unlike her not to argue...

"Bangkok, June 1ˢᵗ1894

This preposterous re-trial of Phra Yoth is to be held in a few days, and admission is only allowed to those who have been granted tickets — exactly as if this were a theatrical performance, and I suppose it is nothing more — it certainly is not justice!

I have persuaded Fanny to apply for two tickets, basing her request on the claim that she has long been opposed to the corrupt Siamese system of justice — ever since her husband was convicted then executed after a mockery of a trial — and has always admired the way France hands down the law.

The French Embassy officials know of her efforts in providing legal and financial assistance to many unfortunate people who are unjustly accused — Hardouin even used the word 'crusade' when describing it to me — and probably will be delighted in having someone who is both a Siamese and British subject as a witness to their undoubtedly superior way of doing things.

She was reluctant at first, but agreed to send the letter I composed, and gradually became caught up in my indignation.

She even suggested adding the quotation 'France, mother of laws' to strengthen the obsequiousness of our missive and we ended up giggling like schoolgirls.

Michael, I believe, does not suspect anything.

He tells me that Scott has delayed his departure to Mong Sing so as to be present at the trial, and that RJ has advised His Majesty not to attend.

Apparently, the organization of the proceedings themselves have been debated in detail and with no small measure of acrimony, the Siamese insisting on having Phra Yoth appear free, and ensuring he is to be informed of the charges against him.

How could it be otherwise? I ask Michael, but he says that coming from Le Myre de Vilers, nothing would surprise him.

I can no longer go to the Palace, and busy myself around the house, for want of anything better to do."

Julie appeared to have emerged from the thrall of her dark and dangerous spell, Michael reflected gratefully as he headed to the Legation early in the cool of the morning, although he certainly would prefer her less obsessed with the latest news about the trial.

She wanted to know everything, the names of the French judges, who was to act as advocate for the accused, and who was to translate.

He couldn't help but feel there was something rather unhealthy about her interest, but, of course, now that she could no longer go to the Palace for her classes, she needed something to occupy her mind.

Were all expectant mothers so passionate about matters outside the realm of their home? Somehow, he doubted it, but then his wife was an unusual woman.

Anyway, Phra Yoth would be tried soon, and found guilty — for such was the foregone conclusion of the coming pantomime — Scott would at long last head off to the hills of Mong Sing, and he himself would, he hoped, come back to a normal life.

If, of course, he thought wryly, one could see as normal a life such as his, in love with a native servant and with a headstrong and unpredictable wife expecting a child by another man ...

"JUNE 2ND 1894.

The admission tickets have been granted — one for Madame la Baronne Preecha, and the other for her unnamed 'advisor'!

The opening session is day after tomorrow, at the French Consulate.

Michael is not attending, thank heavens — although I think he would not dare have me removed forcibly — but Mr Scott is.

If I wear a heavy veil and sit at the back, I think he will not notice me.

"I can barely see or breathe though my veil," Julie muttered as they alighted from the buggy in the *soi* that led to the French Legation and joined the small crowd waiting to be ushered in.

"Still, keep it over your face," Fanny replied looking about nervously. "At least until we are seated."

She was beginning to feel quite out of place, and shook her head. "Although truly, I wonder who you are hoping to fool? Could there be another six-month pregnant woman who might want to be here?"

If the heavily armed marines guarding the doorway at the top of the steps only blinked when they saw the two women present their passes before entering, Julie was aware of a shocked murmur as they passed the door before selecting seats towards the back of the big room.

"So much for being unnoticed," she whispered, laughter in her voice, as she spotted Monsieur Malherbe who stared at her in disapproval when she lifted her veil with a sigh of relief. She gave him a pleasant smile and nodded, and Léonie's husband remembered his manners in time to nod back.

"The main thing is to look as if our presence were absolutely normal," she stated, fanning herself with what she hoped was a confident and careless air.

"The main thing," Fanny hissed back, "is to be quiet."

Other people filed though, the American chargé with a Swedish businessman, Admiral de Richelieu grimacing darkly at everyone, Mr Scott chatting to the German Minister.

Julie lifted her open fan before her face but the British chargé noticed nothing, so busy was he examining the carved wood panels as if to put a price on them. He was shown by a French Consulate employee to an armchair at the very front, where he was joined by Gustave Rolin-Jaequemyns, eyes downcast, a worried expression on his kind and tired face.

Monsieur Hardouin crept in after them, hunched as if under the great weight of his responsibility. He gave RJ and Scott a cold nod and and sat to the very end of the front row, mopping his neck and head and smoothing his sparse stringy hair. A noisy group then followed — "Journalists." Fanny whispered, recognizing Henry Norman, a friend of hers, — but the boisterous press members were curtly hushed by the guards ordering all to rise because finally, sweeping in in their magnificent robes, the French judges made a dramatic entrance, followed by the Siamese judges in drab western attire, and all busily arranged themselves along a long baize-covered table.

"Just like the theatre, isn't it? The one in red with the ermine trim should be Monsieur Mondot, the President of the Court of Appeals in Hanoi. He is to preside over the trial.

"Look at his face, so full of contempt for all of us," Julie commented very low. "I guess the other one in red must be Monsieur Cammate, from Saigon, he's a Counsellor, not so high a grade — so no ermine. Therefore the one in black is Prosecutor Fuynel, from My Tho."

Fanny paled suddenly, as everyone stood once more. "Oh, good Lord... Prince Devawongse."

She made to curtsy, but Julie pulled her back down into her seat.

"No, he hasn't seen you, keep still."

Fanny was shaken, and kept twisting her fingers. "I don't like this, I truly don't like this. We have no business here. I should not have let you talk me into coming. Look, we are the only women."

Julie peered around and whispered back that it wasn't quite true, there were two other women, Mrs Mitchell, the solicitor's wife who was seated by her husband, and behind her, attempting to be as discreet as they themselves were, Emilie Rolin-Jaequemyns, who gave them a diffident smile.

And then both she and Fanny forgot their discomfort because the accused, Phra Yoth, was being escorted in, in a clanging of the chains binding both wrists and ankles, and greeted by a mutter of disbelief and dismay.

"I can't believe this! He was supposed to appear free." Julie gasped over the general, ominous hum of angry protests coming from the Siamese, but also from some Europeans, who were shaking their heads and scowling at the French judges.

Prince Devawongse leapt to his feet, and tried to rush up to the prisoner, but was restrained by Rolin Jaequemyns' hand on his arm.

"Silence! Silence!"

President Mondot rapped on the table with his gavel, glared around the room and announced he would read the act of indictment.

Clearing his throat with a phlegmy cough, he picked up a piece of paper, but did not appear to read it, as if the words it contained were seared in his mind. His voice swelling in indignation, lingering over every detail, he described what he insisted on calling the treacherous and unwarranted ambush that led to Inspector Grosgurin's death.

His eyes glowered unflinchingly as he waved his wide red sleeves and pointed his finger and proceeded to accuse Phra Yoth, Commissioner of Kham Muon, of premeditated murder, assassination, theft and incendiarism and described the rather small and commonplace man standing in irons before him as a veritable blood-thirsty monster.

"What's the difference between murder and assassination?" Fanny muttered behind her fan, while Mr Tilleke, Phra Yoth's Singhalese lawyer translated President Mondot's speech.

Julie shook her head. She did not know.

The prosecutor continued to declaim his charges but seemed to lose vigour as the heat in the room became oppressive; Phra Yoth, seemingly unaware of the gravity of the charges against him was nodding calmly and smiling at his lawyer and a guard dozed off, lulled by the rhythmic swish of the punkah.

A sudden clatter at the door stopped President Mondot's peroration and he scowled at the interruption over his spectacles. With the rest of the audience, Julie turned to look as well and clapped her hand to her mouth in horror and dismay.

Edward Thompson, with an apologetic smile to the judges, had just entered the room and leaned over to right the stool he had upset.

With whispered greetings, and shaking hands here and there, he began to pick his way through the audience, scanning the room to spot a free chair near the other members of the press before finally settling near Henry Norman, oblivious to the prosecutor's ill-contained exasperation as the muted hubbub and the scraping of chairs subsided.

Too late, Julie hunched down in her chair and attempted to hide her face behind Fanny's shoulder, but he had seen her and started as their eyes met, his head snapping back as if he had been slapped.

"What is it? What is the matter?" Fanny demanded, fanning her friend furiously. "Is it the heat? Are you unwell? Do you have pains?"

Julie just moved her hands in denegation, unable to speak.

Gulping hard to attempt to control her nausea, she wanted to give in to her instinct to push everybody aside and flee from the crowded chamber but somehow managed to control herself and not create another disturbance when their presence here appeared to be forgotten if not accepted.

Feeling her heart beating in her throat, she remained frozen in her chair, and finally murmured that it was nothing, just a dizzy spell.

Fanny looked around and spotted Thompson who could not detach his eyes from them, and raised her eyebrows thoughtfully. "Oh. Oh, I see."

Then, as Julie blanched and began to stammer, she said in a soothing voice, "Hush. It's all right."

In her sickening turmoil of emotion, Julie was aware of one thing above all. Edward must not see her standing up, must not notice her ungainly, thickened figure, must not, even for a moment, wonder if the child might be his.

She was not listening to the aggressive questioning of President Mondot, was barely aware of his disparaging comments when one, then two, then three witnesses for the defence were brought before the court then ridiculed and dismissed, hardly heard the hiss of disapproval from the audience when he described in vociferous tones the death of the unfortunate Grosgurin and rejected out of hand any plea of self-defence on the part of the Siamese.

She could only feel her breath coming in ragged sobs, her fingers tight on her fan, the child kicking within her, and waves of shame at the memory of heart-stopping pleasure in Edward's arms.

Finally, Fanny touched her elbow. "Come, they are adjourning until tomorrow." And when Julie shook her head, said kindly, but in a voice that would brook no objection. "You must. Let me help you get up."

Of course, moving against the people filing out towards the verandah and the stairs, Edward was coming up to them, his mouth set in a grim half smile.

"Baroness Preecha, Mrs Crawfurd."

Fanny nodded back, coolly. "Mr Thompson. You have returned from Hong Kong?"

He couldn't miss this trial, the journalist replied with a shrug. His readers lapped up any story of French colonial arrogance and double-dealing.

"But I see you are to be congratulated, Mrs Crawfurd." he added with a sneer. "Was it wise, in your condition, to attend this farcical event?"

Loyal Fanny hastened to exonerate her friend. "I asked Julie to come with me to translate if need be. My knowledge of French is indifferent at best, but I am interested in comparing the French system of justice with the Siamese.

"However," she added, turning to Julie, "I believe we have seen enough, and shall not return tomorrow."

Still speechless, Julie nodded her assent, and moved between the abandoned seats and the group of people who still lingered on the verandah discussing the morning's hearing.

She overheard Scott say in playful tones that Phra Yoth was as cool as the proverbial cucumber, and Monsieur Malherbe growl that France's image would not come out of this untarnished, when Edward grasped her elbow. "You are very pale, Mrs Crawfurd. Come, let me assist you down these stairs."

She could not shake his hand off without making a scene, she could not refuse a gentleman's assistance, she could not scream " Go away, let me be!", so she obediently let herself be guided down the steep and narrow steps, and only pulled away when he whispered that he must see her, speak to her, that he would come by her house in the afternoon.

As he handed her into the waiting buggy, she finally said her first words to him, speaking in a firm and final voice. "You are right, it was unwise to come. I believe this is the last time I shall appear in public, and shall receive no visits at home. So this is farewell, Mr Thompson."

And, moving over to make place for Fanny, she rapped on the window to tell the coachman to go.

They both remained silent during the short ride back, but when they were about to enter the house, Fanny waved away Julie's halting murmur, "Join me for lunch. I must tell you – about Thompson –" with a understanding shrug.

"No need. We all saw how relentlessly Thompson pursued you last winter. You behaved thoughtlessly in allowing it and now feel embarrassed.

"Had I been the subject of his attentions, I might have done the same. It must have been so flattering!"

She gave a dismissive half laugh, and Julie to her immense relief, realized Fanny had imagined her engaged in no more than a harmless flirtation.

Or perhaps, she then thought with a sickening lurch of her stomach, was she simply pretending? "But truly," her friend continued, "the man is quite incorrigible – could he not see you are expecting? Take my arm – Oh dear..." She looked up at the verandah and whispered that Michael was waiting for her and looked unhappy.

"I believe we have some unpleasant explaining to do."

Michael was indeed unhappy.

In fact, he was as angry as his mild and gentle nature enabled him to be, and as he watched Julie remove her hat and give it to Pon, he could not find words to express the depth of his irritation.

Ever since he had heard from the Legation coachman that his wife was seen entering the French Consulate, he had rehearsed the biting things he would say but now found himself unable to utter them, faced with the two women who stood before him, Fanny with a chastened and apologetic expression and Julie looking less defiant and far more upset than he expected.

He shook his head, ruefully.

"I cannot say I am surprised, Julie, although I imagined you more sensible. But I expected better from you, Fanny, than to follow my wife in her foolish schemes."

Fanny earnestly repeated what she had told Thompson: she wanted to see a French trial and had thus applied for tickets and asked Julie to come along.

Michael shook his head again.

"You both wanted to thumb your noses at the French, and saw this as some kind of lark. And please, Fanny, do not lie. I know this was Julie's idea.

"Can you imagine how ridiculous this makes me look, that I am unable to control my wife?

"I told you—" he struggled not to shout, and took a deep breath, "I told you, did I not, that you were not to attend?

"Had I thought for a moment you would ignore my wishes, I would have forbidden you to leave the house."

Julie closed her eyes briefly and sighed.

"You should have learned by now that you cannot forbid me anything, Michael. However, I am very sorry, more than you can imagine, that I defied you. Now may we please come in and sit? I am very tired.

"In fact, I think I need my bed."

When Michael joined her, he found her lying in her darkened room, with Fie bustling about her and glaring at him as if he were to blame for Julie's prostration.

Sitting at her bedside, he took her cold and limp hand.

"I never expected you to be afraid of my displeasure," he whispered with a low laugh. "Have you at last become a proper, husband-fearing wife?"

She pulled her hand from his, and sat up, resting against a mound of pillows and managed to respond in kind, lightly. "My dear. Afraid of you?

"How little you know me," and continued, haltingly, "Truly, Michael, it was not a lark, as you said.

"It's just that — well, France is my country. I felt I needed to take some kind of stand, to be a witness, to show... well, to show that there are honest people amongst us."

He stroked her forehead. Yes, he knew. He understood, although, it did put him in an awkward position, she did realize, this, did she not?

She took a deep breath, and was about to tell him of Thompson's return when they heard Pon bounding up the wooden steps, announcing that a man, yes, Khun Eddod who had often been here, was at the door and asking for Maem. He had told him Maem was unwell, but the man was insisting.

Should he serve him a drink?

Michael rose up from the chair, his face thunderous.

"Who? Eddod? Edward Thompson? Why did you not tell me?"

She was about to, why did she think her so upset? Julie cried, grabbing his arm with both hands, her face ashen.

"You must send him away, Michael, please, send him away, do not let him in, please, please." He shook his arm free and, in silence, his expression grim, he followed Pon to the verandah.

A battered book bag at his feet, Thompson stared levelly at him, looking neither apologetic nor embarrassed, as if he had every right to go up to Julie's bedroom, Michael thought in amazement at the man's utter lack of restraint, or even manners.

He squared his shoulders and forced himself to speak in a calm voice. "You must leave. Julie is resting and does not wish to see you."

The journalist shook his head. "I must see her. Please do not force me to push past you, but if I have to, I will."

Michael was aware of the greater strength of the man before him, and even more aware of how appealing he must have been to Julie, with his tousled mane of dark hair, his rumpled linen suit and his dishevelled and rakish air of energy and adventure.

He was so... so vital, so masculine, so... everything that he, Michael, was not.

He felt completely ineffectual and ridiculous in contrast, with his portly figure, in shirtsleeves and in stocking feet, his wispy curls stuck to his head and his voice wavering as he repeated that Julie was entertaining no visits.

"If need be, I will have you thrown out by the servants."

Thompson gave a short laugh.

"Truly? And what if I were to tell you that the child she is carrying is probably mine?"

How he was able to produce such a contemptuous snort, Michael never knew.

"Thompson, you are either drunk or mad, and insult a lady's reputation.

"So, once again, stop making yourself ridiculous, and let Julie be.

"She will not see you."

Thompson's face seemed frozen in his belligerent sneer, but his voice was hoarse with hurt. "I love her, and I know she loves me. She told me once that if she wanted it, you would release her. Is that true?"

Michael drew himself up to his full height, a good several inches shorter, he realized, than the damnably attractive man before him.

"I am sorry you love her, for she does not love you, she regrets whatever weakness she may have had for you, and no, I shall never release her, or at least, not to one such as you.

"Now, go, Edward, please.

"If indeed you love her as you say, go. And do not come back."

His head to one side, his expression sullen, the journalist considered him at length, and Michael could see a vein throbbing at his neck, the dark stubble on his chin and the frayed and yellowed collar of his shirt. Finally, he hoisted his canvas book bag over his shoulder and shook his head in defeat.

"I do not understand you, and I do not understand her," he muttered, turning on his heel, stumbled down the verandah steps and gave a vicious kick to a toy of Louis' lying on the gravel walk before slamming the garden gate behind him.

Julie was crying quietly in her bed when he came back to sit beside her.

"He left, and I think will not come back." he whispered, but she just stared at the wall.

"Is that what you really wanted? Are you sure?" and when she nodded silently, added, "My darling, can you ever forgive me?"

In surprise, she rose on one elbow to better see his face.

Forgive him? She was going to ask the same of him. He gently took the balled up handkerchief from her hand, and wiped the tears away from her cheeks, then put his hand on her belly so as to feel the baby kick, and remind them both, he thought, of what mattered most.

"It is my fault, mine alone. I never should have ... I

had no idea …," he faltered, but managed to complete his thought, and find the right word, "No idea… how… seductive he could be."

Julie gave him a sad smile, and they remained hand in hand throughout the afternoon until the last rays of the sun flickered over the mango tree and left them in darkness.

"BANGKOK, JUNE 18ᵀᴴ 1894

So it is over, Phra Yoth has been sentenced to twenty years of hard labour and Edward has left.

It is so strange that Michael had never tried to feel the baby move before, and stranger still that we now feel closer, joined in our common longing for a man who shall never return."

Lily Delphine Crawfurd was born on the 25th of August 1894 in the European section of Siriraj Hospital and the birth was duly registered at the British Consulate.

On the same day, at the French Legation, Joseph Pilinski, a diplomat recently arrived from Batavia, was informing the Ministry in Paris that he hoped to soon register 45,000 protégés in Bangkok alone, besides the several thousand Khmers, Laos and Karikali Indians who had already been granted French privileged status.

"These figures," he wrote "do not include the 27,000 Chinese Catholics administered by the French Foreign missionaries or the protégés in our province of Chantaboon. Once the consulates in Nan, Korat and Battambang are operational, we can also expect a massive increase in the numbers.

Thus, when the majority shall owe allegiance to us, we shall accomplish the task Siam thwarted when she capitulated to our second ultimatum and create the conditions for a quiet and bloodless takeover of the entire country."

Chapter XIV

"Bangkok, 15th of September 1894

Lily is perfect in every way."

Julie let the pencil drop on the coverlet, and rested back on her pillows.

She was barely emerging from the aching, restless fever that followed the delivery and every movement seemed to drain whatever little strength she had.

She could hear the baby fretting in the next room and the new wet-nurse's soothing voice. What was her name? Ah, yes, Phim... a young, sturdy girl from Isaan, the Northeast, who had lost her child at birth.

Julie shuddered in horror and sympathy. For all her torment and fears throughout the long, bleak months of her pregnancy, it now seemed impossible to believe that she had often wished a similar fate for the small, dark-haired and rosy beauty who had grasped her finger and opened slate-blue eyes on the world. "She will have grey eyes, like you." Michael had remarked, holding the infant with surprising confidence, and stroked her petal-soft cheek. He looked up at Julie, without even attempting to hide the tear that trickled down his cheek. "I did not know it was possible to be so happy."

Louis burst in noisily, carrying a picture book and climbed on the bed to snuggle next to her. "Read." he ordered.

"Louis, Mama is tired," she protested, then relented when she saw his sad little face, drew him near her, and began to turn the pages, relishing the weight of his head on her shoulder and the feeling that he trusted her once more, after his horrified and betrayed expression when being presented with the swaddled bundle Michael was holding so proudly.

Ever since, the boy had been moody and withdrawn, hiding in corners, whimpering at mealtimes, refusing to share Nhu Dam's games and glaring at Fie when she tried to jolly him out of his moods.

"He feels abandoned," Michael said. He remembered when his sister Dahlia was born; it was as if his world had come to an end.

Perhaps... he had an idea, he said thoughtfully. Give me a few days.

And in the meantime, he spent long hours with him, cutting open frogs and caterpillars, and patiently encouraging him to speak English.

How strange... From being an amused, slightly remote uncle figure, Michael was becoming a devoted father, even to Louis, she reflected with bemused gratitude for the time he spent with her son. Time that should have been devoted to briefing a new Consul-General and Chargé, Maurice de Bunsen, come to replace both Edward French who was returning to England and James Scott who had finally been acknowledged by London as a liability.

"What is he like?"

Well, crisp, fortyish, single, Rugby and Oxford educated. Not particularly friendly. A career diplomat, therefore more cautious than Jones and certainly less prone to erratic and sweeping views than Scott.

"As to whether he'll be able to deal with Pavie... only time will tell."

The shadows were lengthening in her room and though the open windows, the dusk had turned the sky to lilac.

"Mama get up to eat?" Louis asked in a tiny voice, hopeful that life might come back to normal.

She nodded; she would try.

"Listen, do you hear the gate? Michael is home."

The boy bounded down the stairs and she heard his shout of astonished delight float upstairs, "Mama, *ma du, ma du!*" along with Fie's protesting loudly at something and Michael's quiet laugh "No, Louis, remember, in English. Say Mama, come see. No, we can't bring him up."

Him?

She pulled on a wrapper and carefully descended the stairs, feeling dizzy.

"Mama, look!"

It was a monkey, a small gibbon, with little fretful hands and shaggy golden fur. He had a leather collar around his neck, and was perched on Louis' shoulder, his round worried eyes darting around. He looked strangely touching and dignified, as if politely attempting to make the best of his new surroundings whilst hiding his fear.

"Mama, Michael says he's for me!"

She sat down weakly on a rattan armchair. Really?

Fie was grumbling in the background, muttering dire warnings of poisonous monkey bites and damaged property.

No, Michael reassured her. The animal was clean, tame, and friendly. In fact, its name was Pouan, which meant "friend".

"Mama, *ling tua lek ni yu thini dai mai*?"

Both Michael and Louis looked at her beseechingly, and she felt she could not refuse them, after all the heartache she had caused them both these past months; she smiled in surrender. Only if Louis said: "Can the little monkey stay?" But not in the house.

"Where…?" she began to ask, but Michael came to sit beside her and explained, relieved laughter still in his voice.

The gibbon belonged to a Dutch family who was leaving Bangkok, they could not take it with them, and were looking for someone to adopt it. He had seen it at their house, and been amused by its friendly antics — it seemed to him Pouan was just what Louis might need to feel better about life.

Pouan was indeed tame and friendly, but revealed himself to be an accomplished thief, snatching fruit from the kitchen, bread from the breakfast table on the verandah and clothes drying on the line. He was also a tease, pulling the cat's tail, jumping on the gardener's back or tweaking Somboon's turban and soon stole the hearts of the household, even Fie's. He was never far from Louis' arms, and Julie suspected that at night he crept through the boy's window instead of sleeping on his perch at the foot of the big mango tree.

Victor, when he came to meet his new niece, was enchanted with the gibbon, so much so that he wanted one for himself.

"It would be company in Chantaboon and keep me amused, you cannot imagine how boring life is there."

Well, shouldn't the occupation now come to an end? Michael asked reasonably.

After all, Develle had assured Lord Rosebery — and confirmed it in writing — that it was to last only a few weeks, or months at most.

"Yes, I know you did tell us that Pavie and Le Myre never meant it to end, but they cannot force their views upon their ministers, surely.

"With that farce of a re-trial of Phra Yoth, even the most nationalistic Colonial Party die-hard must be satisfied, don't you think?"

Victor raised his eyebrows, obviously wondering whether an insult were hidden in the question, and decided not.

Develle was no longer Foreign Minister, he replied in an equable voice, and for that matter, Lord Rosebery had been replaced as Foreign Secretary. Therefore, any personal agreements they might have had were no longer valid, were they?

As to the re-trial of Phra Yoth, Michael may call it a farce, but the view of France was that justice had been served.

Julie gave an exasperated sigh and slapped rice into her dish.

Farce was the word Michael used, and a farce was what that... she cast about for a word... that piece of humiliating theatre was.

The French judges brought in from Saigon who had already decided the verdict even before hearing the accused, refusing to hear the witnesses for the defence, badgering and bullying Phra Yoth, challenging the interpreter, was that justice?

And sentencing the man to twenty years hard labour, and dragging him away in chains?

"Yes, I was there," she added with an impatient toss of her head, "well, at the first session, not for the sentencing. But I heard all about that, and not just from Michael.

"I went with Fanny, who managed to get two tickets, because — did you realize? — the French Legation was actually requiring tickets to attend as if the trial were the Opéra Comique! Just like the Romans executing the Christians, what you called justice was a spectacle!"

"Please don't compare that man, who was guilty of killing a French official, to Christian martyrs," her brother replied heatedly. "After all, the sentence could have been death. He is lucky to get away with hard labour, and in Siam at that, not in Indochina at Poulo Condor or Cayenne. And furthermore, when you talk of spectacle, I marvel at Michael allowing you to go about and be seen when you were expecting."

Michael rose to pour more wine and attempt to restore peace to the conversation.

Indeed, hard labour in Siam was probably better than the infamous French penal colony of Poulo Condor — he raised his hand, yes, English prisons in India were awful as well, he knew that — but still, what of the continued occupation in Chantaboon? How long did Victor think that...?

"Listen," his brother-in-law said at last, with reluctance, "I don't know.

"And, as there are just the three of us here, I cannot say I am happy about it. No, it is not an unduly harsh rule, but it is designed to humiliate. For instance..."

He shook his head and sighed. "Take the prison that has just been built.

"Once, without meaning any harm, to explain why the Siamese officials want to be placed higher up than their inferiors, I told a fellow officer that for the Siamese, the head is the most sacred part of the body.

"Remember, you both told me that, during one of my visits here?

Well, this man designed the prison as a very small square fort — we don't have that many prisoners, you know — with wire netting instead of a ceiling and chicken are kept there, just under the roof. So they defecate on the men's heads.

"You can't call it torture — and I am sure that the administrators of Poulo Condor would say that we are coddling our prisoners, but still..."

Julie bit her lip.

So if she had not told Victor about this aspect of Siamese beliefs, his fellow-officer would not have come up with such a horrible idea?

She could well imagine how debased the prisoners felt. Torture might have been more acceptable.

"Someone else would have told him, don't feel guilty. I was just trying to explain how we are destroying the good will we created by building a school and a clinic — and no one seems willing to understand. It's almost as if I were being disloyal to France by saying so."

Michael toyed with his bread.

In fact, he ventured, it was preferable from the Siamese point of view to resent the occupation rather than consider French rule as a benefit... So whatever the form the torture took — and yes, he considered that peculiar imprisonment under a chicken coop a torture — then that officer was playing into Siamese hands.

Victor furrowed his forehead, not really understanding, but Fie entered the dining room at that moment, carrying Lily in a lacy shawl and her uncle stretched out his arms to take her, marvelling at her delicate starfish hands and her lovely pursed mouth. "You know, although she has Julie's eyes," he remarked, "I think she takes after you."

Michael beamed. He thought so as well.

The end of the monsoon brought cool dry winds and renewed energy for clashes between Siamese police forces and French troops in Luang Prabang, Battambang and Siem Reap but Rolin-Jaequemyns was scathing and unyielding at each new protest brought to him by Pavie.

Local police forces, he repeated, meant Siamese forces, not Lao or Khmer. Meanwhile, in response, the French press, claiming Treaty violations, lost no occasion to urge its government to simply annex Siam and be done with it.

From Paris, Prince Svasti who had been appointed the Kingdom's ambassador because of his combative nature was reporting frustration by Hanotaux in containing the Colonial Party and general exasperation with the British stance on Mong Sing.

"Is it not enough for them, Prince Devawongse asks me," the Belgian Adviser complained to Maurice de Bunsen and Michael one December morning, "to populate Siam with so-called French protégés exempt from our laws and our taxes? Do they also need our trade, our mines, our very lifeblood?

"And I am tempted to answer yes, but of course, I cannot excite him further.

"It is exhausting for me, and my health is suffering, what with the Crown Council meetings from midnight till dawn, and the burden of work which would be sufficient without having to argue with Pavie over every single case of policemen meeting the Tirailleurs Annamites somewhere along the Mekong. I feel only a trip back home to rest and recover will enable me to continue in the task I have set for myself, which is to make the Kingdom unimpeachable in European eyes.

"His Majesty agrees that he can do without me for several months and if Pavie's complaints aren't addressed, well so much the better. He says he wants me in good health so as to enable us to continue our work together."

Yes, yes, de Bunsen replied patronizingly.

Crawfurd had told him of the new organization of the Royal administration here, a daunting task, which was beginning to yield results, now that the Council only had an advisory role.

And the new *Monthon,* the territorial district subdivisions that were being implemented by Prince Damrong — truly, a remarkable achievement and no one better than His Highness Damrong to see it through.

On the pleasant news front, he had heard that Monsieur Pavie was to leave, was that confirmed?

Yes, Rolin-Jaequemyns smiled, his good humour restored.

His replacement, announced for sometime later in the year, was to be a Monsieur Defrance.

Whoever he might be, he could not be worse than Pavie.

And, thankfully, Hardouin was appointed consul

in Nan, where he would no doubt try to make as much mischief as possible, but at least he would not be underfoot in Bangkok, slithering about trying to convince the bosses of Chinese underworld gangs that being French protégés would enable them to continue their life of lawlessness.

And in the meantime, the chargé was to be Pilinski, that stand-in sent from Batavia. Not a bad man, in fact, he and Pavie, from what was heard, loathed each other. Assisted by that young whippersnapper, what was his name?

Réau, yes.

Bright, very bright in fact, but much too young and impulsive.

How old was he? Twenty-three or twenty-four, at most, but he behaved at times as if he were fourteen and all this were a great game.

Michael chuckled in agreement.

The new French diplomat was not unlike a puppy, tail wagging and indiscriminately friendly, and with no idea how to behave.

They had met him at a dinner party at the Malherbes' and the boy — because really, he could not be called anything else — who was sitting next to Julie had confided to her the price of his suit, that of his shoes, and then his ambition of seizing Siam for France to execute the grand plan devised by his hero, Pavie.

And only then had he inquired about her husband. When told he was a British diplomat, he hadn't even been slightly abashed...

"He just said that he had not really heard her name when they were introduced and thought her to be 'really French', so elegant and at ease in company was she.

"He actually imagined he was paying her a compliment!" he recounted laughingly. "He is so earnest and green, it's almost touching."

Maurice de Bunsen rose to take his leave. "He'll learn, unfortunately. One can only hope it will happen as late as possible and that young Réau shall continue to be so guileless and informative."

Victor returned to Bangkok for Christmas and the round of parties and balls where, notwithstanding diplomatic animosities, all the members of the foreign legations met, danced and drank together.

Raphael Réau was very attentive to Henriette Rolin-Jaequemyns, raising eyebrows and whispers behind feathered fans. It was said her father did not approve. It was also said that Monsieur Pilinski, the French chargé, had a bit of a roving eye, and that his wife did not approve.

At the British Legation's fancy-dress ball held at Customs House, a breathless Fanny came to sit down beside Julie after a fast mazurka with Victor and smoothed out her white cotton skirt trimmed with black pompoms.

"So easy to come as Columbina," she had said on arrival, twirling to show off her costume. "And so cheap, as well! I adore fancy dress balls.

"Lovely as is the gown you gave me for your wedding, I fear it has been seen a bit too often. No, no...," she raised her hand in warning "I absolutely forbid you to give me another under some excuse, such as Lily's christening."

She looked at Julie's dress critically. A gypsy? Again?

At least Victor had made the effort to come as a Hindoo prince, and looked quite handsome with his peacock blue turban. Whereas Michael as a toreador... not terribly convincing.

"That's the point," Michael retorted, swirling his cape. "One should have a costume that goes against one's nature. I for instance, am a coward, and...," he squinted at Madame Pilinski dressed as an Egyptian. "Do you think there's any political meaning to be read there, given our conflict with France over Egypt?"

Fanny fanned herself and, still too breathless to speak, with a movement of her chin wordlessly indicated Monsieur Rolin-Jaequemyns scowling under his Red Indian feathered headdress as he watched his daughter held a bit too closely by the new junior French diplomat, who was prancing about garbed as an Empire colonel with a three-cornered plumed hat.

His costume had come to only ten ticals, he had explained to Fanny, who retorted triumphantly that hers cost even less.

"How nice to be young and sought after," she remarked wistfully. "I do miss it at times... Don't you?"

Julie laughed. No, not really. Well... "You see, I never was actually sought after. Louis was the first man to pay me any attention. But, to be honest, I discouraged all the eligible suitors who..."

She stopped, frowned and looked towards the other end of the room.

"What's happening?" The music had stopped and groups were beginning to cluster by the door, while a guard wearing the Palace uniform was whispering to Rolin-Jaequemyns who blanched as he tore off his headdress.

He said something very low to his wife who crossed herself, and left the room hurriedly after seeking Maurice de Bunsen.

Young Réau, abandoning a startled Henriette on the dance floor, rushed up to Monsieur Pilinski who was standing nearby chatting with Monsieur Malherbe and started to gabble without bothering to lower his voice in his excitement, assuming that no one within earshot understood French and seeing neither Fanny or Julie who were seated in a window enclosure behind.

Both could make out what he was saying and stared at each other in horror.

"Crown Prince... dead, yes... just now....

"Of course, it was a plot... no doubt the king's brother?

"Wasn't he passed over to be next-in line for the throne? Perhaps an opportunity... Maybe get in first to focus on the new heir? Do you know who he might be?"

As the older man looked around in embarrassment, Monsieur Malherbe took Réau by the arm and shook him. "Restrain yourself and show some decency," he snapped. Fanny bit her lips and wiped away a tear.

"I am so sorry for His Majesty... too much grief for one man to bear, even a king. And now... Prince Vajirunhis... such a promising boy..."

Did Fanny know him? Julie asked, surprised.

Yes, she had seen him as a lad of ten or twelve; she was sometimes asked to the Palace, discreetly, of course.

"His Majesty and I really were very good friends, you know. He still does what he can to help me."

Michael came to stand by his wife, followed by Victor, and put his hand on her shoulder. All the guests were frozen in groups and the costumes, Arabs, gypsies, fanciful generals and shepherdesses, so gay and playful but some minutes earlier now seemed ridiculous and almost blasphemous in the face of the death of a sixteen-year-old prince.

Maurice de Bunsen, in his gorgeous dragon-embroidered Chinese robe removed his mandarin hat with the attached pigtail and, stepping to the centre of the ballroom said a few sorrowful words. Some of the musicians were crying openly and women began to collect their shawls.

"I need to get back to the office," Michael muttered, wiping off his toreador moustache. "But I have to get rid of this costume first. Come."

"The supper is yet to be served, and it's still very early, not even midnight." Réau was saying hopefully to Victor, "won't you stay? I shall. I heard it was to be very good and that the British Legation spared no expense. No?"

And holding his hat whose red plumes drooped

disconsolately, he remained alone in the empty room, glancing in wistful longing towards the buffet.

"Bangkok January 25ᵗʰ 1895

The Inner Court mourns the young Prince, but the succession is paramount, and the King has appointed another son, Maha Vajiravudh, as heir to the throne. This was announced during a ceremony at Wat Rajabhopit, with all of the royal family, the Sangha — that is the clergy — and the diplomatic corps there, so that there can be no questions or doubts.

Michael said the King looked pale and ailing but very dignified and resolute as he stood before everyone and made his announcement then listened to the speeches and prayers without faltering.

The new Crown Prince is studying in England at present. One can only wonder how it felt to learn of both his half-brother's death and of the enormous weight that is now resting upon his shoulders.

That is what Keow explained, tears trickling down her cheeks, which she dabbed at with a napkin. 'I do not cry for His Highness who has gone to Paradise while he awaits to be reborn, but for us, who miss him. And especially, for Their Majesties who have lost a son.'

Then she once more becomes her business-like self, and discusses the topknot-cutting ceremony of one of the little princesses, planned for next week although the girl is ill.

We both fervently hope she has not the typhoid fever that killed the young prince.

The epidemic is spreading, as it does very year, with the dry season and the stagnant water, but I cannot help feel that this time it seems worse, probably because the Royal family itself is not spared.

I worry for Louis, who is a great favourite of all the food sellers on the soi and is given bits of fruit and meat each time he goes by. Fie and I make him feed them to Pouan, but I know that he often shares the gardener's meals, not to mention all the titbits on offer at the Palace.

He no longer stays at the school to be petted and tickled by the young princesses but runs off to play with the little princes still young enough to reside with their mothers in the Inner Court, and Heaven knows what he is given to eat by the guards or the servants.

Of course, although Lily cannot totally replace him in my butterfly ladies' hearts — he is a boy, after all — her visits to the Inner Court are always a triumphant procession from the sturdy muscular arms of khlons to the bejewelled ones of Mom Chaos. She coos from her basket with at least one of the Palace resident grandmothers fanning her and hushing us if we chatter too loud.

Keow regrets that she will never be given the opportunity to train Lily in the feminine arts all of her girls display so beautifully — she will walk like a Maem, she bemoans, miming the heavy-footed stride of the European woman while we all collapse in laughter — mine somewhat forced as I make a mental note to be more careful of my deportment."

Monsieur Rolin-Jaequemyns, his wife and daughters, and several young princes bound for British universities departed for Europe in late March, waved off at the dock by His Majesty himself, who seemed to be recovered from his most recent illness.

"Good. While that Belgian prig is away, we can start advancing our own views," Maurice de Bunsen announced, rubbing his hands in busy anticipation. "Get me an appointment with Devawongse."

Whitehall's idea, as the British envoy exposed to His Highness, was that, given the attitude of the French, greater strength needed to be demonstrated by Siam, and not just of the legalistic type advocated by RJ, worthy and indispensable as those legal challenges were.

"Otherwise," he warned ominously, "Siam may well be eaten leaf by leaf like an artichoke."

An artichoke? Indeed. His Highness had seen them but never eaten any. However, to his mind, the image was particularly striking.

So, what did His Excellency de Bunsen recommend?

"To start — and you are the first to know — Lord Kimberley has ordered a detachment from Fort Stedman, in the Shan States, to occupy Mong Sing. As you know France has established a very large garrison nearby, in Chieng Kong, and that is intolerable to Britain."

Inwardly, Michael sighed. Mong Sing, again... Why were the European powers obsessed with that useless little pocket of land?

But de Bunsen was continuing to hector the Siamese Foreign Minister. "What we need is evidence that, contrary to what Pavie is claiming, Mong Sing is not now, or ever was, a vassal of Nan."

The Prince threw up his hands. All those little provinces were vassals of several powers at once, Nan and Luang Prabang inter alia, and paid tribute to all of them. Really, what did it matter?

"It matters. Do you really want France — who, as I may be so bold to remind you, is now allied with Russia — to gain a greater foothold on your land and control Siam's access to China?

And with Russia backing her, decide to invade both Siam and British Burmah?

Yes, I know, you are going to tell me that the Emperor of Russia is a friend of Siam, but truly, what proof of this has he given you thus far?

Words, words and more words."

Prince Devawongse reflected on this for a moment. "Pavie is a most cunning man, as you know."

If he had found any documents to support France's claims, they were bound to be false. The tribute system existed by custom and show of strength, not on paper.

Maurice de Bunsen smiled. Such a statement was all he needed.

He picked up his hat, did a deep *wai*, and, before opening the door added crisply that a show of presence by the Siamese navy in the gulf would not come amiss.

No point in letting the French believe they ruled the waves and possibly harass British shipping, which was so profitable for Siam, was there?

Prince Devawongse nodded in agreement.

He could also tell them that His Majesty, deeply offended by the fact that the French occupation force was using the island of Koh Si Chang as their own private retreat, had decided to dismantle his palace there, teak plank by teak plank, and re-erect it here in Bangkok.

"Perfect. One should never disregard the impact of a symbol. Please congratulate His Majesty on our behalf."

The British diplomat *wai*-ed again and took his leave.

Reactions in Indochina to the occupation of Mong Sing were virulent.

Pavie, along with Armand Rousseau, the new Governor-General of Indochina, called for naval retaliation and the immediate imposition of a protectorate over Siam.

Paris, however, limited itself to a stance of muted contempt to this yet additional example of British high-handedness.

Even London was divided over the wisdom of such a pre-emptive measure, Lord Elgin, the Viceroy of India, complained of the expense involved in holding a border against the French, and Michael, decoding telegrams, could not refrain from wondering aloud if this show of force might not do more harm than good.

"Well, given that France and England cannot agree on what its borders might be, it certainly means the end of the buffer state project," de Bunsen replied carelessly. "And if we want to keep our dominant position in Siam, we're going to need another solution."

Chapter XV

Lily has started to take her first, hesitant steps, a good three months before Louis showed any signs of wanting to walk.

She is a constant delight, a laughing, gurgling, little blossom of a child who has grabbed all our hearts — in fact Fie and all the servants call her 'Dok Mai' — flower.

What never ceases to surprise me is that, remembering Louis' first year, I constantly sought his father in him, his eyes, his smile, the way he turned his head or lifted his chin. But Lily is just herself, or rather, in my mind as in his, she is very much Michael's daughter.

She totters about on her plump bare feet, and when she hears Michael return in the evening, she stretches her arms out, crowing with joy.

Even Louis is reconciled to her existence, and allows her to stroke Pouan's fur and feed the monkey bits of papaya.

It is impossible to imagine how we all lived before her.

Yesterday, there was a garden party at the Legation to honour Queen Victoria's birthday, and it was a most lavish event, attended by "le tout Bangkok", whether Siamese or farang, and ending with a magnificent display of fireworks.

Remembering the paltry and stark receptions given by Captain and Mrs Jones, one could only feel sorry for that well-meaning and hearty, but very austere couple — they are now in Peru, Michael says. But there was a feeling of genuine friendship then, whereas when received by Maurice de Bunsen, one has the impression of being weighed for what one might contribute to his career. Whilst being quite polite, he always looks at me as if thinking, "Hmmm, an heiress. What must I do to get one of those?"

Léonie came to tell me that her husband was informed by Monsieur Réau of his most recent plan to grab Siam for France. It is to enlist the support

*of several Chinese criminal protégés, each commanding the obedience of
several thousand men who would be sent to seize the Palace and overthrow
the King 'at the right moment.'*

*Obviously, I am to pass the message along to Michael; because he had been
sworn to secrecy, Monsieur Malherbe could not do so himself, but knew that
the information would nonetheless reach him through this rather unorthodox
but effective channel — after all, as Léonie says, there are no secrets between
man and wife, are there?— and Réau should have realized that.*

*However, it appears that this mindless plot was already uncovered and
dismissed as preposterous — the Siamese have ways of knowing everything,
and the Chinese are not foolish enough to put their trust in the French — and
young Réau is now viewed by all, even his superior, Monsieur Pilinski, as a
bit of a hothead.*

A man after Pavie's own heart."

Throughout the months of his European tour, Monsieur
Rolin-Jaequemyns sent the Court in Bangkok reports of
the diplomatic contacts he was able to make, and of the
state of public opinion in both Paris and London.

In July, he read with dismay that the French colonial
press was reporting that his visit to England was to sign a
treaty placing Siam under British protectorate.

"Rumours, easily dispelled," Prince Devawongse told
the British minister with a shrug.

He also wrote that a new French ambassador to Britain
had been appointed, a Baron de Courcel, whom he knew,
and was a reasonable man.

And, after the general elections in England that had put
in place a Tory government, with Lord Salisbury once again
as both Prime Minister and Foreign Secretary, and Mr
Curzon, who was a personal friend, as Under-Secretary,
Monsieur Rolin-Jaequemyns had hopes of finally settling
the question of Siam's territorial integrity and neutrality.

"Like Switzerland or Belgium," added the Prince
hopefully. "There are to be talks."

"BANGKOK, OCTOBER 25TH 1895

It would seem that finally France, faced with a revolt in Madagascar, has not the means or the stomach to attempt an annexation of Siam, and in any case, prefers not to clash with Britain while both nations are seeking a solution over their claims to Egypt and, of course, to the Suez Canal which is the gateway to the East.

The territorial integrity of Siam is guaranteed at last.

What a curious world we now live in, where the courage and determination of a small island far away determines the freedom of an Asian kingdom that is practically ignorant of its existence, and a chess move in Suez leads to a pawn taken in Tananarive.

So a treaty is to be signed, dealing with all those problematic countries and dividing up the world…

Michael recounts the many ups and downs of the negotiations — Paris says, Saigon says, London says — the steps forwards, the steps backwards, but I have lost interest, it has been going on for so long, and is so repetitive.

Even Monsieur Réau's schemes, once so amusing in their outrageousness now appear childish to me.

Is it because Pavie has finally been recalled to Paris — somewhat in disgrace, I understand, for endangering relations with England — and I am left with no one to hate?

His replacement, a rather complacent young man, with a Levantine beauty of a wife, inspires only mild boredom — both he and she are perfectly friendly, very elegant, and completely shallow.

Michael suggests that perhaps it is time for me to take a holiday, but Lily and Fie both are unwell, Fie with stubborn coughs and fevers and Lily with stomach ailments, so I dare not take them away.

When they are better, we shall go to Singapore, or perhaps Penang."

"Bangkok, November 16th 1895

My dearest Mother,

I do not know how to write this. Lily died yesterday from dysentery, and I wish it were I lying cold on the bed. She had been ill for several weeks, refusing all food and drink and the doctor could do nothing to help. So many children die here, he said.

Julie is prostrate with grief, and I cannot help her, being as heartbroken as she is.

I shall write later in the week, if I can.

Your loving son,
Michael Crawfurd"

The service at Christ Church had ended, and Lily's little body laid to rest under mounds of white flowers in Bangkok's Christian cemetery on the bank of the great river. Julie and Michael had stood together by the grave, incapable of even holding hands, and stared, unseeing, at the sumptuous wreath of orchids sent by His Majesty the King. Fanny hovered nearby, weeping into a handkerchief, and ready to catch her friend if she showed signs of collapsing, but Julie seemed to be made of stone, stiff and cold and silent.

Finally, their friends had left the house where they had gathered after the funeral, and Julie and Michael were alone, listening to Louis' muted chatter from the garden and Fie's insistent cough from the first floor, while she attempted to console little Phim, Lily's nurse, who after losing her own child had lavished all of her love along with her milk on the enchanting little *farang* girl who had just died. Somboon, they both knew, was sobbing in Michael's bedroom, waiting to offer him solace and oblivion.

Lek and Pon served them dinner, but they toyed with their food.

"Do you want...?" Michael ventured, finally, showing the wine.

She shook her head.

"Listen," he said urgently, "we'll go away. To Saigon, if

you like, or perhaps Penang, which is so picturesque. Just give me a month or so, until this damn treaty is signed."

Julie just shrugged. She did not care.

She cared about nothing.

Fie died on Christmas day, carried away by pneumonia aggravated by the bronchitis that had weakened her all those past months.

Kneeling by the bed, Julie had mopped her forehead and watched as Doctor Hertz listened to Fie's stertorous, ragged breaths. He shook his head.

The heart was failing, he murmured, putting away his stethoscope. She had slipped into a coma and would not emerge. "Did you not know she had a bad heart?" he inquired gently.

Julie pushed herself up on her elbows, biting her lips so as not to scream her despair, and dissolved in the tears that she had not allowed herself for Lily.

She knew nothing, she finally answered. She did not even know how old the poor woman was, and neither did she.

"Oh, old, old, Fie very old," she always replied with a laugh, when asked. She had no family she could remember, an aunt — or was she a neighbour?— had sold her into service as a child, she was beaten and often hungry, but then, "oh, so lucky! First an English family, for ten years, perhaps, then here with Maem Chouli and her Nhu Thong, then Baby flower and every day enough rice, and kind people... Fie visited the Palace and countries across the great oceans, imagine that! Fie was lucky all her life," she always maintained cheerfully.

Julie took the clammy work-roughened hand in hers and stroked it, while Michael thanked the doctor and escorted him back to the gate.

"Take Mrs Crawfurd away," the elderly German whispered urgently. "I fear for her — it is not normal to grieve so for a servant – and on top of the loss of your little girl…"

Tight-lipped, Michael thanked him again and almost pushed him out.

Then he walked heavily indoors to consult Somboon and Pon on organizing the funeral rites.

Julie insisted that Louis attend the several lavish ceremonies at the temple – he would miss Fie dreadfully and needed to say farewell – and had often been brought to Wat Yannawa when she went to pray or make offerings.

The saffron-garbed monks, the statues and the chants were familiar to him, and reminded him of happy moments with her. It was only fitting that he pay tribute to her spirit and pray for her re-birth.

She appeared to be right; the child stopped his daily fits of wild, gasping sobs that no amount of loving words seemed to calm and lit the incense and candles with a steady hand.

"She will be reborn to a beautiful life, I know it," he announced happily after the cremation. "And we will meet again, and go fishing for crab at the sea.

"Fie always wanted to go to the sea."

"*BANGKOK JANUARY 25*TH *1896*

How do we go on?
I do not know. I move as if underwater during the day and at night, I awake suddenly thinking I have heard Lily cry, and Fie's heavy footstep padding across the room to comfort her. And then, I remember, and another day of misery begins.

I try to take Fie's place with Louis, but know I cannot.

Thankfully, he has Nhu Dam to play with and Mali to look after him, and above all Pouan.

I pace the house, I walk to the temple and make offerings — the monks know me there — and occasionally I have the strength to see Fanny.

My days are endless.

When Michael comes back in the evening, he tells me all about the declaration signed earlier this month between England and France that will guarantee the Menam Basin from either a French or a British takeover. It is not all of Siam, but the part that matters most.

It is not a treaty, because a treaty must be ratified by Parliament, and the Colonial Party would therefore scuttle it.

Apparently Monsieur Defrance, he of the well-combed moustache and the frivolous wife, and Monsieur Réau are furious, and claim that it is all an English plot to deprive La République of what is rightfully hers.

Monsieur Defrance says he is so disgusted with France's caving in to London that he has asked to be recalled — he did not accept a posting here to see France's Empire be carved up.

Apparently, he has still not realized that Siam is not and never was part of France's Empire.

Oh, and of course, everybody has lost interest in Mong Sing, which has now been given to France, who seems not to care.

The King is relieved and RJ is satisfied but warns that neither the Siamese part of the Malayan peninsula, nor what Siam has retained of her Khmer and Lao provinces are safe yet — from either England or France, he adds with a dark look — but for the time being, it will have to do.

I make efforts to listen, and to be interested, and for some blessed moments I am... But then something, anything, brings the utter irrelevance of all this to my mind and I can only wonder that Michael is able to deal with it every day, all day long.

Nonetheless, I accepted to attend the official dinner which Mr de Bunsen gave last night to celebrate the signing of the Treaty — Michael practically begged me to accompany both him and Victor who had come from Chantaboon for the event, telling me out of my brother's earshot I could not miss the sour looks on all the French envoys. After all, he said wistfully, there aren't that many things to smile about these days; it's a pity not to witness such discomfiture.

Emilie and RJ were there, and pressed me to their breasts — I had not seen them since their return early this month — and Princes Damrong and Devawongse were most sympathetic and attentive.

Prince Devawongse conveyed the wishes of Keow to see me back at the Palace soon — I don't know, though.

I fear the many memories, I will always see Fie seated in the shade gossiping and glancing about as if she still could not believe her good fortune at being there. But another part of me craves Keow's forthright talk and her firm grasp on reality. I think she is the only one to whom I can confide my dreadful feeling of guilt and the knowledge that I am punished now for wishing Lily dead before she was born.

A very grand representative of the Viceroy of India was sent from Calcutta with an escort of the Duke of York's own Bengal lancers, a Sikh regiment and the Bombay Infantry — purportedly to ensure the requisite pomp and circumstance — but mainly, we take it, to hammer home to the French the point that they are to abide by the terms of the Treaty, and that for all the strength of the French troops in Indochina, the Indian Army is much stronger. And one had to admit the Tirailleurs Annamites looked rather puny compared to those very tall and impressively bearded Indian soldiers who marched to drums and bagpipes.

An officer of the delegation asked to be introduced to Victor and me, one Captain Sir Peter Arneys, whose mother is a friend of Mama's.

Of course we both knew the name — "can't you still hear her say, 'My friend Sophie Meadows, well, that is, Lady Arneys now...?' " Victor muttered.

He expressed his mother's sympathy for our loss, and told us this is his last official mission, he is being decommissioned next month and returns to London — his father died earlier this year and along with the title, he has inherited the estate. Victor was looking thoughtful at that — perhaps foundries, seen from Chantaboon, are now more attractive to him.

Michael invited him to dinner this evening at the Oriental.

Victor declined — "Much as I should like to join you, I cannot be seen dining with the British, unfortunately," he stated with an apologetic shrug"— but I shall force myself to go, the idea of being alone in the house listening to the silence is more than I can bear.

"My dear Mrs Crawfurd", Peter Arneys murmured as he kissed her hand, "I was hoping against hope that you would join us tonight. I am overjoyed."

Julie managed a smile in return and took his arm as they moved towards the dining room.

She did not go out at the moment, except when her presence was required for official events, she said tremulously, but in this case — he was almost family, was he not?

Indeed, was the reply.

After all, he was told by his mother that he and Victor had played together as children, although he had no memories of it, and when Michael added that for his part, his childhood memories of battles with Victor were seared in his mind, Captain Arneys shook his head.

"I would have wished him to be here this evening. This modern world is so strange, how families and friends find themselves divided over matters that truly concern them little."

He was a pleasant man, well read and interesting and for the first time in weeks, Julie was able to escape her bottomless pit of misery for several minutes at a time listening to the British officer describe India which he seemed to find endlessly endearing and exasperating at once.

"Their religion, for instance. One does try to understand, truly. But the caste system, how these intelligent people — for they are indeed intelligent — accept it is beyond me.

"And I still cannot fathom this Brahman business — it's a principle, but also, I gather, a religion, a sacred rite, or a priest or a caste."

Michael asked questions, and described some Brahmin rites that continued to be practiced in Siam and Julie listened, aware that their guest's eyes never strayed very far from her and that despite her wan face and sad, remote eyes, he was attracted to her.

How strange.

Since Edward, she somehow found it easy to read men's minds and lust and, although she knew she would not give the man more than a passing thought beyond tomorrow when she would write to Mama telling of meeting Lady Arneys' son, she began to feel that perhaps, she was not dead inside.

"*BANGKOK, FEBRUARY 11TH 1896*

I finally gathered strength enough to return to the Palace, and it was easier than I thought to lose myself in the good-humoured chatter of the princesses who grieve with me for a few moments but then return to their more pressing concerns of dress, jewels, and gossip.

Princess Erb, one of the royal concubines — who by birth is of the family of the former Regent and therefore has tremendous standing and influence, although, Keow sniffed, she has not yet been able to produce a child — was given a camera by a wealthy relative, and she is experimenting to the tremendous fascination of everyone.

Keow, besides her disparaging comments on the new photography craze, was as I expected, comforting and imperious at the same time.

'Death is life, and life is going to death, never mind. Is to be a human.'

She feels I need a consultation with a fortune-teller, as she said: 'So you know where your life go now.

Life always go somewhere.'

"*BANGKOK FEBRUARY 24TH 1896*

The fortune-teller is a middle-aged woman who regularly comes to the Inner Court, and always is in great demand. The young ladies are keen to know if the marriage being arranged for them will be happy and fruitful, or, in the case of the many concubines, if they might perhaps soon catch His Majesty's eye.

What Keow was anxious to find out was whether Siam shall be safe during the King's tour through European countries next year. According to the seer, there is no danger and His Majesty's health, along with the Kingdom — and its women, she claims, surprisingly — will actually be strengthened.

As to me, she sees change. She stared at my hand for a long time, then said my heart knew what the change should be, and my head will find out soon. Why ask me? she laughed. Ask yourself.

And of course I know. I just need the courage to see it through.

It took several weeks before she was able to muster the courage to finally admit it both to herself and to Michael.

Louis was in bed, after arguing with Mali who definitely did not have Fie's firm manner, and Pon, supervised from the doorway by Lek, was serving the prawns and rice.

Michael had just finished recounting his latest meeting with RJ regarding France's registration of 20,000 additional protégés, who would then, according to some sources, attempt a bloodless takeover "in the name of France, but not by France."

"When will they ever accept that it's over?

"Yes, they probably will manage to acquire Siem Reap and Battambang by hook or by crook, and I think that even the Siamese have grown to realize that, but Defrance and Réau still hope and plot."

Julie remained silent, and just stared at her plate as he was about to tell her of the complicated protocol arrangements for the King's visit to England, when she put down her fork and looked up gravely.

"Michael. I want a divorce."

"BANGKOK MARCH 1ˢᵀ 1896

*So it is done, and, although he pleaded and reasoned, I think somehow
Michael is as relieved as I am.*

*You have Somboon, I told him. I have only Louis, and he needs to go
back amongst his own kind.*

*And he admitted that I am right, but added bitterly, 'I suppose that in
time you will marry someone like Peter Arneys — he looked quite smitten.' "*

Julie had laughed in shocked surprise.

"Michael, you're jealous?"

He spoke without looking up at her. Of course he was
jealous. Could she not realize that despite his... well, the
way he was, she was his wife, whom he loved, and she and
Louis were his family?

"Yes, I agreed, if I could, I probably would remarry.

After all, I am only thirty.

*It is arranged that I shall travel to London next month, and that in time,
the divorce be applied for.*

The grounds are to be abandonment, on his part, not mine.

*I did not know that it was possible for me to grieve yet more than I was
— but I do.*

I think my heart is broken forever."

Chapter XVI

Michael stood at the door of Julie's London flat and hesitated.

"It's furnished, and depressing, but perfectly comfortable, and only temporary," she had written. *"Your family has been very understanding and supportive, staunchly going along with the abandonment story, and I expect whatever interest our divorce may have generated here will soon die down. Your sister Dahlia has introduced me to the 'right' people, and if not exactly fêted, I am still received in society and met Peter Arneys again at her house.*

You were right — of course you were — and I shall marry him when our divorce is final.

If not happy — shall I ever be happy again? — at least, I am at peace."

He had arrived in London the day before to assist in the preparations for the King of Siam's visit and also to sign the last papers severing Julie's life from his own.

A footman ushered him in, and he waited, turning between his hands the small package wrapped in silk a messenger from the Inner Court had brought to the Legation for her, looking at the heavy draperies and massive mahogany furniture, and trying and failing to imagine her in this stifling décor.

But the charmingly polite and remote creature who entered this dark red drawing-room was not the Julie he remembered, and as he listened to her well-bred inquiries as to his health he felt that he was divorcing a stranger. She had changed her hair, he noted — no doubt her ladies' maid was more skilled than poor Fie had been — and her dress, even to his unpractised eye, must have been in the latest fashion.

This could not be the same woman who fought her way through a rioting crowd on New Road, cut open bullfrogs, fed nuts to a pet gibbon and chattered with Siamese princesses in a harem, and certainly not someone who, lust-crazed and wanton, had thrown caution to the winds in a journalist's shabby little room on Windmill Road.

It was a moment before he realized that she was as nervous and frightened as he.

Only when, for want of finding anything to say to her, he thrust the parcel into her hands and she peeled away the silk, did the society lady melt away and she became the Julie he had known in Bangkok.

Tears brimming over, she gazed at the framed group portrait of her students, gathered together before the camera of one of the princesses who had developed a taste for photography and ran her fingers over the sepia-tinted faces, naming each one.

"I dream I am back, almost every night," she murmured. She looked up eagerly with the real Julie's eyes, not the veiled ones of a distant and well-bred hostess, "And tell me...?"

He answered all her questions about her friends, Fanny sent her love, and Léonie, and, of course, Emilie and RJ, and yes, Somboon was well, Pon as erratic and enthusiastic as ever, and Pouan, my God, was his usual mischief. She was much missed by all.

"The fortune-teller was right, you know," he informed her. His Majesty's trip so far was a great success— "Well, the French gave him somewhat of a cold shoulder, and their press was rather snide, but I suppose that was to be expected,"— and Queen Saovabha had been appointed Regent in his absence — a tremendous stride forward in favour of women.

When Louis, wearing a sailor's suit, came in to share their tea and threw himself into Michael's arms and chattered to him in Siamese, she stiffened somewhat. The child always refused to speak Siamese with her, and screamed when she tried. But she hoped this would pass soon. "Peter loves him and will be a good father to him," she said a bit defiantly.

Michael left shortly afterwards, feeling reassured and immeasurably sad.

Two years later, she wrote to say she was expecting a child, then to announce the birth of her daughter Sophie, and Somboon found him in tears when he read her letter.

"We named her for my mother-in-law, and she is fair, and placid and looks just like Peter. He is overjoyed, although I know he would have preferred a son.

Do not think, darling Michael, that this baby has replaced Lily in my heart. She is always there, as are you... Louis, who somehow imagined he would be given a monkey again on this occasion, is very disappointed. He asks me to say he has no interest in his new sister and sends his love."

He answered giving her his best wishes and that of all her friends and telling her he often brought flowers to Lily's grave and sat to tell her of all her mother's news.

"But I am weary of Siam and of all these memories, which I cannot escape. There is little for me to accomplish here — or perhaps I have lost interest.

I have asked to be recalled, or to be given a new posting but there is little hope of it before several years — there is a need, I am told, of someone who knows the country well."

She replied at length, as she always did, and ended with the news that Edward Thompson had died of typhoid fever in Manila the year before, covering the Spanish-American war.

I learned to think of him without bitterness and, whilst I was pained to think of him dying alone, so far from family or friends — although if I know him, he probably had some fair woman mopping his brow and holding his hand at the end —, somehow I could not erase the fear that he might reappear in a London drawing-room and create a scandal in that flamboyant way of his.

So his death marked an end for me, but beside that irrational fear, the end of what, I cannot tell. Guilt, regrets? Or simply my youth?"

He shook his head in sorrow; if vitality and talent such as Edward's were to be cut short, then it should have been gloriously, defiantly, with a bullet to the heart. Not weakened and sweating with typhoid fever in some god-forsaken hospital … He folded the letter carefully and put it with the others in a blue leather pouch, to be reread and savoured and, at times, cried over.

A few months after the beginning of the new century, he received a missive to tell of the birth of a son, and to his delight, he recognized once more the biting and irreverent Julie he knew instead of the conventional lady Peter Arneys seemed to have turned her into.

"FEBRUARY 16ᵀᴴ 1900

You probably think me as prolific as a prize sow surrounded by her piglets, and when I look in the mirror, that is what I see, a woman fat, content, and boring.

I hope that when you next see me, I shall be merely content.

This son — his name is John, and it was all I could do not to have Peter call him Edward — is born to a changing world, and I wonder what his life will be.

Peter is delighted to have an heir, and he and his mother hope for a spare, but I have learned enough at the Palace to ensure that there shan't be.

Enough piglets, my dear!"

She wrote over the years, to announce snippets of news — Sophie was walking, John had two teeth — to cheer him up, congratulate him on his appointment as Minister-Counsellor in Rome, and then an indignant and supportive letter when an spiteful young Monsignor had set spies in his household and revealed his relationship with Somboon.

He had to send the poor man back in tears to Siam with money enough to purchase a house, and the promise that he would come to join him when he could.

"Of course, I was only recalled and the matter was suppressed — heaven knows I am not the only diplomat with such proclivities!" he told her wryly when they met as he was passing through London before taking up his new appointment in Peking, "but any ambition of becoming ambassador has vanished."

And his daily comfort and happiness as well, she added with tears in her eyes as she squeezed his hand. Yes, he could only reply, his happiness as well.

But Somboon had hated Rome — too dirty and unhealthy, he claimed — so in some way, he was happy to be going back home.

She looked at him with clouded eyes. Did he know what she missed most about Siam — well, not most, but most frequently?

The scents — the frangipani outside her window, the garlands of jasmine Mali draped on the spirit house, the perfume of ripe mango, the lemongrass cook pounded into a paste...

"The reek of the *khlong* behind the house," he continued playfully, "the stench of dried fish, the rotting refuse on the streets... Yes, how I understand the power of nostalgia."

She laughed and announced Nanny was about to bring the children in for tea, and Peter should arrive soon. "He does not understand how or why we remain so close, but to please me, he will welcome you."

She rose and rearranged a few flowers in a vase, then turned back to him.

"He's really very good to me, you know. Ah, here come my piglets!" and opened her arms to a fair, shy-looking girl in a starched pinafore and a bustling noisy toddler who snatched a jam tart from the tray, tugged at his mother's skirt, climbed on to her lap and demanded cake, cake, cake in a shrill voice.

"Master John, you must behave. What will Mummy's visitor think?" the nanny chided him mildly.

"Mummy's visitor will think he is a normal boy, once he puts down that tart." Julie laughed. "Sophie, John, you may both have cake after you say hello to Uncle Michael."

When Peter came in a few moments later, Michael saw the love he had for his wife in everything he said and how his eyes followed her every movement, and could not repress a twinge of envy for everything the man had and that once was his.

And he also saw in the surprising gentleness of her hand on his, and the way she offered her jam-smeared cheek up for a kiss that Julie appeared to be, as she had hoped, content.

When France finally returned Chantaboon to Siamese rule, but only in exchange for the coastal province of Trat, Sir Peter Arneys, Baronet, had become the Conservative Member of Parliament for his Devon constituency, Louis was at Winchester, Queen Victoria had died and was succeeded by King Edward VII, and the Entente Cordiale signed between Paris and London, putting an end to the colonial rivalries between the two nations along with Siam's dream of ever regaining the territories it had lost.

"I was appalled to read of this yet further proof of French hypocrisy — truly, what on earth allowed them to demand anything in return for Chantaboon?— and I am glad RJ did not live to see this," she wrote then, *"but then I suppose, that like everything else, peace has a price and Siam must feel stronger in the recognition of its new borders.*

Victor, as you can imagine, is in two minds about it. But then, as usual, he is in two minds about everything.

He finally married according to Mama's wishes, a smart, sharp-edged little Mademoiselle Adelaide Aignier and when we went to Paris for the wedding, Mama confided that now, after the Entente Cordiale, it was at last rather chic to be English. Although, as you know, our relations have never been easy at best, my heart went out to her, and to this need for acceptance I confess I never felt myself.

Meanwhile, upon Papa's death last year, Victor sold the foundries, and promptly regretted both marrying and no longer being a captain of industry, albeit a bored and probably rather incompetent one.

The world has changed, and Peter does not like what it has become, whereas I passionately embrace this new age with its infinite promise.

Louis is doing well at his school, and considering studying medicine.

I took the children to the zoo and showed them that poor tired and downtrodden elephant — they were amazed when I told them I had lived in a land where elephants carry kings to ceremonies, just like the royal carriages here.

It is raining outside, cold and grey... Oh how I miss Siam."

The mails to Peking were unreliable, but when he received the papers, he always looked for the occasional picture of her in the society pages, and was once very amused to find her name amongst those ladies who had marched with Frances Balfour and Lady Strachey for women's suffrage.

His sister Dahlia wrote *"your ex-wife has a reputation for being rather political but she is still very good company, and so with that dishy husband of hers and all the amusing people she attracts, invitations to their soirées are much coveted."*

And he found himself craving the news she sent almost every month.

"MARCH 15ᵀᴴ 1907

Fanny wrote with a most delicious bit of information: Prince Chakrabongse, he, you remember, who was a Hussar in a Saint-Petersburg regiment, eloped with a Russian lady named Catherine and married her in Constantinople. The rumour, Fanny says, is that His Majesty is most displeased — how I wish

I could transport myself to the Inner Court and hear what Keow has to say about that!

In fact, how I wish I could transport myself to the Inner Court and take up residence there.

It's not that I am unhappy, my dear, but the children are now at school, Peter wishes me to spend time in his constituency talking to very worthy women who, I am sure, attempt to guess how much I pay for my hats and I am bored, bored, bored, so I try to remember Keow's lessons in deportment and smile graciously over endless teas.

I miss you. You never would have made me do such things, would you?"

"NOVEMBER 5TH 1910

"I read of His Majesty Chulalongkorn's death last week, and found myself crying for Siam, but also over my own memories. I know he had been ailing for a long time, but it seemed that with his visit to Europe three years ago, he had recovered. Did I ever tell you that he recognized me at a reception at Buckingham Palace then? He was very friendly and called me a 'true friend of Siam'.

At least he lived long enough to see his Kingdom safe from both French and British clutches...

One can only imagine the outpouring of sorrow throughout the kingdom and I think, of course, of all my friends at the Palace and wish I could write to Keow to share her grief.

Many of the illustrated papers have published admiring and dutiful obituaries, but I find none have been able to define what a remarkable reign he had in the face of such adversity."

"FEBRUARY 9TH 1914

Louis is to marry, a perfectly suitable and uninteresting girl who wears very appropriate dresses with commodious pockets.

She, I believe, disapproves of me because I am thrice-married and once-divorced and lived in the East — although she recognizes that some women may be called upon to, they are certainly not to enjoy it.

But all this may well be due to just my imagination and own mild dislike of her.

Peter and I find him too young, only twenty-three, but he will not hear of waiting, with the war-like noises coming from Germany, and of course he will be called up, just the right age for cannon-fodder.

Please Michael, if you still love us, and if there is Buddhist temple near you, do make offerings for him."

Then, many years later, as if she were continuing a conversation they had barely interrupted.

"Do you believe, as do the Siamese, that souls are born again and again and that death and life are but a passage?

After the carnage this war has brought us, I find myself attempting to cling to this idea, especially when I see what Louis has become after serving as an army surgeon in the trenches.

I believe it is only his young son Lawrence who saves him from complete despair.

Increasingly, I also think of Princess Keow, and her wisdom. She must be long dead, now, of course, and happily reborn, I am sure.

Will you do something for me, Michael, please, and don't think I am being maudlin, I have no premonition of death. It is just that you are the only one who can both understand and actually ensure that funeral ceremonies at a Buddhist temple are carried out for my safe rebirth?

And can you pray I am reborn in Siam?"

When she died of a deadly strain of influenza a few years later, Louis wrote, she was babbling in Siamese.

"Her hands were joined together, and my wife, who is devout, was surprised but pleased to think she was praying.

I did not tell her that she was talking to Princess Keow and performing her last wai."

CHIANG MAI 1938

I close young Lawrence's book and indulge in a few old man's tears.

Yes, he was faithful to who we were.

So faithful, in fact, that I wonder how Louis will feel reading about his mother as a young and headstrong and impulsive woman.

But will he truly be surprised?

I believe, as did she in fact, that he married to find the stability that somehow, Julie always denied him.

And will he recognize the Bangkok he knew?

I did, and found it strange to be taken by Lawrence's words to a world that exists no longer but in my mind — Julie's house was torn down to make way for new and ugly buildings, the smelly khlong behind the garden filled in and New Road and Windmill Road full of electric lights and clogged with traffic.

I now recognize nothing on the rare occasions when I go, and am always happy to get back to my lotus-eating haven of Chiang Mai.

I did as she had asked, and the funeral rites were said at Wat Yannawa, where the ceremonies for Fie were also held.

There were actually a few of the older monks who remembered the farang lady who came and cried for her daughter and her servant both.

And I imagine that somewhere, in the Palace or the great households of Bangkok, there are a few middle-aged princesses who can still say a few words of French and smile when they think of their laughing, lovely teacher.

It is a better memorial than most.

Every year on the day of her death, I make offerings for her.

Somboon believes that she must be reborn here, and claims that in fact, in her previous lives she was Siamese as well.

He also says that her spirit is all around, and that I needn't go to Wat Phra Singh to seek her presence.

And I reply that I prefer to go, never mind.

So when I say I talk to myself, I also talk to Julie.

As I sit on the temple floor, I tell her that the kingdom she cared so passionately about has changed beyond recognition, but that, knowing her, she would probably love what it had become; that we, the witnesses to what happened, and what might have happened, are gradually disappearing and that, as Keow taught her, death is life and life is death, and that nobody will remember us.

And that really, it matters not at all.

Bibliography

Printed sources
1894 Directory for Bangkok and Siam, The
Bangkok Times
Bangkok 1996 repr. from 1894
White Lotus Press

*1904 Traveller's Guide to Bangkok and
Siam, The*
Antonio, J
Bangkok 1997 repr. From 1904
White Lotus Press

1905 Siam Boundary Delimitation Album
Department of Provincial
Administration
Bangkok 2015

Around Tonkin and Siam
Orleans, Henri d'
Bangkok 1999 repr. from 1892
White Lotus Press Bangkok

*Atlas of the Pavie Mission, Pavie 2 Laos,
Cambodia, Siam, Yunnan*
Pavie, Auguste,
Bangkok 1999
White Lotus Press

Bangkok in 1892
Fournereau, Lucien
First English translation of 1894
by Tips, Walter E.J.
Bangkok 1998
White Lotus Press
*Contest for Siam, 1889-1902: a study in
diplomatic rivalry*
Chandran Jeshurun
Penerbit Universti Kebangsaan
Kuala Lumur 1977

*L'exploration du Mékong: la mission
Doudart de Lagrée-Francis Garnier*
Gomane, Jean-Pierre,
L'Harmattan Editions 1994

Five Years in Siam (1891-1896)
Smyth, Warington H;
Bangkok 1999 repr. from 1898
White Lotus Press

Four Reigns
Kukrit Pramoj
English version by Tulachandra
Translation by Chancham Bunnag
Silkworm Books
Chiang Mai 1981

French Wolf and the Siamese Lamb, The
Tuck, Patrick
Bangkok 1995
White Lotus Press

*Hidden Histories of War Crimes Trials
(Phra Yoth Tric!)*
Heller, Kevin and Simpson,
Gerry
Oxford University Press, 2013
History of Anglo-Thai Relations
M.L Manich Jumsai
Chalermit 1970

Golden Cherchonese and the Way Thither, The
Bird, Isabella,
Cambridge University Press,
2010

Gustave Rolin-Jaequemyns and the Making of Modern Siam,
Tips, Walter E.J.
Bangkok 1996,
White Lotus Press

In Siam: The Diary of a Legal Adviser of King Chulalongkorn
Jottrand, Emile
First English translation 1905
Tips, Walter E.J.
Bangkok 1996
White Lotus Press

Jeune diplomate au Siam; 1894-1900
Lettres de mon grand-père Raphaël Réau
Marchat, Philippe
L'Harmattan Editions 2013

Mad about the Mekong
Keay, John
Harper Collins 2005

New French Imperialism, 1880-1910:
The Third Republic and colonial expansion
Cooke, James E.
Newton Abbot 1973,
Archon Books, Hamden, Conn.

Pavie Mission Exploration Work, Pavie 1,
Laos, Cambodia, Siam
Pavie, Auguste
Bangkok 1999
White Lotus Press

Procédés de la Commission Franco-Siamoise de la délimitation des Frontières entre le Siam et le Laos, Les (1904-1907) d'après les Archives d'Outre-Mer)
M.L. Manich Jumsai,
Chalermit, Bangkok 1984

Relations entre la France et la Thaïlande, (Siam) au XIXème siècle, d'après les archives des Affaires Etrangères.
Pensri Suvanij Duke
Chalermit
Bangkok 1962

Siam and the Siamese
Lajonquière, Lunet de
Bangkok 2001
White Lotus Press

Siam Directory 1912, The
Anonymous,
Bangkok 2005
White Lotus Press

Siamese Sketches
Buls, Charles
Bangkok 1994
White Lotus Press

Siam's Struggle for Survival
Tips, Walter E.J.
Bangkok 1996
White Lotus Press

Press Archives *1892-1896* :
Le Figaro, Paris
L'Illustration
The New York Times
Le Petit journal
The Singapore Advertizer
The Straits Times